Routledge Studies in Crime and Society

Harm and Disorder in the Urban Space
Social Control, Sense and Sensibility
Edited by Nina Peršak and Anna Di Ronco

Serial and Mass Murder
Understanding Multicide through Offending Patterns, Explanations, and Outcomes
Elizabeth Gurian

Mass Shootings and Civilian Armament
Alexei Ansin

Criminalization of Activism
Historical, Present, and Future Perspectives
Edited by Valeria Vegh Weis

Elderly Sexual Abuse
Theory, Research, and Practice
Eric Beauregard and Julien Chopin

Desistance from Sexual Offending
The Role of Circles of Support and Accountability
Kelly Richards

Oppressed by Debt
Government and the Justice System as a Creditor of the Poor
Edited by Saul Schwartz

A Criminological Biography of an Arms Dealer
Yarin Eski

For more information about this series, please visit: www.routledge.com/Routledge-Studies-in-Crime-and-Society/book-series/RSCS

Desistance from Sexual Offending

This book explores how Circles of Support and Accountability (CoSA) can reduce sexual reoffending. The release of a notorious sex offender from prison strikes fear into members of the public. Media coverage often provokes further panic, casting such offenders as irredeemable monsters and ticking time bombs, destined to continue preying on innocent children and women. In the West, governments have responded by enacting heavily punitive and exclusionary policies, such as public sex offender registers, indefinite detention and lifetime correctional supervision.

A radically different approach – Circles of Support and Accountability – emerged alongside these measures. CoSA are groups of trained volunteers who collectively resist the exclusionary impulse, instead actively supporting those with sexual offence convictions to reintegrate into communities. Despite their seemingly counterintuitive nature, the research is clear that CoSA reduce sexual reoffending far better than more popular draconian sex offender management policies. However, little is understood about how CoSA work.

This book begins to address this gap by proposing a new way of understanding how CoSA reduce sexual reoffending. Drawing on 65 in-depth interviews with CoSA participants, it offers a new theoretically informed empirical explanation of CoSA's capacity to promote desistance from sexual offending and to turn those convicted of sexual offenders into law-abiding and productive members of the community. Ultimately, it is a call to action, demonstrating that we, the community, must play a more central role in integrating people with sexual offence convictions if we desire safer communities for our children and our selves. This work illuminates new directions for research, policy and practice, and is essential reading for academics and students engaged in the study of criminology and criminal justice, restorative justice, sexual violence and reentry

Kelly Richards holds a PhD in criminology from Western Sydney University. She is currently an Associate Professor in the School of Justice at Queensland University of Technology, where her research focuses primarily on those who perpetrate sexual violence. In 2010, she was awarded the ACT Government Office for Women Audrey Fagan Churchill Fellowship to investigate Circles of Support and Accountability in Canada, America and the United Kingdom. She was recently awarded a Fulbright Senior Scholar Award and will use this to further her research at California State University and the University of Vermont. She lives in Brisbane with her husband and Staghound X, and enjoys hiking, music and pub trivia.

Desistance from Sexual Offending

The Role of Circles of Support and Accountability

Kelly Richards

Routledge
Taylor & Francis Group
NEW YORK AND LONDON

First published 2022
by Routledge
605 Third Avenue, New York, NY 10158

and by Routledge
2 Park Square, Milton Park, Abingdon, Oxon, OX14 4RN

Routledge is an imprint of the Taylor & Francis Group, an informa business

Library of Congress Cataloging-in-Publication Data
Names: Richards, Kelly (Lecturer in criminology), author.
Title: Desistance from sexual offending : the role of circles of support and accountability / Kelly Richards.
Description: 1 Edition. | New York, NY : Routledge, 2022. |
Series: Routledge studies in crime and society | Includes bibliographical references and index.
Identifiers: LCCN 2021032776 (print) | LCCN 2021032777 (ebook) |
ISBN 9780367646240 (hardback) | ISBN 9780367646257 (paperback) |
ISBN 9781003125532 (ebook)
Subjects: LCSH: Sex offenders—Rehabilitation. | Self-help groups. |
Community mental health services. | Community psychology.
Classification: LCC HV6556 .R534 2022 (print) | LCC HV6556 (ebook) |
DDC 365/.661—dc23
LC record available at https://lccn.loc.gov/2021032776
LC ebook record available at https://lccn.loc.gov/2021032777

ISBN: 978-0-367-64624-0 (hbk)
ISBN: 978-0-367-64625-7 (pbk)
ISBN: 978-1-003-12553-2 (ebk)

DOI: 10.4324/9781003125532

Typeset in Bembo
by KnowledgeWorks Global Ltd.

Dedication

This book is dedicated to Owen Richards, the best big brother a girl could ask for.

Contents

List of figures and tables

Figures

Tables

Acknowledgements

I am indebted to the Winston Churchill Memorial Trust for providing the initial opportunity to learn about Circles of Support and Accountability (CoSA) through a generous travel grant in 2010. Words cannot express how truly grateful I am for this opportunity; it shaped my career (and life) in ways I could scarcely have imagined. I am also grateful for the funding support provided by the (then) Faculty of Law at Queensland University of Technology, which enabled me to conduct the fieldwork for the current study, to my supportive and inspiring colleagues in the School of Justice, and to my two favourite boys, Adam and Finn.

I am also indebted to the six CoSA programs at which I was supported to collect data for this study, and to all the staff who welcomed me during the research, especially Sheri Wiedenhoefer, David Byrne and Dan McGettigan. Thanks to Sheri, and to CoSA Canada staff for providing feedback on various aspects of the book as it emerged.

Thanks especially to all the tireless CoSA staff, volunteers and stakeholders who agreed to be interviewed for the research, and to the core members for their willingness to share their stories in the pursuit of "no more victims".

Introduction

If you are at all familiar with Circles of Support and Accountability, you're probably expecting this book to start with the story of Charlie Taylor. But this story begins differently. We'll get to Charlie Taylor. This story starts a day or so after I arrived in the town of Fresno, California, for the first time, in late 2010. Fresno is a small regional city by American standards, with a population of about half a million. Located about 300 kilometres southeast of San Francisco and 350 kilometres northeast of Los Angeles in the San Joaquin Valley, it ranks second on a list of American cities for extreme poverty (Calix, 2108). It is one of the most multicultural cities in America (The Business Journal, 2020), with a Latino population of about 50 percent and an Asian population nearing 14 percent according to www.dataus.io. I'd arrived in Fresno after a short domestic hop from my then hometown of Canberra, Australia's capital, followed by a 13-hour flight from Sydney to San Francisco and two train rides totalling about five hours. But it wasn't just my jetlag that made this day memorable.

I'm in a Wendy's restaurant – which to my surprise serves real food, not just ice creams like Wendy's in Australia – with two people I've just met. The first is Clare Ann Ruth-Heffelbower, a Fresno local and then Director of Circles of Support and Accountability Fresno. Clare Ann is immensely welcoming, a slim and energetic woman who makes me feel immediately comfortable in her presence. The second is a man in his late forties who I will call Rory. Like Clare Ann, Rory is warm, articulate and lovely. He too makes me feel welcome immediately. Rory is what I come to learn is known – in the world of Circles of Support and Accountability – as a "core member". Core members are the individuals served by Circles of Support and Accountability programs; in other words, they are the people who have been convicted of and incarcerated for sexual offences, including those committed against children. Rory's story is not atypical in this world. He spent 11 years in prison for sexually abusing two children who had been enrolled in the school at which he was employed. When we meet at Wendy's, he'd been out of prison for about two years. We chat a little about our lives – Rory has all the usual questions about Australian wildlife and the various ways it can kill you – and order food. Before we eat, Rory invites Clare Ann and me to join in a prayer

DOI: 10.4324/9781003125532-1

of thanks. We clasp hands and bow our heads, Rory says grace, and I silently ask myself what on earth I am doing here.

Earlier that year, I had been named the Australian Capital Territory Government Office for Women Audrey Fagan Churchill Fellow for 2010. Churchill Fellowships are awarded to individual Australians with a demonstrated track record of achievement and passion across a wide range of fields and disciplines. In my case, I'd arrived at a Churchill Fellowship via an abiding interest in restorative justice. Although it is a slippery concept, restorative justice generally refers to responses to crime that seek to repair harm rather than merely punish perpetrators. Practices such as victim-offender mediation and reconciliation are usually considered to reflect restorative justice principles. We'll come back to restorative justice a little later too. My research on restorative justice – I'd completed a PhD on the subject in 2007 – had made me aware of a little-known and seemingly somewhat controversial practice being utilised in the United States, Canada and the United Kingdom, called Circles of Support and Accountability. Circles of Support and Accountability, or CoSA for short, would form the focus of my two-month fellowship, during which I would travel to a variety of locations across these three countries, observing CoSA, meeting with those involved and generally learning as much as I could about this practice. The aim of my travels was to return to Australia armed with an in-depth knowledge of this innovative program, ready to improve the way Australian jurisdictions prevent and respond to child sexual abuse.

Prevalence and Criminal Justice Response to Child Sexual Abuse

I mentioned that Rory's story is not atypical. It is not atypical because the sexual abuse of children is not atypical. Indeed, child sexual abuse appears to have always existed (Coldrey, 1996; Mintz, 2012) and appears to exist universally (Shafe & Hutchinson, 2014; Singh et al., 2014). Up to 8 percent of boys and up to 12 percent of girls experience penetrative abuse, and about 12 percent of boys and 27 percent of girls experience non-penetrative abuse (e.g., molestation, exposure to masturbation) before the age of 15 years (Australian Institute of Family Studies, 2017).

Rory is, however, highly atypical in that he was reported, convicted and imprisoned for his crimes. This is rarely the case; sexual offences have the lowest conviction rate of any crime against the person (Christensen et al., 2016). Most sexual violence is never even reported to police (Bouhours & Daly, 2008) for a range of reasons. Kelly et al. (2005) found that victims/survivors of sexual violence may choose not to report offences that occurred some time ago and/or may not want others to know about their victimisation. Others lack trust in the police and/or do not wish to face the criminal justice process (Kelly et al., 2005). Instances of sexual violence and abuse that are reported to police are not routinely recorded or pursued by police or prosecutors. Again, there are a number of reasons for this attrition from the criminal justice process, including evidentiary challenges (Borzycki, 2007) and poor prospects of securing a conviction (Kelly et al., 2005). Securing a conviction in cases of sexual crime is extremely difficult, and many offences of a sexual nature that are adjudicated do not result in a conviction (Fitzgerald, 2006). The reasons for this are "complex and numerous" (Borzycki, 2007, p. 26) but include the fact that individuals who appear in court in relation to sexual offences are less likely to plead guilty than other defendants (Fitzgerald, 2006). Finally, not all of those convicted of sexual offences are sentenced to prison (see Anderson et al., 2012 for an overview). Statistics from the Victoria Sentencing Advisory Council (2009) showed that clear majorities of those convicted of rape (92.2%), sexual penetration of a child aged under 10 years (91.8%) and incest (91.0%) are sentenced to prison. However, only about half of those convicted of sexual penetration of a child aged between 10 and 15 years (inclusive) received a sentence of imprisonment (Victoria Sentencing Advisory Council, 2009). Bouhours and Daly's (2008) study of attrition of sexual violence cases from the criminal justice system across five countries (Australia, Canada, England and Wales, Scotland and the United States) found that only 14 percent of victims/survivors reported the offence to the police. Of these reports, just 30 percent proceeded to prosecution and 20 percent were adjudicated in court. Only 12.5 percent of defendants were convicted and just 6.5 percent were convicted of the original offence (Bouhours & Daly, 2008). Importantly, attrition of sexual violence offences from the criminal justice system occurs differently for particular groups of victims/survivors. For example, First Nations and culturally diverse victims/survivors (Taylor & Putt, 2007) and victims/survivors with disabilities (Fraser-Barbour et al., 2018) face additional barriers to reporting and navigating the criminal justice process.

Child victims/survivors of sexual violence in particular face additional challenges; children may not disclose sexual abuse or delay reporting sexual offences due to self-blame, shame and/or threats by or fear of the perpetrator (Christensen et al., 2015). When children do disclose sexual abuse, whether a report is made to police may depend on whether the child's caregiver believes the child and/or their relationship to the perpetrator. As Christensen et al. (2015) noted, the research suggests that non-offending mothers are less protective of a child when they are in a current relationship with the perpetrator (see also Pintello & Zuravin, 2001). Even when cases of child sexual abuse proceed to court, child complainants face a range of challenges. For example, children may find it difficult to understand legal language and may find giving evidence and being cross-examined scary and even re-traumatising. Child witnesses are also often perceived as unreliable, particularly if they have delayed disclosing sexual abuse (see Richards, 2009 for an overview). As a consequence of these and many other factors, conviction rates in cases of child sexual abuse are low (Cashmore et al., 2020; Christensen et al., 2015, 2016; Richards, 2009). To be clear, while there is little research on whether cases of sexual violence against adults or sexual violence against children have higher levels of attrition, research by Fitzgerald (2006) on New South Wales, Australia, found that offences against children have a higher conviction rate than those against adults. Importantly, however, smaller proportions of incidents involving children resulted in the commencement of court proceedings in the first place. Fitzgerald (2006) found that a higher proportion of defendants charged with a sexual offence against a child (48%) had their charges dismissed without a hearing than those charged with a sexual offence against an adult (27%).

The tide, however, appears to be turning. The number of sexual offence convictions in the United Kingdom has risen year on year since 2012, with a 45 percent increase between 2016 and 2019 alone (Vieira et al., 2020). In Australia, those convicted for sexual offences already comprise 12 percent of the prisoner population and are the third-largest prisoner group (Australian Bureau of Statistics, 2018). The number of people with sexual offence convictions in Australian prisons is increasing rapidly (Australian Bureau of Statistics, 2018), with those convicted of sexual offences increasingly being sentenced to imprisonment rather than community based sanctions. During the year to 30 June 2018 alone, the number of prisoners convicted of sexual offences increased approximately 10 percent; this increase was responsible for a significant proportion of the overall growth in prisoner numbers across Australia (Australian Bureau of Statistics, 2018). The United States Sentencing Commission (2019) reported increases in both the number of federally sentenced individuals convicted in relation to sexual violence and in the length of prison sentences imposed on these offenders, due in part to mandatory minimum sentencing requirements.

Stigmatisation of People Convicted of Sexual Offences

Unlike Rory, the vast majority of those who commit sexual offences are never incarcerated, and therefore do not face the profound stigmatisation and exclusion faced by those who are. This group experiences stigmatisation by and exclusion from the broader community in a way virtually unparalleled in contemporary Western democracies – especially in the United States. Wacquant (2009) detailed the contours of this stigmatisation and exclusion in modern America, but increasingly in other liberal democracies such as Canada, Australia and the United Kingdom (see Blagden et al., 2018; Vieira et al., 2020). Those convicted of sexual offenses no longer merely "do the crime" and "do the time", but are increasingly subject to a wide range of long-term or even permanent measures that "blacklist sex offenders and… deliver them over to the permanent scrutiny and open execration of the public" (Wacquant, 2009, p. 211). These include publicly available offender registries, community notification, severe residency restrictions, so-called "civil" commitment, electronic monitoring and long-term or even lifelong correctional supervision (Bartels et al., 2019; Duwe, 2015). Across the United States, "tent cities" have mushroomed on the outskirts of towns and cities, on the small slivers of land deemed to be a safe enough distance from schools, parks, churches, playgrounds, swimming pools and various other amenities that those convicted of sexual offences are often restricted from frequenting. This has occurred despite evidence showing that such residency restrictions are futile in terms of preventing sexual reoffending (Duwe, 2015). As Soothill, Francis, Sanderson and Ackerley (in Roach & Pease, 2014, p. 166) have argued, a type of "criminal apartheid" exists between responses to sexual and non-sexual offenders in Western jurisdictions.

It is impossible to overstate the public loathing that those convicted of sexual offending against children face (McAlinden, 2007; McAvoy, 2012; Mears et al., 2008; Richards, 2018; Rogers et al., 2011; Viki et al., 2012). This group faces an unparalleled level of stigmatisation; to state that they are "modern-day lepers" or "social lepers" (Thompson, 2015) has become a cliché. As Hacking (cited in Ashenden, 2002, p. 198) claims, "in an age in which we are supposedly drowning in value-relativism, there is striking consensus concerning the wrong of sexual contacts and relationships between adults and children". On numerous occasions, a person suspected of having sexually abused children has been physically attacked by members of the public (see generally Williams, 2006, 2017). The public's suspicions, however, are not always accurate, and on many occasions, an innocent person has been viciously attacked and even killed. In 2013, Iranian immigrant Bijan Ebrahimi was living on a disability pension in Bristol, England, enjoying his passions: gardening and his cat. Verbal attacks – including chants of "paedo, paedo" began to be made on Ebrahimi following rumours that he had taken photographs of children in his local neighbourhood. Ebrahimi had indeed taken photographs of local children – the young people who had repeatedly vandalised the hanging baskets in his garden. Although Ebrahimi was questioned by police about the photographs, he was released without charge. Police accepted that the photographs had only been taken in an attempt to capture evidence of the young people's destruction of his garden. Despite this, two days after being questioned by police, Ebrahimi was viciously beaten and then burned to death by two men who remained convinced that he was a "paedophile" (Morris, 2013).

Similar stories abound. In Jakarta, Indonesia in 2017 a man was beaten to death by a group of civilians after allegedly sexually attacking a five-year-old boy (The Jakarta Post, 2017). In other instances, those (sometimes falsely) accused of grooming minors for sex have died by suicide (Campbell, 2016). "Paedophile hunting" – abetted by the advent of digital technologies – has spread rapidly in recent years. Pedophile hunters are groups of ordinary citizens that work to publicly expose individuals they suspect of sexual offending against children and young people by disseminating their personal information such as photographs, addresses and telephone numbers online (Campbell, 2016; Yardley et al., 2018). In recent years, pedophile hunter groups have materialised in astonishing numbers. Farrell (2018) puts the figure at up to 145 in the United Kingdom alone, but the practice has been documented in countries as diverse as Canada, Cambodia and Kazakhstan (Favarel-Garrigues, 2019). Infamously, the US-based paedophile hunting television program *To Catch A Predator* was taken off the air after Assistant District Attorney Louis Conradt shot and killed himself while being confronted as a suspected sexual offender as part of the show (Woodman, 2015). Despite the cancellation of the program and Conradt's family's successful wrongful death lawsuit against the NBC television network, host Chris Hanson continued to entrap alleged would-be offenders with the financial backing of crowdsourcing platform *Kickstarter* (Woodman, 2015). At least eight suicides of suspects have occurred in the United Kingdom alone as the consequence of paedophile hunting activity (Hadjimatheou, 2019). These online entrapment activities have likewise resulted in physical attacks on targets. One such target, 28-year-old Gary Cleary died by suicide a number of days after he was arrested and released on bail following a sting by paedophile hunting group Letzgo Hunting, in which a decoy posed as a 14-year-old girl (Campbell, 2016). In 2019, Leeds Crown Court found that paedophile hunting group Predator Exposure had "overstepped the mark" when they falsely imprisoned and used unnecessary violence against two men they suspected of sexually abusing children (Adams, 2019). In other cases, the families of suspected offenders have been subjected to threats and abuse despite having no connection with any alleged offending (Hadjimatheou, 2019).

A number of studies in the United States have shown that the presence of a person known to have been convicted of a sexual offence even decreases housing values. Linden and Rockoff (2008) put this figure at 12 percent for homes immediately adjacent to the residence of a person with sexual offence convictions. Navarro and Rabe-Hemp (2018) found that a concentration of two or more registered sex offenders was associated with a $12,750 decrease in sale prices. For sexual predators (i.e., those who received a registerable conviction for the commission of or attempt at certain sexual offences), the decrease was $17,797. A Pennsylvania couple even filed a lawsuit against the neighbour who had molested their daughter, in an attempt to force him to buy their house, which they claimed was now "virtually unmarketable" (Lester, 2013).

Unsurprisingly, then, those in prison for sexual offences often fear their return to the outside world. Many of the core members I interviewed as part of this study felt severely anxious about leaving prison, although they had nearly uniformly experienced prison as terrifying too. They were afraid of everything from seeing their victims or their victims' families, to being physically attacked, to living in a world to which they were no longer accustomed.

As one core member, James, said when I asked him what he was afraid of at this time: "literally everything".

Against this background, the release of those convicted of sexual offences from prison back into the community has become an issue of serious public, and public policy concern. How can we reintegrate those who have committed often heinous sexual crimes? How can we protect the community from the risk that some such individuals may pose and how do we protect them from often outraged communities? They have "done the crime" and "done the time": now what?

The Emergence of Circles of Support and Accountability

This is precisely the question that plagued Correctional Service Canada psychologist Bill Palmer in the summer of 1994, when he discovered that repeat child molester Charlie Taylor was due to be released from prison at the completion of his sentence to the community of Hamilton, Ontario. Charlie had been convicted of numerous sexual offences against children, and had been in and out of prison since his teenage years (Wilson, 2006). Palmer, who had worked with Charlie during his imprisonment, considered him a "marginalised man with few life skills and a persistent sexual interest in children" (Wilson et al., 2008, p. 27). While most prisoners serve around two-thirds of their full sentence in prison and the remainder under correctional supervision in the community, in order to ensure their successful transition back to life on the outside[1], Charlie Taylor was to be released at his Warrant Expiry Date. In other words, he had served the entirety of his sentence in prison, and would be released "cold" into the community – that is, without any supervision (Hannem & Petrunik, 2004). At the time in Ontario, like many comparable Western jurisdictions, offenders considered to be "high risk" – especially those convicted of sexual offences – could be required to serve their whole sentence behind bars rather than undergoing parole supervision for the final portion of their sentence (see Hannem & Petrunik, 2004, 2007; Petrunik, 2002; Petrunik et al., 2008). (Today, detention through to Warrant Expiry Date is much more exceptional, though it still occurs as a regular practice; Canadian CoSA sites thus usually work with offenders still under supervision, at least initially). The primary rationale for this approach is that keeping offenders incarcerated for the entirety of their sentence will increase community safety. Offenders can't commit another offence while incarcerated, so the logic goes, so the longer they are incarcerated, the safer the community will be. An important and overlooked consequence of this approach, however, is that offenders are released into the community without the considerable benefits of correctional supervision and support (Hannem & Petrunik, 2004). As Wilson et al. (2007, p. 6) argued, "paradoxically, these offenders, arguably those in most need of community supervision and professional attention, are those most likely to receive neither". For Charlie Taylor, being released without supervision meant having "no strings attached....he would have no Parole Officer with whom to meet, and he would have no conditions on his community interactions other than those that apply to all citizens (keep the peace and be of good behaviour)" (Wilson et al., 2008, p. 26). Taylor was considered very "high risk" indeed, having been assigned a risk rating of 100 percent chance of reoffending in seven years post-release (Wilson et al., 2008). In other words, authorities were certain that Charlie would reoffend, but had no tools at their disposal to prevent this from occurring. (Changes to legislation and the community management of people with sexual offence convictions occurred in the 2000s leading to greater supervision in the community (Hannem & Petrunik, 2004, 2007; Petrunik, 2002; Petrunik et al., 2008)).

To make the situation even more dire, Charlie Taylor was the subject of considerable media attention: "the local television station ran stories at every possible opportunity, complete with 'mugshot' photographs. Charlie was an instant pariah" (Wilson et al., 2007, p. 7). Numerous newspaper articles from the time attest to this. "Be careful" warned a lead article about Taylor's impending release in local newspaper *The Hamilton Spectator* (Lajoie, 1994). A copy of his mugshot photograph was distributed among local schools to alert the children of Hamilton to Charlie's pending presence in their community.

Correctional Service Canada informed Bill Palmer that they no longer had any capacity or authority to assist Charlie, since he had been released at Warrant Expiry Date, and was thus no longer subject to correctional supervision (Wilson et al., 2008). Palmer made a number of attempts to secure supports for Charlie in the community, but when these were not forthcoming, decided, as a "last ditch effort" (Wilson et al., 2007, p. 7), to contact the Reverend Harry Nigh. Reverend Nigh was the pastor of a small Mennonite congregation in Hamilton. His church, the Welcome Inn Church, was a modest building with a red brick façade adjoining a small parking lot and rundown tennis court. On the day I visit, in late October 2010, a blanket of yellow leaves covers the front yard and walkway, and a sign welcomes local seniors to a Seniors' Diners' Club, which offers a home-cooked meal every Tuesday.

Charlie Taylor had met Reverend Nigh previously:

> He and Nigh had first met in the 1970s, when Nigh ran a one-on-one support program for offenders, called Men to Men, Women to Women. M2/W2 connected each offender with a volunteer, who would help him or her with day-to-day issues and talk them through their problems. If offenders had volunteers they could trust, the thinking went, they might turn to help instead of reoffending. But when Taylor called one on December 26, 1986, the volunteer didn't pick up. Later that day, he lured an eight-year-old boy into his apartment in downtown Toronto and sexually assaulted him.
>
> (Tubb, 2015: np)

Harry Nigh initially had difficulty remembering Charlie Taylor. When he eventually did remember Charlie, he recalled that he had not liked him very much (Wilson et al., 2007). The Reverend Nigh was therefore a little reluctant to become involved, but ultimately, motivated by his concern for the safety of the children in Hamilton (Richards, 2011), he agreed to help Charlie. The Reverend Nigh was painfully aware then that the approach of linking an offender with one volunteer had been far from successful: but "he wondered if Taylor would have reoffended had others been there for him that Boxing Day. With enough people, there might have been a whole community to stop him" (Tubb, 2015).

He did so initially by creating what came to be called a "Circle of Support" around Charlie. "Circles of Support", or groups of trained volunteer supporters, had initially been used in Hamilton, and by the Mennonite church (Hannem & Petrunik, 2007) to foster the social inclusion of people living with disability and/or mental health issues. The "wraparound care" (Hannem & Petrunik, 2007, p. 158) model has been used around the globe to support a diverse range of individuals experiencing social exclusion (see http://www.civilsociety.org.au/Circles.htm). Essentially, the Reverend Nigh hoped that this model of community based support would both protect the community of Hamilton from Charlie and protect Charlie from the community of Hamilton. Nigh described his actions as "accidental courage"; as Wilson (2006: np) explains, "all they [Nigh and his wife] had done was to invite four of their friends over to dinner with Charlie; they wanted to see if they could do anything to help him resettle in the community in the face of public panic".

The original Circle of Support consisted primarily of hand-picked members of Nigh's Mennonite congregation (Wilson et al., 2007, 2008). The group "helped Taylor find a place to stay, welcomed him to attend church services and social functions, and set up a safety net of daily contacts to protect Taylor and minimise his risk to children" (Hannem & Petrunik, 2004, p. 100). Members of the Circle later came to be known as "Charlie's Angels" (Nigh cited in Höing et al., 2015, p. 4; Wilson et al., 2008, p. 27), as newspaper coverage attests (Brooks, 2008; Wilson, 2007). Famously, on spotting the mugshot photograph of Taylor on a flyer distributed at his school, one of Nigh's young sons proclaimed to his teachers and peers that the man on the flyer "came over to our house last night for supper!" (Nigh cited in Höing et al., 2015; Tubb, 2015; Wilson, 2006). As for Charlie Taylor, despite being deemed a particularly high-risk offender, he was never convicted of another sexual offence (Elliott et al., 2013). He remained in contact with his volunteers for over 11 years, before passing away on Christmas Day in 2006 (Tubb, 2015).

The problem of high-risk individuals with convictions for sexual violence being released into the community didn't, of course, begin and end with Charlie Taylor. Four months after Charlie's release, another man, with numerous convictions for sexual crimes against young boys, Wray Budreo, was due to be released in Peterborough, Ontario, also at his Warrant Expiry

Date (Hannem & Petrunik, 2004; Wilson et al., 2008). Budreo was met with the same kind of community response that had accompanied Charlie Taylor's release: "Dan Haley – then prison chaplaincy volunteer – not so fondly tells the story of spiriting Wray out of Kingston Penitentiary in the trunk of his car" (Wilson et al., 2008, p. 27; see also Hannem & Petrunik, 2007, p. 158). A colleague of Harry Nigh's, a community corrections chaplain by the name of Reverend Hugh Kirkegaard, "saw in Harry Nigh's experiment the possibility of a hybrid restorative justice/community safety model that could be applied to the most loathed and feared of offender" (Hannem & Petrunik, 2007, p. 158). Kirkegaard decided to emulate Nigh's approach with Charlie Taylor and formed a Circle of Support for Budreo (Hannem & Petrunik, 2004; Wilson et al., 2008). Based on the apparent success of these two fledgling Circles of Support, Nigh and Kirkegaard sought support from the Chaplaincy Division of Correctional Service Canada and the Mennonite Central Committee of Ontario to extend their experimentation into a more formal pilot program (Hannem & Petrunik, 2007). They managed to obtain a small grant to establish a pilot, to more systematically develop and promote the approach and implement it across Canada (Hannem & Petrunik, 2004). Circles of Support – or Circles of Support and Accountability as they came to be known (see Richards, 2011) – had been born.

Outline of the Book

This book proposes a new way of understanding CoSA, and how CoSA reduce sexual reoffending. Drawing on 65 in-depth interviews with CoSA participants, as well as my broader program of research into CoSA in the United States, Canada and Australia, it puts forward a new theoretically informed empirical explanation of CoSA. Ultimately, this book is a call to action, demonstrating that we, the community, must follow the path set by the Reverend Nigh; we must play a more active role in (re)integrating people with sexual offence convictions if we desire safer communities for our children and our selves.

The remainder of the book is divided into eight chapters. **Chapter 1** explains the aims and purpose of CoSA and describes in detail how they operate in practice. It provides a critical overview of the existing research literature on CoSA from across the globe. In particular, it examines the literature on a range of psychosocial outcomes for core members (e.g., health, housing, employment, relationships) and on CoSA's ability to reduce sexual reoffending. It also provides an overview of existing knowledge about CoSA volunteers and what motivates people to give up their time to support the reintegration of people with sexual offence convictions. The key task of this chapter is to set the scene for the question at the heart of the book: how do CoSA reduce sexual reoffending? **Chapter 2** critically analyses existing theoretical explanations of CoSA. It assesses the most common theoretical explanations for CoSA – the Good Lives and Risk, Needs, Responsivity models, restorative justice and reintegrative shaming – and posits the need for a different theoretical fit. It argues that CoSA ought to be conceptualised as desistance-promotion (following Fox, 2015), and provides an overview of the key components of this theoretical framework. **Chapter 3** describes how the research presented in this book was conducted. It details the project's epistemological assumptions, as well as the methodological approaches of phenomenology and narrative criminology that informed the research. The chapter outlines how the data were collected, how participants were sampled and recruited and how the data were analysed. It also describes the characteristics of the sample, and provides demographic information about participants, with a particular focus on core members.

Chapters 4–7 present the data collected for the book. **Chapter 4** provides an overview of the sparse literature on desistance from sexual offending. This chapter then focuses on the concept of "redemption scripts" (Maruna, 2001) and demonstrates that in contrast to existing understandings (Harris, 2017; Maruna, 2016), narratives of redemption *are* available to people who have sexually offended and CoSA are a key avenue for enabling them. **Chapter 5** introduces the concept of the "110-percenters" and its role in desistance. The 110-percenter refers to the reformed offender who appears to give "110 percent" to this new identity and role (Maruna, 2001). This chapter demonstrates that CoSA provide an opportunity for core members to perform the role of the 110-percenter or super-reformed. It also argues that a critical, yet previously unidentified, role of CoSA volunteers is as sympathetic witnesses to core members' performances of this new identity and role. As such, this chapter begins to position members of the community as key actors in offender reintegration and desistance. **Chapter 6** demonstrates that in a sociopolitical context in which the notion of individuals with sexual offence histories being redeemed is almost unimaginable, CoSA offer a rare avenue that enables exactly that. The chapter fleshes out the key concept of "generativity" (i.e., a "commitment to promoting the next generation, manifested through parenting, teaching, mentoring and generating products and outcomes that aim to benefit youth and foster the development and well-being of individuals and social systems that will outlive the self" (McAdams & de St Aubin, 1998, p. xx)). While generative projects are an important feature of most offenders' redemption scripts, it has become virtually impossible for people with convictions relating to sexual offending to give back or make amends. Against this backdrop, this chapter demonstrates that CoSA provide a unique opportunity for generative projects to be imagined and even realised by core members. **Chapter 7** introduces the concept of the "wounded healer" or "professional ex" – those reformed offenders who recraft their delinquent pasts into a "source of wisdom to be drawn from while acting as a drug counselor, youth worker, community volunteer or mutual-help group member" (Maruna, 2001, p. 117). While it may seem inconceivable in the current climate that any avenue would exist for individuals with sexual offence convictions to coach or mentor others, one of the CoSA programs included in the current study operates on the premise that former core members can, in appropriate circumstances, make a unique contribution to CoSA as volunteers themselves. This chapter presents the first theoretical and empirical examination of the utilisation of former core members as volunteers. It argues that empowering former core members to act as volunteers facilitates the "wounded healer" role and can thus make a substantial contribution in shaping the desistant identities of those with sexual offence convictions.

Chapter 8 makes a series of suggestions about what the key findings outlined in the preceding chapters mean for the practice of CoSA around the globe. It offers guidance on the main ways in which CoSA practice could adopt its key findings to strengthen practice and improve outcomes in the future, as well as providing broader advice for those who engage with people who have perpetrated sexual violence as therapeutic or correctional professionals. Finally, a brief **Conclusion** provides a summary of the theoretical and empirical contribution of the book, before suggesting areas for future research to build on what has been presented here.

Note

1. This is an effective practice; as Weatherburn and Ringland's (2014) research indicated, most offenders do not reoffend while on parole (i.e., receiving correctional supervision in the community), although it appears that a higher proportion reoffend once they have completed their parole period. Furthermore, a higher proportion of those released from prison without supervision reoffend than those released from prison under correctional supervision (Wan et al., 2014).

References

Adams, J. (2019, 22 October). Vigilante paedophile hunters 'overstepped the mark' when they attacked and verbally abused suspects after posing as teens online, court hears. *Daily Mail Australia*. https://www.dailymail.co.uk/news/article-7596653/Vigilante-paedophile-hunters-overstepped-mark-attacked-verbally-abused-suspects.html

Anderson, J., Richards, K., & Willis, K. (2012). *Evaluation of the ACT sexual assault reform program (SARP): Final report.* Australian Institute of Criminology. https://www.aic.gov.au/publications/tbp/tbp51

Ashenden, S. (2002). Policing perversion: The contemporary governance of paedophilia. *Cultural Values, 6*(1–2), 197–222. doi: https://doi.org/10.1080/1362517022019829

Australian Bureau of Statistics. (2018). *Prisoners in Australia 2018, cat. no. 4517.0.* Australian Bureau of Statistics. https://www.abs.gov.au/ausstats/abs@.nsf/Lookup/by%20Subject/4517.0~2018~Main%20Features~Prisoner%20characteristics,%20Australia~4

Australian Institute of Family Studies. (2017). *The prevalence of child abuse and neglect.* Australian Institute of Family Studies. https://aifs.gov.au/cfca/publications/prevalence-child-abuse-and-neglect

Bartels, L., Walvisch, J., & Richards, K. (2019). More, longer, tougher… or is it finally time for a different approach to the post-sentence management of sex offenders in Australia? *Criminal Law Journal, 43*(1), 41–57.

Blagden, N., Mann, R., Webster, S., Lee, R., & WIlliams, F. (2018). "It's not something I chose you know": Making sense of pedophiles' sexual interest in children and the impact on their psychosexual identity. *Sexual Abuse, 30*(6), 728–754. doi: https://doi.org/10.1177/1079063217697132

Borzycki, M. (2007). *Research and public policy series no. 79: Pilot study on sexual assault and related offences in the ACT: Stage 3*. Australian Institute of Criminology. https://www.aic.gov.au/publications/rpp/rpp79

Bouhours, B., & Daly, K. (2008). *Rape and attrition in the legal process: A comparative analysis of five countries*. Griffith University School of Criminology and Criminal Justice.

Brooks, L. (2008, 19 June). Virtuous circles. *The Guardian*, np. https://www.theguardian.com/commentisfree/2008/jun/19/socialcare?gusrc=rss

Calix, B. (2108, 26 April). Fresno's extreme poverty puts the city in a bad spot on a national list. *The Fresno Bee*. https://www.fresnobee.com/news/local/article209826869.html

Campbell, E. (2016). Policing paedophilia: Assembling bodies, spaces and things. *Crime Media Culture, 12*(3), 345–365. doi: https://doi.org/10.1177/1741659015623598?journalCode=cmca

Cashmore, J., Taylor, A., & Parkinson, P. (2020). Fourteen-year trends in the criminal justice response to child sexual abuse reports in new South Wales. *Child Maltreatment, 25*(1), 85–95. doi: https://doi.org/10.1177/1077559519853042

Christensen, L., Sharman, S., & Powell, M. (2015). Professionals' views on child sexual abuse attrition rates. *Psychiatry, Psychology and Law, 22*(4), 542–558. doi: https://doi.org/abs/10.1080/13218719.2014.960036

Christensen, L., Sharman, S., & Powell, M. (2016). Identifying the characteristics of child sexual abuse cases that exit the criminal justice system before the forensic interview. *Police Science & Management, 18*(2), 103–114. doi: https://doi.org/10.1177/1461355716641973

Coldrey, B. (1996). The sexual abuse of children: The historical perspective. *Studies: An Irish Quarterly Review, 85*(340), 370–380. doi: https://www.jstor.org/stable/30091236?seq=1#metadata_info_tab_contents

Duwe, G. (2015). What has worked and what has not with Minnesota sex offenders: A review of the evidence. *Journal of Sexual Aggression, 21*(1), 71–85. doi: https://doi.org/10.1080/13552600.2014.901430

Elliott, I., Zajac, G., & Meyer, C. (2013). *Evaluability assessment of the Circles of Support and Accountability (COSA) model*. Department of Justice. https://www.ojp.gov/pdffiles1/nij/grants/243832.pdf

Farrell, J. (2018). *Perverted justice: An exploration of the origins, operations and future of paedophile hunting in the UK* [Master's thesis, Utrecht University]. Utrecht, The Netherlands.

Favarel-Garrigues, G. (2019). Digital vigilantism and anti-paedophile activism in Russia: Between civic involvement in law enforcement, moral policing and business venture. *Global Crime, 21*(3–4), 306–326. doi: https://doi.org/10.1080/17440572.2019.1676738

Fitzgerald, J. (2006). *Crime and justice bulletin no. 92: The attrition of sexual offences from the new South Wales criminal justice system*. New South Wales Bureau of Crime Statistics and Research. https://www.bocsar.nsw.gov.au/Publications/CJB/cjb92.pdf

Fox, K. (2015). Theorizing community integration as desistance-promotion. *Criminal Justice and Behavior, 42*(1), 82–94. doi: https://doi.org/10.1177/0093854814550028

Fraser-Barbour, E., Crocker, R., & Walker, R. (2018). Barriers and facilitators in supporting people with intellectual disability to report sexual violence: Perspectives of Australian disability and mainstream support providers. *The Journal of Adult Protection, 20*(1), 5–16. doi: https://doi.org/10.1108/JAP-08-2017-0031/full/html

Hadjimatheou, K. (2019). Citizen-led digital policing and democratic norms: The case of self-styled paedophile hunters. *Criminology and Criminal Justice*. doi: https://doi.org/10.1177/1748895819880956

Hannem, S., & Petrunik, M. (2004). Canada's Circles of Support and Accountability: A community justice initiative for high-risk sex offenders. *Corrections Today, 66*(98–101), 98–101.

Hannem, S., & Petrunik, M. (2007). Circles of Support and Accountability: A community justice initiative for the reintegration of high-risk sex offenders. *Contemporary Justice Review, 10*(2), 153–171. doi: https://doi.org/10.1080/10282580701372046

Harris, D. (2017). *Desistance from sexual offending: Narratives of retirement, regulation and recovery*. Palgrave Macmillan. https://www.palgrave.com/gp/book/9783319631998

Höing, M., Duke, L., & Völlm, B. (2015). *Circles of Support and Accountability European handbook*. Avans University of Applied Sciences Centre for Public Safety and Criminal Justice. https://www.circles-uk.org.uk/circles4eu/what-is-circles-4eu

Kelly, L., Lovett, J., & Regan, L. (2005). *A gap or a chasm? Attrition in reported rape cases*. Home Office. https://www.ojp.gov/ncjrs/virtual-library/abstracts/gap-or-chasm-attrition-reported-rape-cases

Lajoie, D. (1994, 15 August). Public interest versus personal rights is focus of media dilemma and debate. The Hamilton Spectator, np.

Lester, P. (2013, 14 May). Judge: Sex offender not required to buy victim's property *The Morning Call*. https://www.mcall.com/news/local/mc-xpm-2013-05-14-mc-upper-milford-oliver-beck-sex-offender-lawsuit--20130514-story.html

Linden, L., & Rockoff, J. (2008). Estimates of the impact of crime risk on property values from Megan's laws. *American Economic Review, 98*(3), 1103–1127. doi: https://www.aeaweb.org/articles?id=10.1257/aer.98.3.1103

Maruna, S. (2001). *Making good: How ex-convicts reform and rebuild their lives*. American Psychological Association. doi: https://www.apa.org/pubs/books/431645A

Maruna, S. (2016, November). *Self-narratives of desisting sex offenders: Where are the redemption scripts?* American Society of Criminology annual meeting New Orleans.

McAdams, D., & de St Aubin, E. (1998). *Generativity and adult development: How and why we care for the next generation*. American Psychological Association. doi: https://www.apa.org/pubs/books/431601A

McAlinden, A. M. (2007). *Public attitudes towards sex offenders in Northern Ireland: Research and statistical bulletin 6/2007*. Northern Ireland Office. https://pure.qub.ac.uk/en/publications/public-attitudes-towards-sex-offenders-in-northern-ireland-resear

McAvoy, J. (2012). *Birds of a feather? Irish public attitudes towards sex crime and sex offender reintegration. Is there a publically perceived scale of sexual deviance?* [Master's thesis, Dublin Institute of Technology]. Dublin.

Mears, D., Mancini, C., Gertz, M., & Bratton, J. (2008). Sex crimes, children, and pornography: Public views and public policy. *Crime & Delinquency, 54*(4), 532–559. doi: https://doi.org/10.1177/0011128707308160

Mintz, S. (2012). Placing childhood sexual abuse in historical context. The Immanent Frame 13 July. https://tif.ssrc.org/2012/07/13/placing-childhood-sexual-abuse-in-historical-perspective/

Morris, S. (2013, 29 November). Vigilante jailed for killing man he mistakenly thought was paedophile. *The Guardian*. https://www.theguardian.com/uk-news/2013/nov/28/vigilante-lee-james-life-murdering-bijan-ebrahimi

Navarro, J., & Rabe-Hemp, C. (2018). The financial impact of registered sex offenders on home sale prices: A case study of McLean county, Illinois. *International Journal of Rural Criminology, 4*(1), 86–109. doi: https://doi.org/doi.org/10.18061/1811/86151

Petrunik, M. (2002). Managing unacceptable risk: Sex offenders, community response, and social policy in the United States and Canada. *International Journal of Offender Therapy and Comparative Criminology, 46*(4), 483–511. doi: https://doi.org/10.1177/0306624X02464009

Petrunik, M., Murphy, L., & Federoff, P. (2008). American and Canadian approaches to sex offenders: A study of the politics of dangerousness. *Federal Sentencing Reporter, 21*(2), 111–123. doi: https://www.jstor.org/stable/10.1525/fsr.2008.21.2.111?seq=1#metadata_info_tab_contents

Pintello, D., & Zuravin, S. (2001). Intrafamilial child sexual abuse: Predictors of postdisclosure maternal belief and protective action. *Child Maltreatment, 6*, 344–352. doi: https://doi.org/10.1177/1077559501006004007

Richards, K. (2009). *Trends & issues in crime and criminal justice no. 380: Child complainants and the court process in Australia.* Australian Institute of Criminology. https://www.aic.gov.au/publications/tandi/tandi380

Richards, K. (2011). *The potential of Circles of Support and Accountability (COSA) to reduce child sexual abuse in Australia.* Winston Churchill Memorial Trust. https://www.churchilltrust.com.au/media/fellows/Richards_Kelly_2010.pdf

Richards, K. (2018). Born this way? A qualitative examination of public perceptions of the causes of pedophilia and sexual offending against children. *Deviant Behavior: An Interdisciplinary Journal, 39*(7), 835–851. doi: https://doi.org/10.1080/01639625.2017.1335526

Roach, J., & Pease, K. (2014). Police overestimation of criminal career homogeneity. *Journal of Investigative Psychology and Offender Profiling, 11*(2), 164–178. doi: https://doi.org/10.1002/jip.1405

Rogers, P., Hirst, L., & Davies, M. (2011). An investigation into the effect of respondent gender, victim age, and perpetrator treatment on public attitudes towards sex offenders, sex offender treatment, and sex offender rehabilitation. *Journal of Offender Rehabilitation, 50*(8), 511–530. doi: https://doi.org/10.1080/10509674.2011.602472

Shafe, S., & Hutchinson, G. (2014). Child sexual abuse and continuous influence of cultural practices: A review. *West Indian Medical Journal, 63*(6), 634–637. doi: https://www.ncbi.nlm.nih.gov/pmc/articles/PMC4663956/

Singh, S., Parsekar, S., & Nair, S. (2014). An epidemiological overview of child sexual abuse. *Journal of Family Medicine and Primary Care, 3*(4), 430–435. doi: https://www.ncbi.nlm.nih.gov/pmc/articles/PMC4311357/

Taylor, N., & Putt, J. (2007). *Trends & issues in crime and criminal justice no. 345: Adult sexual violence in indigenous and culturally and linguistically diverse communities in Australia.* Australian Institute of Criminology. https://www.aic.gov.au/publications/tandi/tandi345

The Business Journal. (2020, 23 January). Fresno among most diverse US cities, though its diversity is falling. *The Business Journal.* https://thebusinessjournal.com/report-fresno-among-most-diverse-us-cities-though-its-diversity-is-falling/

The Jakarta Post. (2017, 21 December). Alleged pedophile dies after being beaten by mob. *The Jakarta Post.* https://www.thejakartapost.com/news/2017/12/21/alleged-pedophile-dies-after-being-beaten-by-mob.html

Thompson, D. (2015). *Moving on after getting out: Support and accountability for convicted sex offenders* [PhD thesis, University of Leeds]. Leeds. https://etheses.whiterose.ac.uk/13410/1/Thompson_D_Law_PhD_2015.pdf

Tubb, E. (2015, 10 May). Minding the monster. *The Walrus.* https://thewalrus.ca/minding-the-monster/

United States Sentencing Commission. (2019). *Mandatory minimum penalties for federal sex offenses.* Office of Public Affairs. https://www.ussc.gov/research/research-reports/mandatory-minimum-penalties-federal-sex-offenses

Victoria Sentencing Advisory Council. (2009). *Sentencing for sexual penetration offences: A statistical report.* Victoria Sentencing Advisory Council. https://www.sentencingcouncil.vic.gov.au/publications/sentencing-sexual-penetration-offences-statistical-report

Vieira, C., Rose, R., Craissati, J., & Campbell, C. (2020). The impact of a community psychological treatment programme on desistance in personality disordered sexual offenders. *The Journal of Forensic Psychiatry & Psychology, 31*(6), 837–853. doi: https://doi.org/10.1080/14789949.2020.1807041?journalCode=rjfp20

Viki, G., Fullerton, I., Raggett, H., Tait, F., & Wiltshire, S. (2012). The role of dehumanization in attitudes toward the social exclusion and rehabilitation of sex offenders. *Journal of Applied Social Psychology, 42*(10), 2349–2367. doi: https://doi.org/10.1111/j.1559-1816.2012.00944.x

Wacquant, L. (2009). *Punishing the poor: The neoliberal government of social insecurity.* Duke University Press. doi: https://www.jstor.org/stable/j.ctv11smrv3

Wan, W.Y., Poynton, S., Van Doorn, G., & Weatherburn, D. (2014). *Trends & issues in crime and criminal justice no. 485: Parole supervision and reoffending.* Australian Institute of Criminology. https://aic.gov.au/publications/tandi/tandi485

Weatherburn, D., & Ringland, C. (2014). *Re-offending on parole.* New South Wales Bureau of Crime Statistics and Research. https://www.bocsar.nsw.gov.au/Pages/bocsar_publication/Pub_Summary/CJB/cjb178-Re-offending-on-parole.aspx

Williams, A. (2006). Paedophiles, panics, and protests: Understanding penal populism. *Japanese Journal of Sociological Criminology, 31,* 52–73. doi: https://researchportal.port.ac.uk/portal/en/publications/paedophiles-panics-and-protests-understanding-penal-populism(074ea298-e9fc-4985-b088-5eabe11caa51).html

Williams, A. (2017). Panic or placebo? Enterprise In the construction of risk and fear of the child sexual offender. In K. McCartan, & H. Kemsahll (Eds.), *Contemporary sex offender risk management volume 1: Perceptions* (pp. 145–178). Palgrave macmillan. doi: https://www.palgrave.com/gp/book/9783319635668

Wilson, D. (2006, 17 June). Saturday comment: The prison trick. *The Guardian*, 25.

Wilson, R. (2007, 19 April). Out in the open. Community Care, np.

Wilson, R., McWhinnie, A., Picheca, J., Prinzo, M., & Cortoni, F. (2007). Circles of Support and Accountability: Engaging community volunteers in the management of high-risk sex offenders. *The Howard Journal of Criminal Justice, 46*(1), 1–15. doi: https://doi.org/10.1111/j.1468-2311.2007.00450.x

Wilson, R., McWhinnie, A., & Wilson, C. (2008). Circles of Support and Accountability: An international partnership in reducing sexual offender recidivism. *Prison Service Journal, 178*, 26–36.

Woodman, S. (2015, 19 October). Chris Hansen is back to catching predators. The New Republic. https://newrepublic.com/article/123138/chris-hansen-back-catching-predators

Yardley, E., Lynes, A., & Wilson, D. (2018). What's the deal with 'websleuthing'? News media representations of amateur detectives in networked spaces. *Crime Media Culture, 14*(1), 81–109. doi: https://doi.org/10.1177/1741659016674045

Chapter 1

Situating Circles of Support and Accountability

Since their emergence in Hamilton, Canada in 1994, following Charlie Taylor's release from prison, Circles of Support and Accountability (CoSA)[1] have spread across the globe. CoSA have been implemented across Canada and in parts of the United States[2] (Bohmert et al., 2018; Chouinard & Riddick, 2014; Duwe, 2013, Duwe, 2018; Elliott et al., 2013; Elliott & Zajac, 2015; Fox, 2013, Fox, 2014, Fox, 2015, Fox, 2016, Fox, 2017), the United Kingdom (Bates et al., 2007; Bates et al., 2012; McCartan, 2016; McCartan et al., 2014a, b, c; Nellis, 2009; Thomas et al., 2014; Thompson, 2015; Thompson et al., 2017; Winder et al., 2020), New Zealand[3] (Lowe, 2017; Lowe et al., 2019; van Rensburg, 2012), parts of Europe (Höing, 2015; Höing, Bogaerts, et al., 2016, 2017; Höing et al., 2010, 2013, 2015; Höing, Petrina, et al., 2016; Höing, Vogelvang, et al., 2017; Petrina et al., 2015), and South Australia (Richards et al., 2020; Richards & McCartan, 2018). CoSA differ considerably by location; while the overview here is designed to offer a general introduction, specifics will inevitably vary.

CoSA have twin objectives: to reintegrate people with sexual offence convictions into the community; and to reduce the sexual victimisation. The aligned twin mantras of CoSA are: "no one is disposable" (or "no one is dispensable") and "no more victims" (Hannem & Petrunik, 2007; Liautaud, 2010). CoSA also have twin methods for reaching these objectives: support and accountability. The collective mission of CoSA according to CoSA Canada is "to substantially reduce the risk of future sexual victimization of community members by assisting and supporting released individuals in their task of integrating with the community and leading responsible, productive, and accountable lives" (see http://cosacanada.com). In McAlinden's (2007, p. 168) terms, CoSA "have a dual responsibility to be caring for the offender often in the midst of wider public hostility, and at the same time to be concerned that community safety is not compromised". (see also Heise et al., 1996).

DOI: 10.4324/9781003125532-2

How Do CoSA Work?

How, then, do CoSA work in practice? This is not an easy question to answer, especially as CoSA practice continues to evolve (see e.g., CoSA Canada, 2020). It is important to note here that CoSA are not a "program" as such, although CoSA advocates and scholars (myself included) often slip into using this shorthand. CoSA are not a "program" in the ordinary sense of the word – i.e. the weekly meetings of the core members and volunteers that form the basis of the approach are not extensively structured or formulaic. Rather, discussion commonly focuses on the core member's progress against his aims, struggles that he may be experiencing, and how these might be addressed. In other words, CoSA may vary considerably from one another, and there is no set content being delivered in the same way that there would be in, for example, a treatment program relating to sexual offending. Volunteers do receive guidance on tools they might use within Circles as well as from their training, codes of conduct and so on (e.g., https://www.edmontoncosa.org/volunteering-with-cosa/volunteer-code-of-conduct/). CoSA programs in some parts of the world also receive operational support from an umbrella agency. For example, an operational framework of good practice has provided guidance and support in Canada since 2017, and both Circles UK (www.circles-uk.org.uk) and CirclesEurope (https://www.circleseurope.eu/) provide support for good practice. For the purposes of this book, I use the term "CoSA program" to refer to the organisations that deliver multiple CoSA rather than to individual Circles (e.g., "the Fresno CoSA program").

As CoSA have developed and matured around the world, they have come to rely on a variety of operating models, receiving funding from a variety of sources (including government and philanthropic) and having varying relationships with the respective criminal justice systems that form their local backdrop. While CoSA historically usually commenced once an offender has been released from prison, as was the case with Charlie Taylor and Wray Budreo, increasingly, staff meet with the offender prior to his release from prison (see e.g., Kitson-Boyce, 2018). This was the case in the flagship Minnesota CoSA ("MNCoSA") model. The Safer Living Foundation in the United Kingdom has likewise recently adopted a model that commences in prison prior to an offender's release to the community (Kitson-Boyce, 2018). Despite such differences, CoSA programs operate on the same premise: that by providing core members with a Circle of community volunteers who provide practical support and accountability, offenders will be better equipped to lead law-abiding lives in the community. As Almond et al. (2015, p. 27) saw it:

> The role of the CoSA is to develop interpersonal contact between the core member and the wider community in order to generate the kind of social capital that militates against future offending; core members

> openly discuss their behaviours and thoughts with the circle volunteers, and are answerable to them for any deviations from their own aspirations to live non-offending lives.

Individual Circles usually meet weekly in the first instance, although the frequency of meetings may decrease over time as a core member becomes reintegrated into the broader community. At least, this is usually the stated aim of CoSA that Circles last for 12–18 months, by which time the core member is sufficiently integrated into other social and community networks that a formal CoSA is no longer necessary or desired (Hanvey et al., 2011). In practice, however, some Circles, such as those run by the Minnesota Department of Corrections, last for a shorter time (Duwe, 2018). More significantly, many others last well beyond the envisaged 12–18 months period, placing significant resource burdens on CoSA programs (Richards, 2011). Some core members simply lack the necessary skills and attributes to form relationships and networks outside of their Circle, and often remain in a formal Circle, or at least in contact with a CoSA program, for a longer time. This is particularly so for core members who have cognitive impairments and/or mental illnesses and is no doubt exacerbated by the very rigid conditions under which some core members live. Such conditions may prohibit offenders from forming new relationships, such as romantic relationships, without disclosing their offending history. In other cases, Circles may end due to core members being recalled to prison for breaches of their statutory conditions or due to concerns raised about their behaviour by volunteers and/or staff[4] (Lowe & Willis, 2019; Quaker Peace and Social Witness, 2005, 2008; discussed further below). Core members may also opt to stop participating in a Circle for a range of practical and personal reasons (Elliott et al., 2013; Quaker Peace and Social Witness, 2005, 2008; Richards, 2011). Importantly, CoSA were initially envisaged to last as long as necessary to mitigate the risk posed by a core member. As Heise et al. (1996, p. 16) stated:

> [Ideally, a Circle] maintains the necessary supports for as long as necessary to reduce the risk effectively. Each Circle and plan has its own personality because it is designed around the unique profile of the Core Member. The life of a Circle extends as long as the risks to the community and the Core Member are above average. The intensity with which members of the Circle are intrusively involved in the life of the Core Member varies and will, hopefully, diminish.

In practice, CoSA last for varying lengths of time. Duwe (2013) initially reported that in Minnesota, CoSA generally lasted for at least one year, but later reported that most CoSA last between 6 and 12 months (Duwe, 2018).

Weekly meetings may be supplemented, especially in the early days of an offender's release from prison (Duwe, 2013), with regular contacts (e.g., 2–3 additional contacts per week) with individual Circle volunteers (Heise et al., 1996), at the discretion of a given CoSA program. This depends on the level of need, availability of other community resources, safety concerns identified by the site, and number and availability of volunteers (L. Joly, personal communication, 16 January 2021). Volunteers commonly help core members with the practical tasks associated with re-entering the community after prison, such as obtaining identification documents, finding or settling into temporary accommodation, shopping for necessary items such as clothing and groceries, and so on (McCartan & Kemshall, 2020). As many individuals convicted of sexual crimes have served very long prison terms, they often also require assistance with technological changes to which they have not been exposed in prison, such as electronic banking, smart telephones and electronic public transport passes. Volunteers also help smooth a core member's transition back to the community by simply offering support and encouragement, meeting for a coffee or meal and offering a listening ear. Historically, Circle volunteers may also have provided a liaison point between the core member and agencies such as police, as well as the media and concerned community groups (Heise et al., 1996); in Canada today, this role is undertaken by paid CoSA staff as a matter of good practice, or by others exceptionally with the agreement of staff (L. Joly, personal communication, 16 January 2021).

CoSA are underpinned by a written agreement between the core member and volunteers, sometimes called a "contract" or "covenant". As Heise et al. (1996, pp. 16–17) explained:

> The Core Member and other members of the Circle enter into a mutual agreement, or covenant. The covenant, signed by all Circle Members and the Core Member, establishes conditions of behaviour and associations for the ex-offender and clarifies the expectations to be met by the Circle. It establishes procedures for dealing with breaches of the agreement and failure to meet the conditions. Consequences may include notification of authorities or potential withdrawal of support. The covenant is reviewed at regular intervals and revised when necessary.

While the specific content of covenants (now called Circle agreements in Canada) will vary according to the individual Circle, these agreements typically cover confidentiality expectations, safety procedures and protocols for responding to "warning signs" in the core member's behaviour (Heise et al., 1996, p. 17). In Canada, a national Circle agreement template is now used as the basis of agreements, which each Circle is able to customise to respond to the specific circumstances and characteristics of the core member.

Who Volunteers in CoSA?

You may be wondering who on earth would volunteer their time to support a person convicted of sexual offences. You certainly wouldn't be the first. Media coverage about CoSA consistently refers to CoSA volunteers in superlative terms, as "courageous, dedicated" (Laycock, 2014), "heroic" ("Walking with the monsters among us", 2015), unique and special. They undertake work that "few Canadians are prepared to do" (Walking with the monsters among us, 2015) and adhere to values that "few would be willing to rise to" (Bongers, 2003).

In practice around the world, CoSA volunteers come from a range of age groups and educational, social, cultural and employment backgrounds (Circles South East, 2012; Elliott et al., 2013; Gilliam et al., 2021; Höing, Bogaerts, et al., 2016, 2017; Hough, 2015; Richards, 2011). The small number of existing studies on the motivations of CoSA volunteers have found that adhering to the principles of "restorative justice" (discussed further in Chapter 2) and wanting to contribute to community safety and wellbeing are important motivating factors for CoSA volunteers (see generally Armstrong et al., 2008; Farrington, 2015; Hannem, 2011; Silverman & Wilson, 2002; Wilson et al., 2005, 2007), as they are having a professional interest in criminal justice stemming from current or intended employment; coming from a faith background and/or having a personal interest in social and/or criminal justice issues (Almond et al., 2015; see further Circles South East, 2012; Lowe, 2017; Richards et al., 2020a).

Thompson et al.'s (2017) research on 20 CoSA volunteers from England and Wales categorised volunteers' motivations as either "inward" (i.e. benefiting the volunteer by providing work skills and experience) or "outward" (i.e. altruistic and wanting to help others in the community) (see further Bellamy & Watson, 2013; Richards et al., 2020). Importantly, while 40 percent of volunteers in Thompson et al.'s (2017) study cited "inward" motivations for joining a CoSA in the first instance, a high degree of "motivational drift" occurred over time (Thompson et al., 2017). In other words, many volunteers may initially take part in a CoSA to build their resumé, but over time become committed to the work due to developing more altruistic concerns. Volunteers often also report multiple, interconnected reasons for participating in CoSA (Armstrong et al., 2008).

An often-overlooked group of CoSA volunteers is those who have experienced sexual violence themselves, and those who have been close to a victim/survivor of sexual violence. Some volunteers report that their own experiences of sexual violence are the main catalyst for their decision to volunteer with CoSA. Indeed, Wager and Wilson (2017) estimated that 20–25 percent of CoSA volunteers in the United Kingdom are victims/survivors of sexual violence (see also Richards, 2011). Almond et al. (2015) found that 13 of the 160 volunteers they surveyed reported that personal experience as a survivor of sexual violence was a factor that motivated them to join a CoSA, and McCartan's (2016) research found that knowing victims/survivors of sexual abuse was a motivating factor for some volunteers (see also Kerr et al., 2018). As one volunteer (cited in Richards et al., 2020, p. 43) in the Adelaide, South Australia CoSA program described her motivation to volunteer in CoSA:

> Actually, it's very personal – I wanted to work within the CoSA program because I'm a victim myself. So I can look at it from a way that children need to be kept safe…I think from a victim's point of view, the program was really important, and I could look at the program in a really positive way….Being a victim, it's so important to me – that's why I grabbed on to this [CoSA] when it came along, because nothing else is helping…We need to start focusing on something that's going to stop the problem… we need to start concentrating on what we can do to minimise what's happening to children.

There has been some reticence about including victims/survivors as CoSA volunteers (McWhinnie & Wilson, nd), due to concerns that volunteering may retraumatise victims/survivors and that they will be "drawn into this field in order to resolve their own traumas" (Wager & Wilson, 2017, p. 265). In some cases, it appears that victims/survivors of sexual violence are screened out as volunteers as they are deemed too vulnerable to participate in CoSA (Armstrong et al., 2008). Hinton (2008) even argued that "I doubt that any survivor can participate in COSA without experiencing some degree of re-victimization or triggering of our past abuse". The sole research study that has been conducted specifically on victims/survivors as CoSA volunteers, conducted by Wager and Wilson (2017), involved interviewing 13 CoSA volunteers from one CoSA program, five of whom identified as victims/survivors of sexual violence, and the remainder of whom did not. The authors found that while other volunteers tended to be concerned that victim/survivor volunteers would be retraumatised by CoSA, this was not the case. They also found that the victim/survivor volunteers in the study were not "seeking self-healing or [volunteering] in order to undergo a process of meaning-making. Rather they come to CoSA once they have transitioned from victim to survivor" (Wager & Wilson, 2017, pp. 279–280). Whatever the reason for their participation, research shows that volunteers gain satisfaction from participating in CoSA (Höing et al., 2015a; Hough, 2015). Indeed, many CoSA programs rely on volunteers returning to take part in subsequent Circles, and on word-of-mouth from current to prospective volunteers to ensure they have sufficient volunteer numbers (Richards, 2011, p. 26).

All prospective CoSA volunteers are screened and receive training prior to being assigned to a Circle, although this training varies in scope and content across the globe (Richards, 2011). Volunteers are usually informed about the core member's offending history to equip them to identify any thought or behaviour patterns that might lead to the core member reoffending (Hanvey et al., 2011). For example, if a core member had a particular offending *modus operandi* that resulted in offending in the past, volunteers are informed of this so that they can identify it before reoffending occurs. Training might also cover topics such as offender typologies, the criminal justice process, understanding group dynamics, monitoring of the offender and volunteer self-care (Circles South East, 2012; Heise et al., 1996; Thomas et al., 2014; Wilson, McWhinnie, et al., 2007; Wilson, Picheca, et al., 2007a); again, this varies according to location.

Of course, the proverbial buck does not stop with volunteers. Instead, CoSA volunteers are supported by a range of criminal justice and other professionals (e.g., therapists, probation and parole officers, police, CoSA program staff, etc.) to whom they can turn if issues arise in a Circle and/or they need to seek professional advice. (Furthermore, volunteers are sometimes former criminal justice professionals themselves (Thompson et al., 2017)). This may be done on a formal or informal basis. Typically, CoSA are managed by a paid program staff member acting in the role of Circles Coordinator (see Figure 1.1), who is the primary contact point between CoSA volunteers and a network of criminal justice and related professionals (Heise et al., 1996). In other cases, one of the Circle volunteers is appointed to this role. Where necessary, volunteers report back to the Circle Coordinator about the activities of the Circle and the attitudes and behaviours of the core member. The Circle Coordinator may in turn report any concerns to statutory authorities such as a probation and parole officer, if required. As noted above, this has resulted on some occasions in an offender being recalled to prison (Bates et al., 2007; Quaker Peace and Social Witness, 2005, 2008). (In other cases, issues may be dealt with in the Circle. For example, my recent research (Richards et al., 2020, p. 55) documents an incident in the Adelaide CoSA program in which

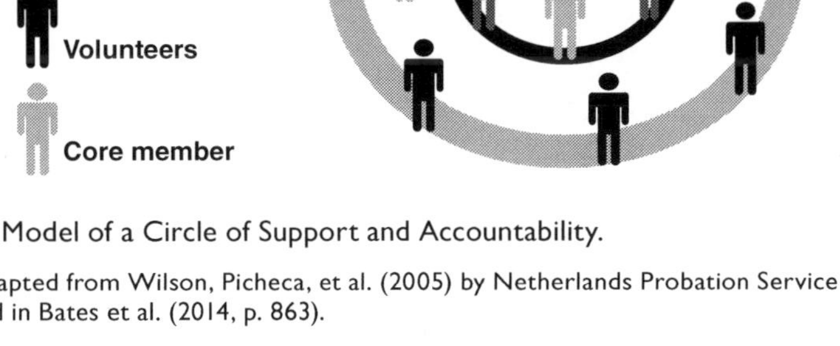

Figure 1.1 Model of a Circle of Support and Accountability.

Source: Adapted from Wilson, Picheca, et al. (2005) by Netherlands Probation Service and reproduced in Bates et al. (2014, p. 863).

a core member showed a volunteer photographs of a child he claimed was his granddaughter. Perturbed about this, Circle volunteers reported the incident to CoSA program staff; it was subsequently dealt with in collaboration with the core member). In the United Kingdom in particular, CoSA volunteers are thus conceptualised as forming an "Inner Circle" around the core member, while a dedicated team of professionals forms an "Outer Circle" (see also Elliott et al., 2013), with the Circles Coordinator being the point of contact between the two (see Figure 1.1).

Do CoSA Work?

CoSA may sound all warm and fuzzy – supporting prisoners to reintegrate into communities, giving power back to ordinary members of the community – but we need to ask: do they work? This question has engaged researchers for nearly as long as CoSA have existed. There is now a substantial body of research about the effectiveness of the CoSA model. A key consideration, however, is: what do we mean when we ask whether CoSA "work"? Does this mean that CoSA help core members reintegrate into the community? Or that CoSA prevent core members from reoffending, thereby protecting the community? The burgeoning body of research from around the globe suggests that CoSA can do both.

A number of research studies have measured the impact that CoSA have on psychosocial outcomes for core members. It has already been well-documented that a range of psychosocial factors, such as access to suitable accommodation, employment and healthy relationships, can reduce reoffending. Investigating whether CoSA meet such aims can therefore provide insight into their contribution towards reducing recidivism. A number of studies, predominantly those conducted in the United Kingdom and Western Europe, document significant improvements for core members across the life of a CoSA. For example, studies have documented improvements in core members' relationships (Bates et al., 2012; Elliott et al., 2017; Winder et al., 2020), education and employment (Bates et al., 2012; Clarke, Warwick, et al., 2017; McCartan et al., 2014a), access to suitable accommodation (Bates et al., 2007; Clarke, Warwick, 2017; Winder et al., 2020), health (Bates et al., 2012), prosocial attitudes (Höing, Vogelvang, et al., 2017), perceptions of social support (Elliott et al., 2017), participation in prosocial activities (McCartan et al., 2014; Winder et al., 2020), emotional regulation and self-esteem (Höing, Vogelvang, et al., 2017), general wellbeing (Winder et al., 2020), sense of hope (Elliott et al., 2017) and goal-setting (Elliott et al., 2017). While this evidence is encouraging, these studies did not use comparison or control groups, meaning that it is not possible to conclude that CoSA caused these changes. In other words, these changes occurred during the core members' involvement in a CoSA but may have occurred as a result of something unrelated to their involvement.

Another group of studies compare individual core members' risk scores at the commencement of their CoSA and again during or at the completion of their CoSA. These studies have produced mixed results. McCartan (2016) analysed data on 27 core members' dynamic risk reviews (DRRs); a 17-point checklist used in the United Kingdom based on four domains of dynamic risk: (1) offence-related sexual interests; (2) pro-offending attitudes; (3) problems in social and emotional functioning; and (4) self-management issues (Bates & Wager, 2012, p. 6) by periodically collecting qualitative and quantitative data from core members and their Circle Coordinators. McCartan (2016) found that the vast majority of core members were considered to have reduced risk of offending at the conclusion of their Circles than at their commencement (although risk fluctuated over the life of Circles). Four of the core members – who were higher risk at the outset – however, had *increased* risk levels. Earnshaw (cited in Clarke, Brown, et al., 2017) reported similar variations in a study of 52 core members' DRRs. Bates and Wager (2012) reported a decrease in the risk posed by core members based on the DRR of 13 core members in the United Kingdom but acknowledged that these reductions may not have been caused solely by core members' participation in CoSA and could be attributable to other factors (as is the case with other similar studies). Höing et al. (cited in Clarke, Brown, et al., 2017) measured the risk of 13 core members in the Netherlands but did not find a significant decrease between 6 and 12 months from the commencement of a CoSA. Most recently, Winder et al. (2020) measured changes in 59 core members' DRR scores and found an 18 percent reduction in risk between their participation in CoSA at three months and nine months.

Another body of research demonstrates that core members report experiencing CoSA in positive terms (McCartan, 2016; McCartan et al., 2014a; Thompson et al., 2017), as do volunteers (Höing, Bogaerts, et al., 2016, 2017; Weaver, 2013). CoSA also reduce criminal justice costs. In the United Kingdom, Elliott and Beech (2012) demonstrated a cost-benefit ratio of £1.04 for every pound spent, and in the United States, Duwe (2018) found that every dollar spent on the Minnesota CoSA program generated an approximate benefit of US$3.73, a 273 percent return on investment (see also Chouinard & Riddick, 2014).

For most of us, however, the most pressing question is whether CoSA can reduce the likelihood that a core member will sexually reoffend once released from prison back into the community. As one CoSA program coordinator whom I met during my Churchill Fellowship put it: "The main thing is preventing reoffending. If the offender gets a life, that's gravy, but it's not the meat and potatoes of CoSA". While others adhere to a different view, championing CoSA as inherently worthwhile regardless of their capacity to reduce reoffending, law- and policy-makers and funding bodies (rightly, in my view) want hard evidence about reoffending rates.

Such evidence is difficult to produce, for a number of reasons. CoSA are, by design, "high-impact, low-volume" (Duwe, 2013, p. 162); in other words, they work intensively with small cohorts of offenders (Richards, 2011). This can mean that there are too few units of analysis (i.e. research participants in the form of core members) for the results of a quantitative study to be able to be generalised (Richards, 2011). As noted above, CoSA also vary significantly across program sites and international contexts, making larger, multi-site evaluations challenging. Furthermore, official rates of sexual recidivism are typically low (Falshaw et al., 2003; Hanson & Bussiere, 1998; Hanson & Morton-Bourgon, 2005), making comparisons among groups of offenders difficult (see Richards, 2011 for a discussion).

Nonetheless, a number of researchers have attempted to overcome these challenges and examine the effect of CoSA on recidivism rates. The first of these studies were conducted by Robin Wilson and his colleagues in Canada. These studies were quasi-experimental in design. In other words, the researchers compared the "treatment" group (i.e. core members) with a matched group of offenders (i.e. a group of offenders who are similar but who did not participate in a CoSA). In the first of these studies, Wilson, Picheca, et al. (2005; Wilson et al., 2007) evaluated the original CoSA pilot program in South Central Ontario. They matched 60 high-risk offenders with sexual offence convictions who participated in a CoSA with 60 high-risk offenders with sexual offence convictions who did not participate in a CoSA. Participants were matched on a number of relevant factors, including their age, risk level, release date, victim profile, prior involvement in treatment specific to sexual offending, and length of time "at large" in the community, and followed for an average of 4.5 years. The study found that recidivism among core members was statistically significantly lower than for the matched group of offenders who did not take part in a CoSA. Compared with the matched group, core members had: 70 percent less sexual recidivism (5% [n = 3] versus 16.7% [n = 10]); 57 percent less violent recidivism (including sexual recidivism) (15% [n = 9] versus 35% [n = 21]); and 35 percent less recidivism of any kind (including sexual and violent recidivism) (28.3% [n = 17] versus 43.4% [n = 26]) (Wilson, Picheca, et al., 2005; Wilson et al., 2007). This study also documented a harm reduction effect – when sexual reoffending did occur, core members had committed offences of a less serious or violent nature than the comparison group members.

Wilson, Cortoni, et al. (2009) later replicated Wilson, Picheca, et al.'s (2005) study using data from CoSA programs across Canada. The researchers again matched a group of core members (n = 44) with offenders (n = 44) who did not participate in a CoSA. The average follow-up time was 35 months. This study found that compared with the matched group of offenders, core members had: 83 percent less sexual recidivism (2.3% [n = 1] versus 13.7% [n = 6]); 73 percent less violent recidivism (including sexual recidivism) (9.1% [n = 4] versus 34.1% [n = 15]); and 71 percent less recidivism of any kind (including sexual and violent recidivism) (11.4% [n = 5] versus 38.9% [n = 17]). While the differences in reoffending rates between CoSA participants and the control group appear substantial in these two studies, Elliott and Zajac (2015) queried whether these might be the result of differences between the two groups (i.e. an example of selection bias). They note that the reason(s) that the control group members did not participate in a CoSA were not explicated in either study and that "If the reason was that they were not suitable candidates for CoSA, it raises questions about potential confounding differences between the experimental and control groups" (Elliott & Zajac, 2015, p. 115). Furthermore, the post-release conditions to which the groups were subject were not described, again potentially meaning that the two groups may have reoffended at different rates for reasons unrelated to their participation in a CoSA (or lack thereof) (Elliott & Zajac, 2015).

More recently, Bates et al. (2014) compared 71 core members involved with Circles South East in the United Kingdom with 71 broadly similar offenders who had been referred to Circles South East but who ultimately had not taken part in a CoSA (e.g., because the program was not available in their local area). The average follow-up period for core members was 53 months; for the comparison group, it was 55 months. Bates et al.'s (2014) analysis found statistically significantly higher violent and higher sexual reoffending among the comparison group than the CoSA group. Harm reduction was again found among the core members (i.e. the small number who did reoffend sexually committed offences of a less serious nature than their previous offending). Elliott and Zajac (2015, p. 115) pointed out, however, that the difference between CoSA participants and control group members is only statistically significant when violent and sexual reoffending are grouped together, and that differences between the two groups in terms of sexual reoffending only would not reach statistical significance.

A limitation of these studies – indeed, any study that uses a quasi-experimental design by matching program participants with a comparison group – is that they do not control for the *motivation* of core members. It is always voluntary for an offender to participate in a CoSA, and while voluntariness may exist along a spectrum (Richards, 2011), it is possible that the treatment and comparison groups in the above studies are not matched on one critical feature – whether participants are motivated not to reoffend once they are released. In other words, it is possible that those who volunteer for CoSA are simply more committed to not reoffending than other offenders, and as a corollary, that reductions in recidivism are an artefact of this commitment rather than of CoSA.

A randomised controlled trial (RCT) is required to test whether CoSA have an impact on recidivism rates while controlling for motivation. RCTs are considered the "gold standard" in evaluation research as they are able to determine causality, not just correlation (Hough, 2010; Wilcox et al., 2005). Only one RCT has been conducted on CoSA to date, in part due to the difficulties associated with evaluating CoSA, as noted above. The RCT was part of an ongoing evaluation of the Minnesota MnCoSA program.

It circumvented the issue of offender motivation by randomly assigning potential core members (i.e. people convicted of sexual offending *who indicated a desire to participate in a CoSA*) into either a CoSA or a control group, and comparing the recidivism of these two groups (Duwe, 2013). The first study published from this RCT (Duwe, 2013) compared 31 core members with 31 control group members and measured the reoffending rates of the two groups for an average of two years. Members of both groups were categorised as Level 2 or "moderate" risk offenders (see Duwe, 2013, for a discussion), and were subject to intensive post-release supervision, curfews, electronic monitoring, sexual offender treatment and alcohol and other drug treatment (Duwe, 2013). This study found significant reductions in rearrests, reincarceration for technical violations as well as reincarceration among the CoSA participants compared with control group members. As there was a very low rate of officially recorded sexual reoffending among both groups, however (i.e. no new sexual offences among CoSA participants and only one among the control group), statistically significant differences were not demonstrated in relation to sexual reoffending (Duwe, 2013). The study did, however, find significantly lower violent recidivism among CoSA core members (Duwe, 2013) and has been widely cited in support of CoSA's efficacy. Nonetheless, the study does not, as Elliott and Zajac (2015) pointed out, provide evidence that CoSA can reduce sexual recidivism – a key aspect of Circles' purpose.

More recent findings from the MnCoSA evaluation (Duwe, 2018) have, however, demonstrated statistically significant differences between core members and the control group. Duwe (2018) compared 50 core members with 50 individuals with sexual offence convictions who were not assigned a CoSA and measured the recidivism of the two groups over an average of 6 years. Duwe (2018) found lower rates of recidivism among core members than among the control group for all six measures of recidivism (rearrest; rearrest for a sexual offense; reconviction; reconviction for a sexual offence; resentence; and technical violation revocation). A statistically significant difference in sexual recidivism was found between the CoSA core members and the control group, with only one core member being rearrested for a new sexual offence compared with seven in the control group (Duwe, 2018, p. 475). The rate of rearrest for a new sexual offence was 88 percent lower for core members than control group members. No CoSA core members were reconvicted (or resentenced) compared with four from the control group (Duwe, 2018, p. 475).

This study thus provides the most rigorous and the most promising evidence about CoSA to date: in Duwe's (2018, p. 48) words, it provides "the strongest evidence to date the CoSA model can be effective in reducing sexual recidivism". As I have argued elsewhere (Richards et al., 2020), the difference in recidivism rates documented by Duwe (2018) may even be an underestimate, if we consider that core members are subject to more scrutiny than their control group counterparts. If core members and control group members committed the same number of reoffences, it stands to reason that more of the offences committed by core members would be detected, as they have CoSA volunteers scrutinising their actions.

A number of caveats should be borne in mind, however. First, the MnCoSA program had a number of key differences from other CoSA programs across the globe. As noted earlier, in Minnesota, CoSA started a number of weeks prior to a core member's release from prison, to ensure that the core member already had a network of support in place prior to his release. This model is not widely used elsewhere, largely for practical reasons (but see Elliott et al., 2017; Kitson-Boyce, 2017, 2018; Kitson-Boyce et al., 2019). Second, the MnCoSA program relied mainly on university students as volunteers, which is not always the case (for a discussion see Elliott et al., 2017; Höing et al., 2015; 2016; Kitson-Boyce, 2017; Lowe, 2017; Thomas et al., 2014). Finally, the MnCoSA program was operated directly by the Minnesota Department of Corrections. Elsewhere, it is typical for governments to fund CoSA programs, but for service delivery to be undertaken by community based non-government organisations. The results of the MnCoSA RCT thus may not be generalisable to CoSA elsewhere (Duwe, 2018). Further, Duwe (2018, p. 480) cautions that the statistical differences between the two groups in terms of sexual recidivism took a number of years to emerge, due primarily to the low rates of recidivism in both the CoSA and control groups: therefore, for other CoSA programs, "a great deal of patience is likely needed to see whether its impact on sexual recidivism ever comes to fruition" (Duwe, 2018, p. 480).

Duwe (2018) also argued that the MnCoSA program was able to successfully reduce sexual reoffending because it targeted higher-risk offenders, and that differences between the two groups may not have emerged if CoSA had been used for individuals deemed lower risk. This is an important point. CoSA emerged as a response to high-risk offenders like Charlie Taylor and Wray Budreo, and many programs claim that CoSA are primarily used for this high-risk population (see e.g., Chouinard & Riddick, 2014). In practice, however, it appears that lower-risk offenders are increasingly recruited into CoSA programs, at least in some locations (McCartan et al., 2014b; Richards et al., 2020); CirclesEurope states that CoSA support medium- and high-risk individuals (https://www.circleseurope.eu/). This is understandable, because CoSA programs may lack the resources to support only very high-risk individuals, and it is likely easier to recruit volunteers for lower-risk offenders. Indeed, McAvoy (2012) found that the less serious a core member's offence, the more likely members of the public would be to volunteer in his CoSA[5]. Nonetheless, if CoSA are primarily effective with high-risk individuals, it stands to reason that CoSA programs should focus on this group of offenders.

Astute readers may be wondering how accurate the studies described above are, given that sexual offending typically occurs in secret. It has been well-documented that sexual offences against children, in particular, have one of the highest rates of attrition from the criminal justice process of any offence (see Introduction). Cases "drop out" of the system at a variety of points along the way, from reporting to conviction, resulting in only a very small proportion of all perpetrators being convicted (Bouhours & Daly, 2008). To some extent these concerns are less relevant in relation to the above studies, as the core members and control group participants were subject to very strict correctional supervision, making reoffending less of a possibility. In Duwe's (2013, 2018) study, for example, participants were subject to intensive post-release correctional supervision, curfews, electronic monitoring, treatment specific to sexual offending and substance abuse treatment. Nonetheless, research in the United Kingdom has sought to circumvent this issue by documenting not only official rearrests and/or reconvictions, but "pro-offending behaviour" among core members (see Richards, 2011 for a discussion). For example, a study by Quaker Peace and Social Witness (2005) on CoSA in the Thames Valley found that none of the 20 core members was reconvicted of a new sexual offence during the period of the research (April 2002–March 2005). However, volunteers identified "pro-offending behaviour" among eight of these core members. One was in possession of pornographic material in which adults were dressed like children, and another had developed a relationship with a single mother who had three underage children (Quaker Peace and Social Witness, 2005; see further Bates et al., 2007). Collectively, these studies suggest that while most core members do not reoffend sexually (at least in the short to medium term), some demonstrate problematic behaviours that might be considered "warnings" or "red flags". As Bates et al. (2007; see also Clarke, Brown, et al., 2017; Nellis, 2009) argued, this should still be considered a success of the CoSA model since by identifying these red flags, volunteers were able to mobilise additional supports or other interventions for the core member. In some cases, the core member was returned to prison for having breached his parole or licence conditions. This may not be how we hope a CoSA will end, but with a goal of increased community safety – no more victims – it may sometimes be a necessary step.

Taken together, the existing body of research on CoSA from around the globe appears promising but does not yet conclusively show that CoSA reduce sexual recidivism. This does not mean that CoSA are ineffective, but rather that, as Clarke, Brown, et al. (2017, p. 469) argue, "we need studies with a sufficiently long follow-up" in order to more conclusively determine CoSA's effectiveness. Nonetheless, the existing research should be considered promising in terms of CoSA's ability to reduce sexual reoffending (Clarke, Brown, et al., 2017; Elliott & Zajac, 2015; Richards et al., 2020).

We understand much less, however, about how CoSA work – about the mechanisms via which CoSA change the behaviour of core members. In short, while it appears that CoSA reduce sexual recidivism, it remains unclear *how* they do so. This book is the first detailed step towards an explanation. The following chapter considers the main existing explanations about how

CoSA work. It introduces and critically analyses the primary theoretical explanations for CoSA's success, and makes a case for a new approach. In doing so, it examines the theoretical and conceptual terrain of restorative justice, reintegrative shaming, and the Risks, Needs, Responsivity and Good Lives models of offender rehabilitation. Most significantly, it situates CoSA within the conceptual domain of desistance-promotion, and outlines the key elements of this position, to lay the groundwork for the chapters that follow.

Notes

1. The term "Circles of Support and Accountability" is variously shortened to "CoSA" or "COSA" in the international body of literature. These acronyms sometimes refer to an individual Circle, and sometimes to plural Circles. Throughout this book, I use the terms "a CoSA" to refer to an individual Circle and "CoSA" to refer to Circles in the plural.
2. In late 2019, the Minnesota Department of Corrections announced that CoSA would not be continued in Minnesota.
3. Funding for CoSA was halted in New Zealand in 2014 after a core member failed to return to prison from temporary release and subsequently absconded from New Zealand (Lowe & Willis, 2019). Following a review of the program, a new pilot was established targeting individuals subject to determinate sentences only (Lowe & Willis, 2019).
4. Staff of CoSA programs in some locations supplement unpaid volunteers and/or regularly participate in Circle meetings to monitor progress.
5. Using an online survey to examine public support for CoSA in Ireland, McAvoy (2012) used vignettes of fictional offenders to determine whether members of the community agreed that a CoSA would be a good idea (for example, "George is 34. He is convicted of raping a 10-year-old boy while working as a school caretaker"; "Karl is 19. He has a sexual relationship with a 15-year-old girl. He is convicted of statutory rape"). The 84 participants in the survey were asked to indicate whether they thought the offender should be provided with a CoSA, and whether they would volunteer to be part of the CoSA. In all cases, a majority of respondents agreed (or strongly agreed) that the offender should be provided with a CoSA. However, much smaller proportions of respondents indicated that they would personally volunteer in a CoSA with any of the fictional offenders. Importantly, smaller proportions indicated that they would volunteer in a CoSA for the most serious offenders. In other words, an inverse relationship appears to exist between the seriousness of a core member's offending, and the likelihood that members of the community would opt to volunteer in a CoSA to support him (see also Höing, Petrina, et al., 2016).

References

Almond, P., Bates, A., & Wilson, C. (2015). Circles of Support and Accountability: Criminal justice volunteers as the 'deliberative public'. *British Journal of Community Justice, 13*(1), 25–40. doi: https://mmuperu.co.uk/bjcj/articles/circles-of-support-and-accountability-criminal-justice-volunteers-as-the-deliberative-public/

Armstrong, S., Chistyakova, Y., Mackenzie, S., & Malloch, M. (2008). *Circles of Support & Accountability: Consideration of the feasibility of pilots in Scotland*. Scottish Centre for Crime & Justice Research. https://www.sccjr.ac.uk/publications/circles-of-support-accountability-consideration-of-the-feasibility-of-pilots-in-scotland/

Bates, A., Macrae, R., Williams, D., & Webb, C. (2012). Ever-increasing circles: A descriptive study of Hampshire and Thames valley Circles of Support and Accountability 2002–09. *Journal of Sexual Aggression, 18*(3), 355–373. doi: https://www.tandfonline.com/doi/abs/10.1080/13552600.2010.544415

Bates, A., Saunders, R., & Wilson, C. (2007). Doing something about it: A follow-up study of sex offenders participating in Thames valley Circles of Support and Accountability. *British Journal of Community Justice, 5*(1), 19–42. doi: https://mmuperu.co.uk/bjcj/wp-content/uploads/sites/2/2020/08/Bates.pdf

Bates, A., & Wager, N. (2012). Assessing dynamic risk in the community: The DRR and Circles of Support and Accountability. *Forensic Update, 108*, 8–16.

Bates, A., Williams, D., Wilson, C., & Wilson, R. (2014). Circles south east: The first 10 years 2002–2012. *International Journal of Offender Therapy and Comparative Criminology, 58*(7), 861–885. doi: https://journals.sagepub.com/doi/10.1177/0306624X13485362

Bellamy, C., & Watson, A. (2013). Reversing the roles: An examination of Circles of Support and Accountability as an example of non-traditional criminal justice groupwork. *Groupwork, 23*(3), 15–31.

Bohmert, M. N., Duwe, G., & Hipple, N. K. (2018). Evaluating restorative justice Circles of Support and Accountability: Can social support overcome structural barriers? *International Journal of Offender Therapy and Comparative Criminology, 62*(3), 739–758. doi: https://doi.org/10.1177/0306624X16652627

Bongers, A. (2003, 9 September). Embracing lowest of the low. *The Spectator*, A.04.

Bouhours, B., & Daly, K. (2008). *Rape and attrition in the legal process: A comparative analysis of five countries*. Griffith University School of Criminology and Criminal Justice. https://www.jstor.org/stable/10.1086/653101?seq=1#metadata_info_tab_contents

Chouinard, J., & Riddick, C. (2014). *An evaluation of the Circles of Support and Accountability demonstration project: Final report*. Collaborative Centre for Justice and Safety. https://www.justiceandsafety.ca/rsu_docs/cosa-final-report-with-cover.pdf

Circles South East. (2012). *Ten years, one hundred circles: Community safety – what can be done*. Circles South East. http://circlessoutheast.org.uk/wp-content/uploads/2016/06/HTV-10-Year-Report.pdf

Clarke, M., Brown, S., & Völlm, B. (2017). Circles of Support and Accountability for sex offenders: A systematic review of outcomes. *Sexual Abuse, 29*(5), 446–478.

Clarke, M., Warwick, L., & Völlm, B. (2017). Circles of Support and Accountability: The characteristics of core members in England and Wales. *Criminal Behaviour and Mental Health, 27*(2), 191–206. doi: https://doi.org/10.1011/cbm.2003

CoSA Canada. (2020). *2019–20 annual report*. CoSA Canada. https://assets.website-files.com/602ac6c7bf34e81b6e0e9121/606490539cc69fe1e503b2b7_Annual%20Report%20-%202019-20.pdf

Duwe, G. (2013). Can Circles of Support and Accountability (COSA) work in the United States? Preliminary results from a randomized experiment in Minnesota. *Sexual Abuse: A Journal of Research and Treatment, 25*(2), 143–165. doi: https://journals.sagepub.com/doi/10.1177/1079063212453942

Duwe, G. (2018). Can Circles of Support and Accountability (CoSA) significantly reduce sexual recidivism? Results from a randomized controlled trial in Minnesota. *Journal of Experimental Criminology, 14*(4), 463–484.

Elliott, H., Winder, B., Lievesley, R., Blagden, N., Kitson-Boyce, R., & Dwerryhouse, M. (2017). Evaluation of safer living foundation Circles of Support and Accountability. Nottingham. file:///H:/Desktop/SLF-CoSA-Evaluation-Update-Report-June-2017.pdf

Elliott, I., & Beech, A. (2012). A UK cost-benefit analysis of Circles of Support and Accountability interventions. *Sexual Abuse: A Journal of Research and Treatment, 25*(3), 211–229. doi: https://journals.sagepub.com/doi/10.1177/1079063212443385

Elliott, I., & Zajac, G. (2015). The implementation of Circles of Support and Accountability in the United States. *Aggression and Violent Behavior, 25*, 113–123. doi: https://www.sciencedirect.com/science/article/pii/S1359178915000993?via%3Dihub

Elliott, I., Zajac, G., & Meyer, C. (2013). *Evaluability assessment of the Circles of Support and Accountability (COSA) model.* Department of Justice. https://www.ojp.gov/pdffiles1/nij/grants/243832.pdf

Falshaw, L., Friendship, C., & Bates, A. (2003). *Sexual offenders – Measuring reconviction, reoffending and recidivism.* Home Office. doi: https://bpspsychub.onlinelibrary.wiley.com/doi/abs/10.1348/135532503322362979

Farrington, P. (2015). *Circles of Support and Accountability: the role of social support in preventing sexual offender recidivism* [PhD thesis, University of Birmingham]. Birmingham.

Fox, K. (2013). *Circles of Support and Accountability: Final report prepared for the state of Vermont department of corrections.* Vermont Department of Corrections. https://legislature.vermont.gov/Documents/2020/WorkGroups/Senate%20Institutions/Dept.%20of%20Corrections/State%20Workforce%20Development/W~Susan%20Russell~Circles%20of%20Support%20and%20Accountability,%202013,%20Kathryn%20Fox,%20Ph.D.%20UVM~1-10-2020.pdf

Fox, K. (2014). Restoring the social: Offender reintegration in a risky world. *International Journal of Offender Therapy and Comparative Criminology, 38*(3), 235–256. doi: https://www.tandfonline.com/doi/abs/10.1080/01924036.2013.848221

Fox, K. (2015). Theorizing community integration as desistance-promotion. *Criminal Justice and Behavior, 42*(1), 82–94. doi: https://doi.org/10.1177/0093854814550028

Fox, K. (2016). Civic commitment: Promoting desistance through community integration. *Punishment & Society, 18*(1), 68–94. doi: https://journals.sagepub.com/doi/abs/10.1177/1462474515623102?journalCode=puna

Fox, K. (2017). Contextualising the policy and pragmatics of reintegrating sex offenders. *Sexual Abuse: A Journal of Research and Treatment, 29*(1), 28–50. doi: https://journals.sagepub.com/doi/10.1177/1079063215574711

Gilliam, M., Novak, M., Bohmert, M. N., & Duwe, G. (2021). Desires and desirability of volunteers in CoSA programs. *Sexual Abuse, 33*(4), 406–433. doi: https://journals.sagepub.com/doi/abs/10.1177/1079063220912454?journalCode=saxb

Hannem, S. (2011). Experiences in reconciling risk management and restorative justice: How Circles of Support and Accountability work restoratively in the risk society. *International Journal of Offender Therapy and Comparative Criminology, 57*(3), 269–288. doi: https://journals.sagepub.com/doi/10.1177/0306624X11432538

Hannem, S., & Petrunik, M. (2007). Circles of Support and Accountability: A community justice initiative for the reintegration of high-risk sex offenders. *Contemporary Justice Review, 10*(2), 153–171. doi: https://doi.org/10.1080/10282580701372046

Hanson, K., & Bussiere, M. (1998). Predicting relapse: A meta-analysis of sexual offender recidivism studies. *Journal of Consulting and Clinical Psychology, 66*(2), 348–362. doi: https://psycnet.apa.org/doiLanding?doi=10.1037%2F0022-006X.66.2.348

Hanson, K., & Morton-Bourgon, K. (2005). The characteristics of persistent sexual offenders: A meta-analysis of recidivism studies. *Journal of Consulting and Clinical Psychology, 73*(6), 1154–1163. doi: https://doi.apa.org/doiLanding?doi=10.1037%2F0022-006X.73.6.1154

Hanvey, S., Philpot, T., & Wilson, C. (Eds.). (2011). *A community-based approach to the reduction of sexual reoffending*. Jessica Kingsley Publishers

Heise, E., Horne, L., Kirkegaard, H., Nigh, H., Peters Derry, I., Steinmann, V., Yantzi, M., & Worth, D. (1996). *Community reintegration project: A pilot project meeting the needs of communities for enhanced safety by providing circles of support for released sex offenders discharged at warrant expiry from federal Institutions*. Mennonite Central Committee Ontario.

Hinton, A. (2008). *Circles of Support and Accountability: Are you ready to be a volunteer? Information for survivors*. Fresno Pacific University Center for Peacemaking and Conflict Studies.

Höing, M. (2015). *Empowering circles: CoSA and their contribution to a safer society* [PhD thesis, Tilburg University]. Tilburg.

Höing, M., Bogaerts, S., & Vogelvang, B. (2013). Circles of Support and Accountability: How and why they work for sex offenders. *Journal of Forensic Psychology Practice, 13*(4), 267–295. doi: https://www.tandfonline.com/doi/abs/10.1080/15228932.2013.808526

Höing, M., Bogaerts, S., & Vogelvang, B. (2016). Helping sex offenders to desist offending: The gains and drains for CoSA volunteers – A review of the literature. *Sexual Abuse, 28*(5), 364–402. doi: https://journals.sagepub.com/doi/abs/10.1177/1079063214535816?journalCode=saxb

Höing, M., Bogaerts, S., & Vogelvang, B. (2017). Volunteers in Circles of Support and Accountability: Job demands, job resources, and outcomes. *Sexual Abuse, 29*(6), 541–562. doi: https://doi.org/10.0077/1079063215612441

Höing, M., Duke, L., & Völlm, B. (2015). *Circles of Support and Accountability European handbook*. Avans University of Applied Sciences Centre for Public Safety and Criminal Justice. https://www.circles-uk.org.uk/circles4eu/what-is-circles-4eu

Höing, M., Petrina, R., Duke, L., Völlm, B., & Vogelvang, B. (2016). Community support for sex offender rehabilitation in Europe. *European Journal of Criminology, 13*(4), 491–516. doi: https://journals.sagepub.com/doi/abs/10.1177/1477370816633259

Höing, M., Snatersen, Y., & Pasmans, V. (2010). *COSA in Belgium: Summary Circles Europe*. http://www.iga-bg.org/proekti/rates/Prevencia/10-0379_COSA_in_Belgium_summary_def.pdf

Höing, M., Vogelvang, B., & Bogaerts, S. (2017). "I am a different man now" – sex offenders in Circles of Support and Accountability: A prospective study. *International Journal of Offender Therapy and Comparative Criminology, 61*(7), 751–772. doi: https://doi.org/10.1177/0306624X15612431

Hough, A. (2015). *Examining resilience, motivation and impact in volunteers working with sexual offenders* [PhD thesis, University of York]. York.

Hough, M. (2010). Gold standard or fool's gold? The pursuit of certainty in experimental criminology. *Criminology and Criminal Justice, 10*(1), 11–22. doi: https://journals.sagepub.com/doi/10.1177/1748895809352597

Kerr, N., Tully, R., & Völlm, B. (2018). Volunteering with sex offenders: The attitudes of volunteers towards sex offenders, their treatment, and rehabilitation. *Sexual Abuse: A Journal of Research and Treatment, 30*(6), 659–675. doi: https://doi.org/10.1177/10790663217691964

Kitson-Boyce, R. (2017). *A prison-based model of Circles of Support and Accountability: Exploring core member and volunteer experience* [PhD thesis, Nottingham Trent University].

Kitson-Boyce, R. (2018). The prison-based model of Circles of Support and Accountability and its application in transitioning to the community. In H. Elliott, K. Hocken, R. Lievesley, N. Blagden, B. Winder, & P. Banyard (Eds.), *Sexual crime and circles of support and accountability* (pp. 71–104). Palgrave Macmillan. doi: https://www.palgrave.com/gp/book/9783319748221

Kitson-Boyce, R., Blagden, N., Winder, B., & Dillon, G. (2019). Supporting desistance through ambiguous practice: What can be learned from the first prison-based model of CoSA in England and Wales? *Journal of Forensic Psychology Research and Practice, 19*(2), 186–209. doi: https://www.tandfonline.com/doi/full/10.1080/24732850.2019.1571362

Laycock, M. (2014, 1 October). *Volunteers helping to stop child sex abusers are praised.* York Press.

Liautaud, M. (2010). Sex offenders in the pew. *Christianity Today September*, 48–53. https://www.christianitytoday.com/ct/2010/september/21.49.html

Lowe, G. (2017). *Circles of Support and Accountability: An investigation of volunteer motivation and experiences, and the effect of the "sex offender" label on community attitudes towards individuals who have sexually offended* [PhD thesis, University of Auckland]. Auckland.

Lowe, G., & Willis, G. (2019). Looking inside a circle: Volunteer experiences of Circles of Support and Accountability. *Psychiatry, Psychology and Law, 26*(1), 129–149. doi: https://www.tandfonline.com/doi/full/10.1080/13218719.2018.1485521

Lowe, G., Willis, G., & Gibson, K. (2019). You do what? A qualitative investigation into the motivation to volunteer with Circles of Support and Accountability. *Sexual Abuse, 31*(2), 237–260. doi: https://doi.org/10.1177/1079063217729157

McAlinden, A. M. (2007). *The shaming of sexual offenders: Risk, retribution and reintegration.* Hart Publishing. doi: https://www.bloomsburyprofessional.com/uk/the-shaming-of-sexual-offenders-9781841135922/.

McAvoy, J. (2012). *Birds of a feather? Irish public attitudes towards sex crime and sex offender reintegration. Is there a publically perceived scale of sexual deviance?* [Master's thesis, Dublin Institute of Technology]. Dublin.

McCartan, K. (2016). *Circles of Support and Accountability social impact evaluation: Final report.* Cabinet Office. https://1library.net/document/zkwvj01z-circles-support-accountability-social-impact-evaluation-final-report.html

McCartan, K., & Kemshall, H. (2020). The potential role of recovery capital in stopping sexual offending: Lessons from Circles of Support and Accountability to enrich practice. *Irish Probation Journal, 17*, 87–106. doi: https://www.pbni.org.uk/wp-content/uploads/2020/11/Kieran-McCartan-and-Hazel-Kemshall.pdf.

McCartan, K., Kemshall, H., Westwood, S., Cattel, J., MacKenzie, G., & Solle, J. (2014a). *Circles of Support and Accountability: A qualitative analysis.* Ministry of Justice.

McCartan, K., Kemshall, H., Westwood, S., Solle, J., MacKenzie, G., Cattel, J., & Pollard, A. (2014b). *Circles of Support and Accountability (CoSA): A case file review of two pilots.* Ministry of Justice. https://assets.publishing.service.gov.uk/government/uploads/system/uploads/attachment_data/file/293400/cosa-research-summary.pdf

McCartan, K., Kemshall, H., Westwood, S., Solle, J., MacKenzie, G., Cattel, J., & Pollard, A. (2014c). *Circles of Support and Accountability (CoSA): A case file review of two pilots (Annexes).* Ministry of Justice. https://assets.publishing.service.gov.uk/government/uploads/system/uploads/attachment_data/file/293401/cosa-research-summary-annexes.pdf

McWhinnie, A., & Wilson, R. (nd). *A quick reference guide for new CoSA coordinators.* Counseling & Psychotherapy Centers of America.

Nellis, M. (2009). Circles of Support and Accountability for sex offenders in England and Wales: Their origins and implementation between 1999–2005. *British Journal of Community Justice*, 7(1), 23–44. doi: https://www.proquest.com/docview/203787263?pq-origsite=gscholar&fromopenview=true

Petrina, R., Alards, A., & Höing, M. (2015). *Best practices in COSA*. Circles4EU. https://jimdo-storage.global.ssl.fastly.net/file/ee4ad48e-d8ec-49d2-b33a-241314920ab6/Best-practices-in-COSA.pdf

Quaker Peace and Social Witness. (2005). *Circles of Support and Accountability in the Thames valley: The first three years April 2002 to March 2005*. Quaker Peace and Social Witness. https://docu.tips/preview/circles-of-support-and-accountability-first-3yrs-5c15e1771626e

Quaker Peace and Social Witness. (2008). *HTV circles – six years of safer communities: Six year report April 2002 to March 2008*. Quaker Peace and Social Witness. https://www.yumpu.com/en/document/read/24121118/htv-circles-six-years-of-safer-communities-quakers

Richards, K. (2011). *The potential of Circles of Support and Accountability (COSA) to reduce child sexual abuse in Australia*. Winston Churchill Memorial Trust. https://www.churchilltrust.com.au/media/fellows/Richards_Kelly_2010.pdf

Richards, K., Death, J., & McCartan, K. (2020). *Community-based approaches to sexual offender reintegration*. Australia's National Research Organisation for Women's Safety. https://www.anrows.org.au/project/community-based-approaches-to-sexual-offender-reintegration/

Richards, K., & McCartan, K. (2018). Public opinion about Circles of Support and Accountability: A qualitative analysis. *Deviant Behavior: An Interdisciplinary Journal, 39*(3), 400–416. doi: https://www.tandfonline.com/doi/abs/10.1080/01639625.2017.1304800

Silverman, J., & Wilson, D. (2002). *Innocence betrayed: Paedophilia, the media and society*. Polity. doi: https://www.wiley.com/en-us/Innocence+Betrayed%3A+Paedophilia%2C+the+Media+and+Society-p-9780745628899

Thomas, T., Thompson, D., & Karstedt, S. (2014). *Assessing the impact of Circles of Support and Accountability on the reintegration of adults convicted of sexual offences in the community*. University of Leeds Centre for Criminal Justice Studies

Thompson, D. (2015). *Moving on after getting out: Support and accountability for convicted sex offenders* [PhD thesis, University of Leeds]. Leeds. https://etheses.whiterose.ac.uk/13410/1/Thompson_D_Law_PhD_2015.pdf

Thompson, D., Thomas, T., & Karstedt, S. (2017). *The resettlement of sex offenders after custody: Circles of Support and Accountability*. Routledge. doi: https://www.routledge.com/The-Resettlement-of-Sex-Offenders-after-Custody-Circles-of-Support-and/Thompson-Thomas/p/book/9780367227111

van Rensburg, J. (2012). The dawn of Circles of Support and Accountability in New Zealand. *Sexual Abuse in Australia and New Zealand, 4*(2), 30–35. doi: https://search.informit.org/doi/10.3316/INFORMIT.032330761147853

Wager, N., & Wilson, C. (2017). Circles of Support and Accountability: Survivors as volunteers and the restorative potential. In E. Zinsstag, & M. Keenan (Eds.), *Restorative responses to sexual violence: Legal, social and therapeutic dimensions* (pp. 265–282). Routledge. doi: https://www.routledge.com/Restorative-Responses-to-Sexual-Violence-Legal-Social-and-Therapeutic/Zinsstag-Keenan/p/book/9780367226480

Walking with the monsters among us. (2015, 24 July). *National Post*, A8.

Weaver, M. (2013). *From the prison of stereotype to the freedom of relationship: Welcoming the otherwise despised in a Circle of Support and Accountability* [Doctor of Ministry, St Stephen's College]. Edmonton.

Wilcox, A., Hoyle, C., & Young, R. (2005). Are randomised controlled trials really the 'gold standard' in restorative justice research? *British Journal of Community Justice, 3*(2), 39–49.

Wilson, R., Cortoni, F., & McWhinnie, A. (2009). Circles of Support and Accountability: A Canadian replication of outcome findings. *Sexual Abuse: A Journal of Research and Treatment, 21*(4), 412–430. doi: https://journals.sagepub.com/doi/10.1177/1079063209347724

Wilson, R., McWhinnie, A., Picheca, J., Prinzo, M., & Cortoni, F. (2007). Circles of Support and Accountability: Engaging community volunteers in the management of high-risk sex offenders. *The Howard Journal of Criminal Justice, 46*(1), 1–15. doi: https://doi.org/10.1111/j.1468-2311.2007.00450.x

Wilson, R., Picheca, J., & Prinzo, M. (2005). *Circles of Support and Accountability: An evaluation of the pilot project in South-Central Ontario*. Correctional Service Canada. https://www.csc-scc.gc.ca/research/092/r168_e.pdf

Winder, B., Blagden, N., Lievesley, R., Dwerryhouse, M., Kitson-Boyce, R., & Elliott, H. (2020). *UK national evaluation of big lottery funded Circles of Support and Accountability*. Nottingham Trent University Sexual Offences Crime and Misconduct Research Unit. https://www.circles-uk.org.uk/images/documents/SOCAMRU_BL_final_report_1_April_2020_v82.pdf

Chapter 2

Theorising Circles of Support and Accountability

This Chapter outlines and critically analyses existing theoretical explanations that relate to Circles of Support and Accountability (CoSA). It unpacks the related but distinct concepts of rehabilitation, reintegration and desistance, which are frequently conflated in CoSA scholarship, and makes a case for how CoSA should be situated within this conceptual terrain. It also critically discusses different types of theory (explanatory versus normative) and demonstrates the varying ways in which existing attempts to theorise CoSA align with these. It assesses the most common theoretical explanations for CoSA – the good lives model and risk, needs, responsivity model, restorative justice and reintegrative shaming – and posits the need for a better theoretical fit. Building on the work of Fox (2015), it makes a case that CoSA ought to be conceptualised as desistance-promotion, and provides an overview of the key components of this theoretical framework.

Existing Theorisations of CoSA

Like a number of other criminal justice measures, such as victim-offender mediation (Peachey, 1989), CoSA emerged organically. In other words, they emerged from below – CoSA were "developed by practitioners and can be regarded as a truly practice-based intervention" (Höing et al., 2013, p. 269). As a result, CoSA were not, and to a large extent are still not, informed by theory. As described in the introduction to this book, the first CoSA was formed when the reverend Harry Nigh put together a circle of volunteers for Charlie Taylor on a hunch that providing this type of support would help Charlie reintegrate into the community and limit his likelihood of reoffending. He did not, nor would anyone in his position have, design a practice or model based on an explicit theory of behavioural change and/or risk reduction. Since their emergence in 1994, a number of scholars from various backgrounds have attempted to theorise CoSA – to draw on existing theories in an effort to explain CoSA's ability to reduce sexual reoffending. This is an undertaking of paramount importance. Explicating the mechanism(s) via

DOI: 10.4324/9781003125532-3

which CoSA decrease sexual reoffending will enable CoSA staff and volunteers to shape practise in ways that most effectively support this goal into the future.

The extant scholarly literature on CoSA is, however, characterised by confusion about how and why CoSA work. In particular, scholars appear confused about whether CoSA are (and/or should be) a *reintegration* or *rehabilitation* measure. This is perhaps unsurprising given that the aims of rehabilitation and reintegration are frequently conflated by correctional authorities, who often "lack a clear *theoretical* basis for reintegration services, and have an unclear distinction between the obligations of rehabilitation and reintegration" (Fox, 2014, p. 251; italics in original). Fox's (2014) work is especially helpful in disentangling these distinct but related concepts (see further Ward et al., 2014). She argued that while rehabilitation is largely *psychological* in focus, reintegration is largely *social*. Essentially, rehabilitation is best understood as those programs and measures that are delivered by correctional and/or therapeutic professionals with the aim of addressing psychological deficits among offenders, and thus reducing their risk of reoffending. For example, cognitive behavioural therapy (CBT) is one common approach to offender rehabilitation. Graham (2016, p. 3) further distinguished between "rehabilitation" – i.e. the lived experience of an individual (ex-)offender, and "rehabilitation work" – i.e. the professional intervention and services provided by criminal justice workers such as probation and parole agents and drug and alcohol workers. Reintegration (often also called re-entry, especially in the United States, or resettlement in the United Kingdom) refers to those processes concerned with an individual's release from prison and subsequent settlement in the community. Davis et al. (2012, p. 448) defined reintegration as "the process of transitioning from incarceration to the community, adjusting to life outside of prison or jail, and attempting to maintain a crime-free lifestyle". For Scheirs (2016, p. 83), reintegration involves "enhancing the ability of offenders to return to and function normally in civil society after release".

As Maruna (2011, p. 18) has argued, while corrections officers undertake rehabilitative work with offenders, reintegration is a social concern and requires a consideration of the role of ordinary citizens and civil service organisations; it is "something that happens between the returning prisoner and the wider community". A sole focus on rehabilitation over reintegration "implies that...the offender's psychology was at the root of re-offending; once the internal problems were fixed, then reintegration would be unproblematic" (Fox, 2014, p. 242). As one corrections authority in Fox's (2014, p. 240) study eloquently argued, rehabilitation "is like fixing the car, but leaving the rocks in the road". In this analogy, rehabilitation (the goal of correctional intervention) is concerned with fixing the car, while reintegration (the mutual responsibility of the ex-prisoner, correctional staff, community service organisations and the wider community) is concerned with ensuring the road is sufficiently well-maintained to be safely travelled. Rehabilitation and reintegration are thus discrete but twin aims: "Repairing the car is necessary but not sufficient – the rocks are the tangible sorts of obstacles that make reentry difficult" (Fox, 2014, p. 240).

Confusion exists about whether CoSA are designed to fix the car or the road. In the edited text, *Sexual crime and Circles of Support and Accountability* (Elliott et al., 2018), for instance, contributors variously situate CoSA as designed to rehabilitate and reintegrate the core member. The book's Foreword, by Circles UK CEO Riana Taylor (2018, p. v) stated that the book showcases the "contribution CoSA makes to the rehabilitation of those who have committed sexual crime". Wilson's (2018) chapter argued that CoSA (in the United Kingdom at least) are a rehabilitative measure, albeit also reflecting elements of desistance-promotion, restorative justice and reintegration practice (see also Blagden, Elliott, et al., 2018). It is of paramount importance to establish, as a global community of CoSA scholars and practitioners, whether CoSA are designed to fix the car, fix the road, do some combination of these or something else altogether. As noted above, articulating the mechanism(s) that inform CoSA will more effectively support CoSA staff and volunteers to achieve the aims of Circles.

The Risk, Needs, Responsivity Model, the Good Lives Model and CoSA

In addition, CoSA are frequently theorised as manifestations of the risk, needs, responsivity model and/or the good lives model (GLM). This section considers each of these models in turn.

The risk, needs, responsivity (RNR) model of offender assessment and treatment has long dominated approaches to offender rehabilitation in Western criminal justice systems (Bonta & Andrews, 2017). Originally developed by Andrews et al. (1990), the model developed from a growing recognition that some approaches to offender rehabilitation were more effective than others. Andrews et al. (1990) thus undertook a thorough analysis of the existing empirical literature on offender rehabilitation in an attempt to identify the factors that made some approaches more effective than others. The patterns they identified form the basis of the RNR model (Bonta & Andrews, 2017). The model posits three principles for the assessment and treatment of offenders: (1) risk; (2) need and (3) responsivity. Other, broader, principles – such as respect for the person – have subsequently been incorporated into the model (Bonta & Andrews, 2017), but the principles of risk, need and responsibility remain at its core.

According to the *risk* principle, which is premised on the notion that criminal behaviour can be predicted, the level of service provided to an individual offender should match their level of risk of reoffending (Bonta & Andrews, 2017). Accordingly, treatment interventions should be reserved for those who present the highest risk (Harkins & Beech, 2007), with this cohort of offenders receiving more intensive and extensive treatment than lower-risk offenders (Bonta & Andrews, 2017). The risk principle, therefore, offers guidance as to both *who* interventions should target (Andrews & Bonta, 2010; Looman & Abracen, 2013) and the intensity of the required treatment (Bonta & Andrews, 2017). This is vital as research demonstrates only a small positive treatment effect for low-risk offenders, and in some cases, negative effects of intensive treatment for low-risk offenders (Bonta & Andrews, 2017).

The *need* principle acknowledges that while offenders – especially high-risk offenders – will possess a variety of needs, not all needs were created equal. Bonta and Andrews (2017) distinguished between criminogenic needs and non-criminogenic needs. The former refers to dynamic risk factors that when targeted are associated with reductions in recidivism (Bonta & Andrews, 2017). The latter refers to needs that are unlikely to reduce future recidivism, such as health and self-esteem (Andrews & Bonta, 2010). As Andrews and Bonta (2010, p. 45) pointed out, enhancing some non-criminogenic needs may actually be counterproductive: "increasing an offender's self-esteem without regard to procriminal attitudes may result in a self-confident criminal". Importantly, while non-criminogenic needs may not be directly related to reduced recidivism, they may be targeted in order to enhance an offender's motivation to engage with treatment, or on humanitarian grounds (Bonta & Andrews, 2017). For example, while treating an offender's anxiety is unlikely to reduce his likelihood of reoffending in and of itself, such treatment may help the offender to more actively engage in treatment designed to address needs directly related to his offending.

According to the RNR, the major categories of criminogenic offender needs are as follows:

- Antisocial personality pattern;
- Procriminal attitudes;
- Procriminal associates;
- Substance abuse;
- Family/marital;
- School/work and
- Leisure/recreation (Bonta & Andrews, 2017).

Together with an offender's criminal history, which is a static risk factor (i.e. cannot be changed), antisocial personality, attitudes and associates form what Andrews and Bonta (2010, p. 45) termed the "big four" risk factors. The RNR thus asserts that addressing these needs should form the primary focus of treatment intervention. The *need* principle thus offers guidance as to *what* treatment interventions should target (Andrews & Bonta, 2010; Looman & Abracen, 2013). Table 2.1, adapted from Bonta and Andrews (2017) provides examples of indicators of domains of criminogenic need, as well as the treatment goals that flow logically from their identification.

Table 2.1 Criminogenic need domains, indicators and treatment goals (adapted from Bonta & Andrews, 2017)

Need	*Indicators*	*Treatment goals*
Procriminal attitudes	• Lack of respect for the law • Rationalisations and justifications for offending	• Counter rationalisations and justifications
Family/marital	• Poor parental discipline • Poor familial relationships	• Build parenting skills
Leisure/recreation	• Lack of involvement with leisure and recreation activities	• Encourage prosocial participation in sports, hobbies and interests

According to the *responsivity* principle, offender treatment programs should be delivered in a style that is compatible with the learning style and ability of the individual offender (Bonta & Andrews, 2017; Harkins & Beech, 2007). The responsivity principle is comprised of two related principles: general and specific responsivity (Bonta & Andrews, 2017). General responsivity asserts that as cognitive-behavioural and cognitive learning interventions have been shown to be the most effective in addressing offenders' behaviour, interventions ought to be premised on these approaches (Bonta & Andrews, 2017). Specific responsivity refers to the notion of "differential treatment" (Bonta & Andrews, 2017). Offenders vary according to a wide range of characteristics (e.g., age, maturity, sex, cognitive capacity, ethnicity/cultural background, mental health, strengths, personality, intelligence) and by identifying personality and cognitive styles, treatment can be better matched to the individual (Bonta & Andrews, 2017). As Looman et al. (2015) stated, in those who have sexually offended, specific responsivity factors may include psychopathy and deviant sexual arousal. The responsivity principle, therefore, offers guidance about *how* interventions should be targeted (Andrews & Bonta, 2010; Looman & Abracen, 2013).

The RNR model of offender rehabilitation has been rigorously analysed, and the resulting evidence clearly supports the approach. The RNR model has been found to significantly reduce recidivism among general offender populations (Andrews & Bonta, 2010; Andrews et al., 2011; Harkins & Beech, 2007; Looman & Abracen, 2013) and specific offender cohorts such as women, young people and offenders from ethnic minority cultural backgrounds (Andrews & Bonta, 2010). It has also been found to reduce reoffending in relation to specific offence types, such as violence, gang involvement and sexual offending (Andrews & Bonta, 2010). Hanson et al. (2009) conducted a meta-analysis of 23 studies and found that programs designed to reduce sexual recidivism demonstrated the largest reductions if they adopted the RNR model (see further Andrews & Bonta, 2010).

Despite the demonstrated effectiveness of the RNR model, it has not gone without criticism. In recent years, the model has been criticised for minimising the multifaceted and complex nature of individual human beings, and instead positioning offenders as disembodied bearers of risk (Ward et al., 2012). A key criticism is that the RNR model views offenders through a deficits lens. Ward and Stewart (2003, p. 355; italics in original) claimed that the RNR model focuses on "the *elimination* of negative attitudes, the *reduction* of cognitive distortions, the *extinction* of deviant sexual interests, and the generation of a list of people, activities, and places to *avoid*". This, Ward (2002b, pp. 172–173) argues, leaves practitioners little to go on: "a therapist is left with a depiction of an individual's psychological vulnerability factors and problems....What is missing is the integration of this knowledge with different, concrete ways of living... Negative goals such as the reduction of risk do not provide constructive guidance for therapists" (see further Ward & Brown, 2004). The key focus of the good lives model, which was developed by Ward (2002b) as a response to, and extension of, the RNR model, is the *strengths*, rather than deficits, of individual offenders (Ward, 2002b; Ward & Laws, 2010). This model promotes the enhancement of offenders' strengths, abilities and skills with the aim of supporting offenders to develop a "good life" (Ward & Stewart, 2003).

The model works from the assumption that all individuals will seek out activities or experiences that will provide them with a sense of wellbeing (i.e. "primary human goods"). Primary human goods are "actions, states of affairs, characteristics, experiences, and states of mind that are viewed as intrinsically beneficial to human beings and are therefore sought for their own sake rather than as means to some more fundamental ends" (Ward, 2002b, p. 174). The scholarship on the GLM proposes 11 categories of primary human goods across the three broad domains of the *body*, *self* and *social life* (Ward, 2002a), as follows:

- Life (i.e., healthy living and optimal physical functioning, sexual satisfaction);
- Knowledge;
- Excellence in work;
- Excellence in play;
- Excellence in agency (i.e., autonomy and self-directedness);
- Inner peace (i.e., freedom from emotional turmoil and stress);
- Relatedness (e.g., intimate, romantic and family relationships);
- Community;
- Spirituality (in the broad sense of finding meaning and purpose in life);
- Happiness and
- Creativity (Yates & Willis cited in Looman & Abracen, 2013).

The GLM posits that offending occurs when an individual utilises maladaptive (i.e. unhealthy) strategies to achieve these primary human goods (Connelly & Ward, 2008). For example, an individual may use the maladaptive strategy of consuming child sexual abuse material to achieve the goal of sexual satisfaction rather than the adaptive goal of seeking out a healthy adult relationship with a consenting partner. The aim of therapeutic intervention would thus be "to identify the types of relationships an offender finds satisfying (providing they are socially acceptable) and to equip them with the necessary internal (skills) and external conditions to increase their chances of establishing these relationships" (Ward, 2002b, p. 174). The model, therefore, encourages practitioners to support offenders to develop goals that are personally meaningful, and to strive towards meeting these – i.e., to develop a "good life" (Ward & Gannon, 2006; Whitehead et al., 2007; Wilson & Yates, 2009) – in adaptive (i.e. healthy and law-abiding) ways.

The GLM thus does not dismiss the importance of risk factors. Rather, it views risk factors as obstacles that impede an individual from living a good life (Whitehead et al., 2007; Willis & Ward, 2013). As Ward (2002, p. 172) explains: "Essentially, risk factors function as indicators or markers that an individual's pursuit of primary human goods is compromised in some way". This has important implications for professionals working with offenders: "the therapeutic focus should be on implementing offender's [sic] good lives conceptualisation rather than simply managing risk. The modification of criminogenic needs, or dynamic risk factors, will occur as a consequence of implementing a good lives plan". The model thus does not stand in opposition to the RNR model as such. Rather, Ward (2002b, p. 176) argued that the RNR ought to be embedded *within* the GLM: "the focus of therapy should be on instilling the capabilities to achieve human goods in ways that are socially acceptable and personally meaningful and satisfying. Risk analysis only informs therapists that there are problems in the way offenders seek human goods". To this end, the GLM "retains the merits of the RNR while addressing its limitations" (Willis & Ward, 2013, p. 309).

Ward (2002) does not discount the evidence that treatment programming based on the RNR is effective (Ward & Brown, 2004). Rather, he argued that this effectiveness is partly a consequence of these programs supporting individuals to adopt good lives: "one of the reasons cognitive-behavioural programs are effective is that they partially install the internal and external conditions necessary to live more prosocial lives" (Ward, 2002b, p. 178). In other words, the success of the RNR may well be a reflection of the extent to which it embeds the GLM.

As the GLM emerged more recently than the RNR model, it has been the subject of fewer evaluation studies to date. However, Willis and Ward's (2013) overview of the evidence showed that rehabilitation programs consistent with the GLM, or explicitly based on the GLM, appeared promising, especially in relation to promoting offender motivation and engagement with treatment. As the GLM reconceptualises the core elements of the RNR model and incorporates these, Willis and Ward (2013, p. 309) argued that "the large body of empirical literature supporting the RNR also supports the main basis comprising the GLM".

CoSA emerged well before the development of the GLM, and as noted above, emerged independently of any theoretical framework. They are, however, commonly considered in the literature to reflect the GLM. For example, McCartan et al.'s (2014) case file review of two CoSA pilot programs in the United Kingdom claims that CoSA are grounded theoretically in the GLM. Blagden, Elliott et al. (2018, p. 36) similarly argue that: "Cosa are well aligned to the GLM, in that it aims to support Core Members in achieving human goods via pro-social methods in order to construct a balanced, fulfilled and socially supported crime free life". Recent CoSA scholarship – including my own (Richards et al., 2020) – however, frames CoSA as reflecting a hybrid of the GLM and RNR models (Chouinard & Riddick, 2014; Höing et al., 2015, 2017) (although Thompson et al. (2017) have queried the extent to which CoSA (at least in the UK context) successfully balance the two models).

Importantly, however, both the GLM and RNR are predominantly models of offender *rehabilitation* (see discussion above) (Ward et al., 2014); they provide guidance to correcto-therapeutic professionals about intervening with identified perpetrators to reduce their likelihood of recidivism. CoSA are, however, uniquely "delivered" by non-professionals. While both the RNR and GLM include a focus on family relationships and the GLM specifically addresses the domain of "community", neither model seeks to explain the role of ordinary members of the community in reducing the likelihood of recidivism. The "something that happens between the returning prisoner and the wider community" (Maruna, 2011, p. 18) is thus left largely unexplained. As such, the RNR and GLM provide a helpful but partial explanation for the efficacy of CoSA.

CoSA as Restorative Justice

It is also widely accepted that CoSA are a restorative justice practice or at least reflect restorative justice philosophy or principles. This is typically stated as a fact in the CoSA literature. For example, McCartan and McKenzie (2014, p. 137) claim that "Cosa is a form of restorative justice with sex offenders" (see also Bohmert et al., 2018; Gilliam et al., 2021; Kerr et al., 2018).

Restorative justice is notoriously difficult to define (Daly, 2016). The problematic nature of defining restorative justice is often attributed to the fact that it is "not a unified concept" (Moxon cited in Miers, 2001, p. iii). Restorative justice is thus described as an "umbrella concept" or "rubric" (Daly, 2000) that encompasses a diverse range of practices and concepts (Zehr, 2002). When it comes to defining restorative justice, McCold (1998, p. 19) claims, "the image of the blind-folded group describing an elephant comes to mind". Many, however, happily adopt Marshall's (1996, p. 37) definition of restorative justice – that it is "a process whereby all the parties with a stake in a particular offence come together to resolve collectively how to deal with the aftermath of the offence and its implications for the future". This definition "has come closest to general acceptance" (Strang, 2000, p. 23). Restorative justice is also – for better or worse (Richards, 2014) – often constructed in opposition to retributive justice. As Zehr (1990) claimed, in the restorative justice paradigm, rather than asking *who should be punished* (as per the retributive paradigm), the question becomes: *what can be done in order to repair harm to victims, offenders and communities*? (see further Bazemore & Schiff, 2001; Ward et al., 2014; Zehr & Mika, 2003).

CoSA are often considered aligned with restorative justice due to a common focus on offender accountability, the creation of a community of care for the offender and the involvement of community members in the aftermath of a crime (Fox, 2014; McAlinden, 2007). CoSA can, however, be distinguished from restorative justice in that they do not seek to *repair harm* to victims/survivors, but rather prevent harm occurring to new victims. Furthermore, CoSA do not involve either direct or indirect encounters between victims/survivors and offenders, which is central to restorative justice practice (Daly, 2016; Zehr & Mika, 2003). CoSA are thus best conceptualised as only "quasi-restorative" (Fox, 2014).

Moreover, while CoSA share some commonalities with the restorative justice paradigm, I argue that understanding CoSA as a restorative practice cannot alone explain their efficacy. This is because restorative justice is a *normative* rather than *explanatory* theory (to the extent that it can be understood as a theory at all). As Braithwaite (2000a, p. 87; italics added) delineates, "explanatory theories are ordered sets of propositions about the way the world *is*; normative theories, ordered sets of propositions about the way the world *ought to be*" (see further Abend, 2008; Braithwaite, 2000b). My contention here is that while a restorative justice lens may guide CoSA practice – i.e. inform what we desire CoSA to be like in normative terms – it is less useful in explaining how CoSA work. As Ward et al. (2014, p. 32) argued, restorative justice lacks a theory of behavioural change: "although R[estorative] J[ustice] has had some success in reducing reoffending, it is not entirely clear how or why the effect occurs". In short, simply understanding CoSA as a restorative justice practice does not elucidate the specific mechanics via which CoSA work to shape the behaviour of core members and thus reduce sexual recidivism. (Indeed, many proponents of restorative justice do not consider reduced reoffending to be a goal of restorative justice and instead characterise reduced crime as a by-product or "added bonus" (Ward et al., 2014, p. 31) of restorative practices (see Claes & Shapland, 2016)).

A limited body of scholarship has attempted to tease out the specific mechanisms via which restorative justice processes might (be expected to) reduce reoffending. These are the reinforcement of shared norms (Petrich, 2016; Ward et al., 2014); the acquisition of empathy (Ward et al., 2014); the development of human and social capital that fosters identity transformation

(Horan, 2015; Petrich, 2016); the opportunity to make sense of one's offending (Horan, 2015); the opportunity to make amends (Horan, 2015); and the opportunity to develop a "redemption script" (see further Chapter 4) (Petrich, 2016). Scholarship on CoSA is yet, however, to examine in detail whether and/or how these mechanisms lead to reduced sexual recidivism among core members.

CoSA as Reintegrative Shaming

A number of CoSA scholars position CoSA as a reflection of Braithwaite's (1989) theory of reintegrative shaming. While the theory of reintegrative shaming and the restorative justice movement emerged independently of one another, they have become closely aligned (see generally Braithwaite, 2000b). Reintegrative shaming is an integrated theory of crime control in that it builds on components of a number of existing criminological theories (control, subcultural and strain theories, differential association and some elements of labelling theory) to posit a general theory of crime control. By "general" theory, Braithwaite (1989) meant that the theory can explain all types of offending, including types of offending usually neglected by criminological theories (e.g., white-collar crime). His argument is that while crimes such as rape, burglary and fraud may well be highly disparate, all such acts are poorly regarded by members of the community, and this poor regard is institutionalised (i.e., there is a formal criminal justice response). Such crimes thus have enough in common to be able to be explained by the same theoretical premise. Acts that are crimes but are not held in near-universal poor regard by the community (e.g., marijuana use) thus cannot be explained by the theory (Braithwaite, 1989).

Braithwaite (1989) argued that in the West, consecutive paradigms of criminal justice policy have, for a variety of reasons, sought to minimise the involvement of members of the community (see also Simon, 1998). The general community has long been cast as not sufficiently skilled and/or potentially too arbitrary to play a role in preventing and responding to crime. Braithwaite (1989, p. 6) contends, however, that the community is key to crime control, and indeed that members of the community have "preventive obligations". Specifically, as the name of the theory suggests, shaming by the community in ways that are *reintegrative* rather than degrading or *disintegrative*, is the key to crime control:

> Crime is best controlled when members of the community are the primary controllers through active participation in shaming offenders, and, having shamed them, through concerted participation in ways of reintegrating the offender back into the community of law abiding citizens.
>
> (Braithwaite, 1989, p. 8)

Reintegrative shaming is thus a *normative theory* of crime control: its claim is that moralising rather than repression is inherently good (Braithwaite,

1989, p. 10). Moreover, Braithwaite contends that shaming by fellow citizens, rather than a repressive response from the state, will more effectively control crime: "shaming is a route to freely chosen compliance, while repressive social control is a route to coerced compliance" (Braithwaite, 1989, p. 10). Repressive or stigmatising responses to crime (e.g., punishment) "erects barriers between the offender and punisher through transforming the relationship into one of power assertion and injury" (Braithwaite, 1989, p. 73). As a consequence, offenders subject to stigmatisation become susceptible to involvement in criminal subcultures, as these provide the offender with the opportunity to "reject her rejectors" (Braithwaite, 1989, p. 14).

In order for shaming to be effective, it must be delivered with dignity, and in a context of social embeddedness. For Braithwaite (1989, p. 55), "shame is more deterring when administered by persons who continue to be of importance to us"; in other words, we may be mortified that we have upset our parents with our unlawful behaviour but care considerably less about what some stuffy old magistrate has to say about the matter. Interpersonal interdependencies are thus central to the theory of reintegrative shaming; such interdependencies must be "attachments which invoke personal obligations to others within a community of concern. They are not perceived as isolated exchange relationships of convenience but of profound group obligation" (Braithwaite, 1989, p. 85).

Shaming will thus be most effective in "communitarian" rather than "individualistic" societies. In the former, individuals are seen as whole persons by other members of the community: "offenders are not confronted as criminals but as whole persons" (Braithwaite, 1989, p. 88). In highly anonymised, urban societies, it is easier for members of the community to adhere to one-dimensional labels or stereotypes of "criminals", "lumping them into crude master categories" (Braithwaite, 1989, p. 88).

In policy terms, then, Braithwaite (1989, p. 163) recommends injecting the "repentant role" into criminal justice programming and developing and implementing measures that include opportunities for ritual or ceremony associated with repentance, and that "decertify deviance". Braithwaite (1989) rightly pointed out that our contemporary criminal justice response actively discourages perpetrators from adopting the "repentant role". Nowhere is this more evident than in cases of sexual misconduct, in which perpetrators have nothing to gain from repenting and everything to gain from maintaining their innocence, even in the face of overwhelming evidence and/or a finding of guilty by the court (as in the case of Harvey Weinstein for example (Wagmeister & Nichols, 2020)). The policy solution, according to the theory, is therefore to create or support the mobilisation of groups of concerned and caring individuals with whom the offender has ties of interdependency, to lovingly shame and then carefully reintegrate the offender back into their fold:

> A responsibility of the probation officer could be to convince representatives of a young person's school, employer, sporting clubs, and other

> groups that are important to the offender to attend the court and offer their opinion on what they would be able to contribute to monitoring the offender's behavior in future and to her rehabilitation. This would heighten communitarian obligations for informal social control among those present; it would also enhance shaming in the eyes of reference groups, and secure practical commitments to reintegration from those same groups.
>
> (Braithwaite, 1989, p. 173)

Astute readers may see some obvious parallels between the theory of reintegrative shaming and the practice of CoSA. In recent years, the notion that CoSA are a manifestation or reflection of the theory of reintegrative shaming has begun to be asserted in the international CoSA literature. Typically, this notion is stated as a fact not requiring further explanation. For example, McCartan and McKenzie (2014, p. 137) simply asserted that CoSA are "closely aligned to concepts of reintegrative shaming". Harper et al. (2019, p. 125) even claimed that a number of jurisdictions "have established models of CoSA that have successfully translated Braithwaite's (1989) theory of 'reintegrative shaming'...into the effective practice of managing such individuals within community settings", although it does not appear that any CoSA program has deliberately applied specific tenets of this theory (McAlinden, 2007, p. 165).

Three pieces of scholarship examine the relationship between reintegrative shaming and CoSA in more detail. Blagden, Elliott et al. (2018, p. 33) argued that CoSA mirror two key tenets of Braithwaite's (1989) theory. First, they argued that Braithwaite's theory suggests that the stigmatisation typically experienced by individuals with sexual offence convictions increases that individual's likelihood of reoffending, since "if the reactions and reflected appraisals of others are negative, self-change may be impaired or hindered" (Blagden, Elliott, et al., 2018, p. 33). By extension, CoSA ought to reduce the likelihood of reoffending as they counteract this stigmatisation. This is, however, a simplification of the theory of reintegrative shaming. As outlined above, Braithwaite (1989, pp. 65–68) does not contend that stigmatisation inhibits self-change, but rather that it renders the individual susceptible to involvement in criminal subcultures. Becoming susceptible to involvement in a criminal subculture does not, however, mean that an individual will necessarily become involved in one. As Braithwaite (1989) pointed out, such subcultures must be readily available and of interest to the offender in order for this to occur, and this is unlikely to often be the case. As he argued, criminal subcultures do not have recruitment centres, and most of us would have no idea how to join the Mafia or Hell's Angels (Braithwaite, 1989, p. 66). This is an important distinction because it highlights the role of social circumstances in an individual's likelihood of reoffending, rather than the role of internal, psychological change (as Blagden, Elliott et al.'s (2018) reading of the theory would have it). It is also important to recognise given that in most western jurisdictions, the strict conditions to which individuals convicted of sexual offending are usually compelled to adhere severely restrict their opportunities to join criminal subcultures in most cases. Second, Blagden, Elliott et al. (2018, p. 33) argued – correctly in my view – that another key tenet of reintegrative shaming that is aligned with CoSA is the importance of significant others in preventing reoffending: "shame associated with letting those close to us down and causing disapproval can serve to promote desistance".

McAlinden (2007) argued in better detail that CoSA are a reflection of the theory of reintegrative shaming. She claims that, in accordance with the central tenets of reintegrative shaming, CoSA "control wrong doers within a communitarian society and informally sanction deviance by reintegration into cohesive networks, rather than by formal restraint" (McAlinden, 2007, p. 171; see further McAlinden, 2005). More specifically, McAlinden (2007, p. 172) contended that CoSA mirror reintegrative shaming due to: the central role of community members in place of statutory authorities; the enmeshment of the core member within interdependent relationships and the shaming of the core member's criminal act(s) within these intimate and supportive relationships. McAlinden (2007, p. 172) also argued that CoSA assist core members with reintegration into the community following prison, including providing assistance with housing and employment, which formal correctional programs have long failed to achieve. A point of note here, however, is that despite the name "reintegrative shaming", Braithwaite's (1989) theory is not a theory of reintegration as this term is typically conceptualised in the criminological literature (see discussion above). The "reintegration" envisaged by Braithwaite is reintegration into families and/or communities in the aftermath of a crime, not (necessarily) in the aftermath of imprisonment. Reintegration in this sense is conceptually distinct from prisoner re-entry or resettlement. Thus, while McAlinden's (2007) point here is no doubt accurate – i.e., CoSA do consistently support core members to reintegrate into the community after prison (see Bates et al., 2012, 2007; Clarke et al., 2017) – this does not necessarily mean they reflect the tenets of reintegrative shaming.

Finally, Hannem and Petrunik (2007), both of whom have extensive experience as CoSA volunteers and researchers, argued that CoSA mirror Braithwaite and Mugford's (1994) 14 conditions of reintegration ceremonies, which build on Braithwaite's (1989) theory of reintegrative shaming to make sense of restorative justice conferences for youth offenders. Hannem and Petrunik (2007) argued convincingly that CoSA meet the first two conditions: 1) "The event, but not the perpetrator, is removed from the realm of its everyday character and is defined as irresponsible, wrong, a crime" and 2) "Event and perpetrator must be uncoupled rather than defined as instances of profane uniformity. The self of the perpetrator is sustained as sacred rather than profane" (Braithwaite & Mugford, 1994). In other words, like McAlinden (2007), Hannem and Petrunik (2007) argued that CoSA reflect reintegrative shaming theory by insisting on the denunciation of the core member's acts but not the actor himself. They are, however, considerably less convincing in arguing that CoSA echo many of the other conditions of successful reintegration ceremonies. In particular, and unsurprisingly, they struggle most significantly to demonstrate those conditions that require the involvement of victims, especially condition 9: "The separation of the victim, any fear or shame experienced by victims, must be terminated by rituals of reintegration" (Braithwaite & Mugford, 1994). While Hannem and Petrunik (2007, p. 162) rightly argued that CoSA aim to "ensure that the C[ore]M[ember] recognizes the broader harms resulting from his offences", given that CoSA do not directly involve victims, it would not be possible (or desirable) for CoSA to meet these conditions. While this point is skirted over in their analysis, this is not necessarily fatal, particularly given the different context and aims of CoSA on the one hand and youth justice conferencing in Australia and New Zealand (on which Braithwaite and Mugford's (1994) work is based) on the other. Indeed, a critically overlooked point here is that the very fact that CoSA do not directly involve victims does not discount their alignment with reintegrative shaming. While Braithwaite and Mugford (1994) emphasised the importance of responding to the needs of victims, the theory of reintegrative shaming as originally conceptualised (Braithwaite, 1989) was heavily offender-oriented. As victimologist Garkawe (cited in Richards, 2009, p. 309) notes, Braithwaite's (1989) book includes very few references to victims of crime. Understanding CoSA as reflective of reintegrative shaming nonetheless provides a helpful starting point. In particular, the shared principle of non-stigmatising shaming carried out within caring interdependent relationships (as per Blagden, Elliott, et al., 2018; Hannem & Petrunik, 2007; McAlinden, 2007) provides a useful lens for understanding CoSA's capacity to reduce sexual reoffending.

Recently, however, a number of CoSA scholars – in particular Fox, 2015, 2014 – have suggested that CoSA might be best understood as situated in the theoretical terrain of *desistance*. Fox (2015) encourages the use of a desistance lens to better understand the specific mechanisms via which CoSA work (see also Blagden, Elliott, et al., 2018; Fox, 2013; Höing et al., 2013, 2015; Richards, in press; Richards et al., 2020; Thompson, 2015) – in other words, how CoSA translate into behavioural change among core members.

Understanding Desistance

Desistance refers to the processes through which offenders turn away from crime and become productive members of society (Cooley & Sample, 2018) – to the process of stopping crime and staying stopped (Maruna, 2001). Although there is no uniformly accepted definition of desistance (Harris, 2017b), a commonly utilised one is Maruna's (2001, p. 26) definition that desistance refers to "the long-term abstinence from crime among individuals who had previously engaged in persistent patterns of criminal offending". While desistance is not a new focus within criminology, concentrated attention to desistance – especially desistance from sexual offending – has only come about quite recently (Blagden, Mann, et al., 2018; Harris, 2017a; Vieira et al., 2020). While much of the criminological canon is devoted to understanding why some people commit offences, desistance scholars are concerned with the conditions under which individuals engaged in offending "go straight" (Maruna, 2001).

As has been rehearsed at length elsewhere, desistance is notoriously difficult not only to define but also to measure (Harris, 2017b; Ward & Laws, 2010). The cessation of crime is rarely linear, with individuals "zig-zagging" (Fox, 2014; Laub & Sampson, 2003) or "drifting" (Matza, 1964) in and out of offending over time. Nor can desistance be understood as binary; as Harris (2017b) argued, we ought not to consider an individual to either have desisted or not, but rather to consider desistance as a *process* (Farmer et al., 2016; Lussier et al., 2016; Ward & Laws, 2010) that might be characterised by periods of desistance, relapse and so on. It may be particularly difficult to capture the contours of desistance from sexual offending specifically, given low rates of reporting and conviction, as well as the secrecy that often characterises sexual offence perpetration (see Chapter 1).

Desistance from crime can be understood in a number of ways. First, desistance is often conceptualised as primary, secondary or tertiary. *Primary* desistance refers to initial behavioural change or short periods in which an offender refrains from crime. *Secondary* desistance refers to more substantial change to an individual's identity, often occurring as a result of a period of primary desistance. *Tertiary* desistance refers to a lasting desistance alongside a genuine reintegration into a prosocial environment (Fox, 2016; Walker et al., 2015). Desistance is also often categorised as occurring as a result of *ontogenetic* or *sociogenic* factors (Kras, 2014; Maruna, 2001). As Sullivan (2012) explained, desistance that occurs as a result of ontogenetic factors involves biological or physiological processes such as maturation, whereas desistance that occurs sociogenically involves interaction between the individual and their social context. None of these categories is absolute; an individual's desistance may display elements of more than one.

An important distinction exists between an *absence of reoffending* on one hand and *desistance from crime* on the other. As Cooley and Sample (2018) argued, these are discrete constructs. Desistance from crime inherently involves some type of cognitive and/or affective transformation, and a genuine commitment to a prosocial lifestyle, whereas the absence of reoffending could simply reflect the natural aging process or a lack of opportunity to reoffend (Cooley & Sample, 2018). Incarcerated offenders and those subject to extremely strict surveillance and supervision in the community are severely restricted from reoffending, but their lack of reoffence could only be considered "forced desistance" (Harris, 2017b, p. 28) unless a genuine desire to desist can be observed (Bullock et al., 2019; Harris, 2017b). Similarly, Laub and Sampson

(2003) recognised that in some cases, desistance occurs by default. By this they mean desistance that occurs passively rather than as a result of a deliberate undertaking on the part of the individual (see further Sullivan, 2012). As Rocque et al. (2016, p. 50) explain, "desistance by default" occurs when "former offenders find themselves in conventional social roles, most often without their intention, and the social role changes them for the better, usually by restricting their opportunity to commit crime".

The more specific concepts of "turning points", "knifing off" and "hooks for change" provide a more finely-grained lens through which to understand desistance processes. Turning points (precipitated by a "disorienting episode" (Lofland, 1969) or "triggering event" (Laub & Sampson, 2001)) refer to significant life events or changes in circumstances that foster desistance (Kirk, 2012) or activate the desistance process (Walker et al., 2015). Turning points serve as catalysts for behavioural change by creating "a sense of crisis in offenders and ultimately prompt[ing] them to reevaluate their lives and reconstruct their identities" (Ward & Laws, 2010, p. 19). Turning points may include marriage or the formation of a new family (Laub & Sampson, 1993), a new work opportunity or environment, the disintegration of an existing peer network (Carlsson, 2012; Maruna, 2001), participation in a treatment program (Farmer et al., 2012) and/or new situations that provide the opportunity for identity transformation (Sampson & Laub, 2016). As "nothing inherent in a situation makes it a turning point" (Maruna, 2001, p. 25), and as turning points may present advantageous or disadvantageous possibilities to an offender (e.g., a marriage may be beneficial, but not if a new partner shares an offender's propensity to abuse illicit substances), they are *necessary* but not *sufficient* to foster desistance (Göbbels et al., 2012, p. 455).

"Knifing off" generally refers to an offender "severing bonds to [a] criminal past" (Willis et al., 2010, p. 547). A range of things might be "knifed off", including former associations, social roles, stigma and opportunities to offend (Maruna & Roy, 2007). As Harris (2017b) understands it, knifing off occurs when an offender conceptualises their life or self in two separate halves: a former (criminal) self/life and a new (non-criminal) self/life (see also Maruna, 2001; Ward & Laws, 2010). Turning points can thus give rise to knifing off: "turning points make it possible for an individual to 'knife off' the (criminal) past from the present" (Göbbels et al., 2012, p. 454).

Finally, the concept of "hooks for change" refers to an offender's own role in capitalising on advantageous changes in their environment (Giordano et al., 2002; Schinkel, 2015). Here, the emphasis is on the offender's use of agency – what Giordano et al. (2002, p. 992) term "agentic moves". Giordano et al.'s (2015) study found that hooks for change for perpetrators of intimate partner violence include becoming a parent or embarking on a new relationship and/or the threat of arrest (see generally Marchetti & Daly, 2017). Offenders may make use of one or more hooks for change in their journeys toward desistance (Giordano et al., 2015).

These concepts – turning points, knifing off and hooks for change – are not mutually exclusive but can be applied in combination to aid in understanding offenders' desistance journeys. For example, a specific turning point could be used by a desisting offender as a hook for change (Farmer et al., 2012) or provide contexts in which knifing off can be practised (Laub & Sampson, 2001).

The concept of "assisted desistance" (Rex, 1999) has emerged to describe the range of measures adopted by state, non-state and other actors to activate, support and help sustain desistance. Assisted desistance speaks to the actions that other parties can engage in to facilitate desistance (see Blagden, Elliott, et al., 2018; Harris, 2017b; Marchetti & Daly, 2017).

Theorising Desistance

Three main theoretical explanations exist that attempt to account for desistance from crime. Theories of *natural desistance* are concerned with biological and physiological processes via which individuals desist from crime. These theoretical explanations take as their starting point the well-established criminological fact that breaking the law is predominantly a youthful endeavour (Harris, 2014). They therefore argued that the maturation process is the key driver of desistance, and that offenders simply "age out" of crime (although for seminal scholars Glueck and Glueck (1968), desistance transpired as a result of "maturation" rather than biological aging *per se*). Theories of *informal social controls* assert that desistance transpires because informal controls such as marriage and employment inhibit an offender's opportunities to continue committing crimes (Laub & Sampson, 1993). Such events increase the individual's "stakes in conformity" (Toby, 1957) and thus serve as a catalyst for behavioural change (Sampson & Laub, 2016). In other words, people desist from crime once they possess "something to lose" by continuing to commit offences.

These two sets of theoretical perspectives have been criticised for casting individuals as automatons who are passively acted upon by life events such as maturation, marriage or work opportunities and failing to explain how opportunities such as marriage and jobs arise, as well as failing to explain whether these precede or follow desistance from crime (see Paternoster et al., 2015). Moreover, as Harris (2017b) and Kras (2014) have argued, since people convicted of sexual offences are increasingly restricted from obtaining employment or entering marriage relationships (see also Vieira et al., 2020), informal social controls may be less salient to understanding desistance from sexual offending specifically. These explanations also assume a link between reasons for the *onset* of crime and *desistance* from it. For example, a lack of informal social controls is posited as the cause of the commencement of crime, and the emergence of informal social controls is posited as the cause of desistance from crime. As Fagan (1989) pointed out, however, the reason(s) that one stops offending may be entirely unrelated to the reason(s) one commenced. The experiences of getting caught and being punished, for instance, may instigate desistance.

The third group of theoretical explanations for desistance emerged in this context, and view *cognitive transformation* as central to desistance. These explanations highlight the role of the personal agency and conscious decision-making on the part of the (ex-)offender in the desistance process. Rather than positioning the offender as a passive subject who simply grows too old for crime or desists from crime as a consequence of external life events, cognitive transformation explanations give credence to the individual's own expression of agency in appropriating elements in their environment or in significant life events (Giordano et al., 2002) to develop a non-offending identity and lifestyle. Cognitive transformation explanations thus highlight the role of an individual's internal meaning-making about external events in the desistance process, rather than assuming that external events themselves instigate desistance (Maruna, 2001). Doing "narrative repair" work (Stone, 2016) is a key aspect of the process of cognitive transformation (Presser, 2008; Rocque et al., 2016). According to this perspective, individuals who desist from crime engage in a process of "rebiographing" (Maruna, 2001) in which they craft believable self-stories about why they are desisting from crime and "going straight" (Maruna, 2001; Presser, 2008). This process of narrative repair is used by offenders to maintain a positive sense of self-worth and moral identity, which is vital to desistance (Larsson, 2019). Correctional and reintegration practice across the West has recently recognised the importance of this and has therefore shifted from a focus on "fixing" offenders to fostering desistance-promotion through narrative repair (Kras & Blasko, 2016). Indeed, it is increasingly recognised that desistance from crime must involve an internal shift and the adoption of an *identity* consistent with a non-offending future (Liem & Richardson, 2014). As Harris (2017b) and Kras (2014) have argued, furthermore, since people convicted of sexual offences are increasingly restricted from employment and marriage, theories of cognitive transformation are especially relevant to understanding desistance among this population.

CoSA as Desistance-Promotion

This book builds on this observation and on the suggestion of Fox 2014, 2015 and other scholars who, as noted above, have recently suggested that CoSA might be most fruitfully understood as desistance-promotion. In doing so, it adds to the nascent body of research literature on desistance from sexual offending (see Chapter 4). It offers the most fleshed-out examination of CoSA as desistance-promotion to date. As argued above, other ways of theoretically situating CoSA may also be useful in developing an understanding of how CoSA reduce sexual reoffending. This book does not disavow these theoretical premises altogether; rather, it makes an argument for situating CoSA in the conceptual landscape of desistance as a complementary way of understanding how CoSA work and critically, how they might work better. It is important to note that the desistance framework shares commonalities with some of the theoretical approaches outlined above. In particular, the concept of *identity* is central to both desistance and the GLM. As a number of scholars (Göbbels et al., 2012; Ward, 2002a; Wilson, 2018) have pointed out, the GLM is compatible with theories of desistance, as the two theoretical lenses share a similar premise about the relationships between human beings and their social world (Ward & Laws, 2010). Furthermore, in positioning CoSA as supporting *desistance*, my argument does not imply that CoSA ought not to be understood as supporting *reintegration*. Like the concepts of rehabilitation and reintegration, discussed above, desistance and reintegration are distinct but related. As Davis et al. (2012, p. 448) note, a person might desist from crime but still have difficulty adjusting to life outside prison. Indeed, both Harris (2017b) and Lussier and McCuish (2016) found that for people with sexual offence convictions, desistance may occur independently of community reintegration. Nonetheless, ideally, all three processes – rehabilitation, reintegration and desistance – will be mutually reinforcing (Fox, 2016, p. 70; see also Göbbels et al., 2012). In relation to CoSA specifically, a focus on reintegration without desistance could harm the image of CoSA, and a focus on desistance without reintegration would undermine the community-based nature of the measure.

Conclusion

This Chapter has outlined the major existing theoretical explanations that relate to CoSA. It argued that while each of these offers insight into CoSA, that an explanatory theory – that is, one that explains *the way things are* – is required for us to understand how CoSA reduce sexual recidivism. Specifically, it has posited the theoretical grounding of desistance as the most promising way of accounting for the efficacy of CoSA. The remainder of this book is dedicated to fleshing out how understanding CoSA as promoting desistance can offer new insights into their operation and efficacy.

References

Abend, G. (2008). The meaning of 'theory'. *Sociological Theory*, *26*(2), 173–199. doi: https://journals.sagepub.com/doi/10.1111/j.1467-9558.2008.00324.x

Andrews, D., & Bonta, J. (2010). Rehabilitating criminal justice policy and practice. *Psychology, Public Policy, and Law*, *16*(1), 39–55. doi: https://psycnet.apa.org/doiLanding?doi=10.1037%2Fa0018362

Andrews, D., Bonta, J., & Hogue, R. (1990). Classification for effective rehabilitation: Rediscovering psychology. *Criminal Justice and Behaviour*, *17*(1), 19–52. doi: https://journals.sagepub.com/doi/10.1177/0093854890017001004

Andrews, D., Bonta, J., & Wormith, J. (2011). The risk-needs-responsivity (RNR) model: Does adding the good lives model contribute to effective crime prevention? *Criminal Justice and Behavior, 38*(7), 735–755. doi: https://journals.sagepub.com/doi/10.1177/0093854811406356

Bates, A., Macrae, R., Williams, D., & Webb, C. (2012). Ever-increasing circles: A descriptive study of Hampshire and Thames valley Circles of Support and Accountability 2002–09. *Journal of Sexual Aggression, 183*, 355–373. doi: https://www.tandfonline.com/doi/abs/10.1080/13552600.2010.544415

Bates, A., Saunders, R., & Wilson, C. (2007). Doing something about it: A follow-up study of sex offenders participating in Thames valley Circles of Support and Accountability. *British Journal of Community Justice, 5*(1), 19–42. doi: https://mmuperu.co.uk/bjcj/wp-content/uploads/sites/2/2020/08/Bates.pdf

Bazemore, G., & Schiff, M. (2001). Understanding restorative community justice: What and why now? In G. Bazemore, & M. Schiff (Eds.), *Restorative community justice: Repairing harm and transforming communities* (pp. 21–46). Anderson Publishing Co. doi: https://www.routledge.com/Restorative-Community-Justice-Repairing-Harm-and-Transforming-Communities/Bazemore-Schiff/p/book/9781583605066

Blagden, N., Elliott, H., & Lievesley, R. (2018). Circles of Support and Accountability, assisted desistance and community transition. In H. Elliott, K. Hocken, R. Lievesley, N. Blagden, B. Winder, & P. Banyard (Eds.), *Sexual crime and Circles of Support and Accountability* (pp. 25–42). Palgrave Macmillan. doi: https://www.palgrave.com/gp/book/9783319748221

Blagden, N., Mann, R., Webster, S., Lee, R., & WIlliams, F. (2018). "It's not something I chose you know": Making sense of pedophiles' sexual interest in children and the impact on their psychosexual identity. *Sexual Abuse, 30*(6), 728–754. doi: https://doi.org/10.1177/1079063217697132

Bohmert, M. N., Duwe, G., & Hipple, N. K. (2018). Evaluating restorative justice Circles of Support and Accountability: Can social support overcome structural barriers? *International Journal of Offender Therapy and Comparative Criminology, 62*(3), 739–758. doi: https://doi.org/10.1177/0306624X16652627

Bonta, J., & Andrews, D. (2017). *The psychology of criminal conduct* (6th ed.). Elsevier Science. doi: https://www.routledge.com/The-Psychology-of-Criminal-Conduct/Bonta-Andrews/p/book/9781138935778?gclid=Cj0KCQjw5uWGBhCTARIsAL70sLIUa5ocjU-dTGudtHQWp9oXaYXPIZ8clafUuEjwCzci0RdbePOnhPsaAl3NEALw_wcB

Braithwaite, J. (1989). *Crime, shame and reintegration*. Cambridge University Press. doi: https://www.cambridge.org/core/books/crime-shame-and-reintegration/5F40BF6C9DFC3D5752888BC73034A1BA

Braithwaite, J. (2000a). Republican theory and crime control. In K. Bussmann, & S. Karstedt (Eds.), *Social dynamics of crime and control: New theories for a world in transition* (pp. 87–104). Hart Publishing. doi: https://www.bloomsburyprofessional.com/uk/social-dynamics-of-crime-and-control-9781841131641/

Braithwaite, J. (2000b). Shame and criminal justice. *Canadian Journal of Criminology, 42*(3), 281–298. doi: https://psycnet.apa.org/record/2000-02140-002

Braithwaite, J., & Mugford, S. (1994). Conditions of successful reintegration ceremonies: Dealing with juvenile offenders. *British Journal of Criminology, 34*(2), 139–171. doi: https://psycnet.apa.org/record/1994-42899-001

Bullock, K., Bunce, A., & McCarthy, D. (2019). Making good in unpromising places: The development and cultivation of redemption scripts among long-term prisoners. *International Journal of Offender Therapy and Comparative Criminology, 63*(3), 406–423. doi: https://journals.sagepub.com/doi/10.1177/0306624X18800882

Carlsson, C. (2012). Using "turning points" to understand processes of change in offending: Notes from a Swedish study on life courses and crime. *British Journal of Criminology, 52*, 1–16. doi: https://academic.oup.com/bjc/article/52/1/1/372083

Chouinard, J., & Riddick, C. (2014). *An evaluation of the Circles of Support and Accountability demonstration project: Final report.* Collaborative Centre for Justice and Safety. https://www.justiceandsafety.ca/rsu_docs/cosa-final-report-with-cover.pdf

Claes, B., & Shapland, J. (2016). Desistance from crime and restorative justice. *Restorative Justice: An International Journal, 4*(3), 302–322. doi: https://www.tandfonline.com/doi/full/10.1080/20504721.2016.1245912

Clarke, M., Warwick, L., & Völlm, B. (2017). Circles of Support and Accountability: The characteristics of core members in England and Wales. *Criminal Behaviour and Mental Health, 27*(2), 191–206. doi: https://doi.org/10.1011/cbm.2003

Connelly, M., & Ward, T. (2008). *Morals, rights and practice in the human services: Effective and fair decision-making in health, social care and criminal justice.* Jessica Kingsley Publishers.

Cooley, B., & Sample, L. (2018). The difference between desistance from sexual offending and not reoffending. *Journal of Crime and Justice, 41*(5), 483–503. doi: https://www.tandfonline.com/doi/full/10.1080/0735648X.2018.1479286

Daly, K. (2000). Restorative justice in diverse and unequal societies. *Law in Context, 17*(1), 167–190.

Daly, K. (2016). What is restorative justice? Fresh answers to a vexed question. *Victims & Offenders, 11*(1), 9–29. doi: https://www.tandfonline.com/doi/full/10.1080/15564886.2015.1107797

Davis, C., Bahr, S., & Ward, C. (2012). The process of offender reintegration: Perceptions of what helps prisoners re-enter society. *Criminology and Criminal Justice, 13*(4), 446–469. doi: https://journals.sagepub.com/doi/abs/10.1177/1748895812454748?journalCode=crjb

Elliott, H., Hocken, K., Lievesley, R., Blagden, N., Winder, B., & Banyard, P. (Eds.). (2018). *Sexual crime and Circles of Support and Accountability.* Palgrave Macmillan. doi: https://www.palgrave.com/gp/book/9783319748221

Fagan, J. (1989). Cessation of family violence: Deterrence and dissuasion. In L. Ohlin & M. Tonry (Eds.), *Family violence* (pp. 377–425). University of Chicago Press. doi: https://psycnet.apa.org/record/1989-98016-000

Farmer, M., Beech, A., & Ward, T. (2012). Assessing desistance in child molesters: A qualitative analysis. *Journal of Interpersonal Violence, 27*(5), 930–950. doi: https://journals.sagepub.com/doi/10.1177/0886260511423255

Farmer, M., McAlinden, A. M., & Maruna, S. (2016). Sex offending and situational motivation: Findings from a qualitative analysis of desistance from sexual offending. *International Journal of Offender Therapy and Comparative Criminology, 60*(15), 1756–1775. doi: https://journals.sagepub.com/doi/10.1177/0306624X16668175

Fox, K. (2013). *Circles of Support and Accountability: Final report prepared for the state of Vermont Department of Corrections.* Vermont Department of Corrections. https://legislature.vermont.gov/Documents/2020/WorkGroups/Senate%20Institutions/Dept.%20of%20Corrections/State%20Workforce%20Development/W~Susan%20Russell~Circles%20of%20Support%20and%20Accountability,%202013,%20Kathryn%20Fox,%20Ph.D.%20UVM~1-10-2020.pdf

Fox, K. (2014). Restoring the social: Offender reintegration in a risky world. *International Journal of Offender Therapy and Comparative Criminology, 38*(3), 235–256. doi: https://www.tandfonline.com/doi/abs/10.1080/01924036.2013.848221

Fox, K. (2015). Theorizing community integration as desistance-promotion. *Criminal Justice and Behavior, 42*(1), 82–94. doi: https://doi.org/10.1177/0093854814550028

Fox, K. (2016). Civic commitment: Promoting desistance through community integration. *Punishment & Society, 18*(1), 68–94. doi: https://journals.sagepub.com/doi/abs/10.1177/1462474515623102?journalCode=puna

Gilliam, M., Novak, M., Bohmert, M. N., & Duwe, G. (2021). Desires and desirability of volunteers in CoSA programs. *Sexual Abuse, 33*(4), 406–433. doi: https://journals.sagepub.com/doi/abs/10.1177/1079063220912454?journalCode=saxb

Giordano, P., Cernkovich, S., & Rudolph, J. (2002). Gender, crime, and desistance: Toward a theory of cognitive transformation. *American Journal of Sociology, 1077*, 990–1064. doi: https://www.journals.uchicago.edu/doi/10.1086/343191

Giordano, P., Johnson, W., Manning, W., Longmore, M., & Minter, M. (2015). Intimate partner violence in young adulthood: Narratives of persistence and desistance. *Criminology, 53*(3), 330–365. doi: https://onlinelibrary.wiley.com/doi/abs/10.1111/1745-9125.12073

Glueck, S., & Glueck, E. (1968). *Delinquents and nondelinquents in perspective*. Harvard University Press. doi: https://www.hup.harvard.edu/catalog.php?isbn=9780674188754

Göbbels, S., Ward, T., & Willis, G. (2012). An integrative theory of desistance from sex offending. *Aggression and Violent Behavior, 17*, 453–462. doi: https://www.sciencedirect.com/science/article/pii/S1359178912000651?via%3Dihub

Graham, H. (2016). *Rehabilitation work: Supporting desistance and recovery*. Routledge. doi: https://www.routledge.com/Rehabilitation-Work-Supporting-Desistance-and-Recovery/Graham/p/book/9781138499454

Hannem, S., & Petrunik, M. (2007). Circles of Support and Accountability: A community justice initiative for the reintegration of high-risk sex offenders. *Contemporary Justice Review, 10*(2), 153–171. doi: https://doi.org/10.1080/10282580701372046

Hanson, K., Bourgon, G., Helmus, L., & Hodgson, S. (2009). The principles of effective correctional treatment also apply to sexual offenders. *Criminal Justice and Behavior, 36*(9), 865–891. doi: https://journals.sagepub.com/doi/10.1177/0093854809338545

Harkins, L., & Beech, A. (2007). A review of the factors that can influence the effectiveness of sexual offender treatment: Risk, need, responsivity, and process issues. *Aggression and Violent Behavior, 12*, 615–627. doi: https://www.sciencedirect.com/science/article/pii/S1359178907000365?via%3Dihub

Harper, C., Wilson, C., Hocken, K., Awan, T., & Lievesley, R. (2019). Religiously responsive treatment for people convicted of sexual offences. In B. Winder, N. Blagden, K. Hocken, H. Elliott, R. Lievesley, & P. Banyard (Eds.), *Sexual crime, religion and spirituality* (pp. 115–138). Palgrave Macmillan. doi: https://www.palgrave.com/gp/book/9783030260392

Harris, D. (2014). Desistance from sexual offending: Findings from 21 life history narratives. *Journal of Interpersonal Violence, 29*(9), 1554–1578. doi: https://journals.sagepub.com/doi/abs/10.1177/0886260513511532?journalCode=jiva

Harris, D. (2017a). Desistance from sexual offending: Behavioral change without cognitive transformation. *Journal of Interpersonal Violence, 32*(20), 3049–3070. doi: https://journals.sagepub.com/doi/abs/10.1177/0886260515596537

Harris, D. (2017b). *Desistance from sexual offending: Narratives of retirement, regulation and recovery*. Palgrave Macmillan. doi: https://www.palgrave.com/gp/book/9783319631998

Höing, M., Bogaerts, S., & Vogelvang, B. (2013). Circles of Support and Accountability: How and why they work for sex offenders. *Journal of Forensic Psychology Practice, 13*(4), 267–295. doi: https://www.tandfonline.com/doi/abs/10.1080/15228932.2013.808526

Höing, M., Duke, L., & Völlm, B. (2015). *Circles of Support and Accountability European handbook*. Avans University of Applied Sciences Centre for Public Safety and Criminal Justice. doi: https://www.circles-uk.org.uk/circles4eu/what-is-circles-4eu

Höing, M., Vogelvang, B., & Bogaerts, S. (2017). "I am a different man now" – sex offenders in Circles of Support and Accountability: A prospective study. *International Journal of Offender Therapy and Comparative Criminology, 61*(7), 751–772. doi: https://doi.org/10.1177/0306624X15612431

Horan, R. (2015). Restorative justice: The relevance of desistance and psychology. *Safer Communities, 14*(3), 147–155. doi: https://www.emerald.com/insight/content/doi/10.1108/SC-06-2015-0025/full/html

Kerr, N., Tully, R., & Völlm, B. (2018). Volunteering with sex offenders: The attitudes of volunteers towards sex offenders, their treatment, and rehabilitation. *Sexual Abuse: A Journal of Research and Treatment, 30*(6), 659–675. doi: https://doi.org/10.1177/1079063217691964

Kirk, D. (2012). Residential change as a turning point in the life course of crime: Desistance or temporary cessation? *Criminology, 50*(2), 329–357. doi/10.1111/j.1745-9125.2011.00262.x

Kras, K. (2014). *Redemption or condemnation? A long-term follow-up of the desistance patterns of sex offenders* [PhD thesis, University of Missouri]. St Louis.

Kras, K., & Blasko, B. (2016). Pathways to desistance among men convicted of sexual offenses: Linking post hoc accounts of offending behavior and outcomes. *International Journal of Offender Therapy and Comparative Criminology, 60*(15), 1738–1755. doi: https://journals.sagepub.com/doi/abs/10.1177/0306624X16668178

Larsson, B. (2019). Morality tales: Young women's narratives on offending, self-worth and desistance. *Probation Journal, 66*(3), 318–334. doi: https://journals.sagepub.com/doi/10.1177/0264550519860560

Laub, J., & Sampson, R. (1993). Turning points in the life course: Why change matters to the study of crime. *Criminology, 31*(3), 301–325. doi: https://onlinelibrary.wiley.com/doi/abs/10.1111/j.1745-9125.1993.tb01132.x

Laub, J., & Sampson, R. (2001). Understanding desistance from crime. *Crime & Justice, 28*, 1–69.

Laub, J., & Sampson, R. (2003). *Shared beginnings, divergent lives: Delinquent boys to age 70*. Harvard University Press. doi: https://psycnet.apa.org/record/2003-88395-000

Liem, M., & Richardson, N. (2014). The role of transformation narratives in desistance among released lifers. *Criminal Justice and Behavior, 41*(6), 692–712. doi: https://psycnet.apa.org/record/2014-16649-002

Lofland, J. (1969). *Deviance and identity*. Prentice-Hall.

Looman, J., & Abracen, J. (2013). The risk need responsivity model of offender rehabilitation: Is there really a need for a paradigm shift? *The International Journal of Behavioral Consultation and Therapy, 8*(3–4), 30–36. doi: https://psycnet.apa.org/fulltext/2014-12592-007.html

Looman, J., Dickie, I., & Abracen, J. (2015). Responsivity issues in the treatment of sexual offenders. *Trauma, Violence, & Abuse, 6*(4), 330–353. doi: https://pubmed.ncbi.nlm.nih.gov/16217120/

Lussier, P., Harris, D., & McAlinden, A. M. (2016). Desistance from sexual offending: A policy and research agenda whose time has come. *International Journal of Offender Therapy and Comparative Criminology*, *60*(15), 1711–1716. doi: https://journals.sagepub.com/doi/abs/10.1177/0306624X16668174

Lussier, P., & McCuish, E. (2016). Desistance from crime without reintegration: A longitudinal study of the social context and life course path to desistance in a sample of adults convicted of a sex crime. *International Journal of Offender Therapy and Comparative Criminology*, *60*(15), 1791–1812. doi: https://journals.sagepub.com/doi/abs/10.1177/0306624X16668179

Marchetti, E., & Daly, K. (2017). Indigenous partner violence, indigenous sentencing courts, and pathways to desistance. *Violence against Women*, *23*(12), 1513–1535. doi: https://journals.sagepub.com/doi/abs/10.1177/1077801216662341

Marshall, T. (1996). The evolution of restorative justice in Britain. *European Journal on Criminal Policy and Research*, *4*(4), 21–43. doi: https://link.springer.com/article/10.1007/BF02736712

Maruna, S. (2001). *Making good: How ex-convicts reform and rebuild their lives*. American Psychological Association. doi: https://www.apa.org/pubs/books/431645A

Maruna, S. (2011). Reentry as a rite of passage. *Theoretical Criminology*, *13*(1), 3–28. doi: https://journals.sagepub.com/doi/10.1177/1462474510385641

Maruna, S., & Roy, K. (2007). Amputation or reconstruction? Notes on the concept of "knifing off" and desistance from crime. *Journal of Contemporary Criminal Justice*, *23*(1), 104–124. doi: https://journals.sagepub.com/doi/10.1177/1043986206298951

Matza, D. (1964). *Delinquency and drift*. Routledge.

McAlinden, A. M. (2005). The use of 'shame' with sexual offenders. *British Journal of Criminology*, *45*, 373–394. doi: https://academic.oup.com/bjc/article-abstract/45/3/373/505380?redirectedFrom=fulltext

McAlinden, A. M. (2007). *The shaming of sexual offenders: Risk, retribution and reintegration*. Hart Publishing. doi: https://www.bloomsburyprofessional.com/uk/the-shaming-of-sexual-offenders-9781841135922/

McCartan, K., Kemshall, H., Westwood, S., Solle, J., MacKenzie, G., Cattel, J., & Pollard, A. (2014). *Circles of Support and Accountability (CoSA): A case file review of two pilots*. Ministry of Justice. https://assets.publishing.service.gov.uk/government/uploads/system/uploads/attachment_data/file/293400/cosa-research-summary.pdf

McCartan, K., & McKenzie, N. (2014). Restorative justice, community action and public protection. In S. Maile, & D. Griffiths (Eds.), *Public engagement and social science* (pp. 127–144). Bristol University Press.

McCold, P. (1998). Restorative justice - variations on a theme. In L. Walgrace (Ed.), *Restorative justice for juveniles: Potentialities, risks and problems for research* (pp. 19–53). Leuven University Press.

Miers, D. (2001). *An international review of restorative justice*. Home Office. https://restorativejustice.org.uk/sites/default/files/resources/files/An%20International%20Review%20of%20Restorative%20Justice.pdf

Paternoster, R., Bachman, R., Bushway, S., Kerrison, E., & O'Connell, D. (2015). Human agency and explanations of criminal desistance: Arguments for a rational choice theory. *Journal of Developmental and Life-Course Criminology*, *1*(3), 209–235. doi: https://link.springer.com/article/10.1007/s40865-015-0013-2

Peachey, D. (1989). The Kitchener experiment. In M. Wright, & B. Galaway (Eds.), *Mediation and criminal justice: Victims, offenders and community* (pp. 14–26). SAGE.

Petrich, D. (2016). Theorising desistance-promotion in circle processes: The role of community in identity transformation. *Restorative Justice: An International Journal*,

4(3), 388–409. doi: https://www.tandfonline.com/doi/full/10.1080/20504721.2016.1245905

Presser, L. (2008). *Been a heavy life: Stories of violent men*. University of Illinois Press. doi: https://www.jstor.org/stable/10.5406/j.ctt1xcj9k

Rex, S. (1999). Desistance from offending: Experiences of probation. *The Howard Journal*, *38*(4), 366–383. doi: https://onlinelibrary.wiley.com/doi/abs/10.1111/1468-2311.00141

Richards, K. (2009). Taking victims seriously? The role of victims' rights movements in the emergence of restorative justice. *Current Issues in Criminal Justice*, *21*(2), 302–320. doi: https://www.tandfonline.com/doi/abs/10.1080/10345329.2009.12035847

Richards, K. (2014). A promise and a possibility: The limitations of the traditional criminal justice system as an explanation for the emergence of restorative justice. *Restorative Justice: An International Journal*, *2*(2), 124–141. doi: https://www.tandfonline.com/doi/abs/10.5235/20504721.2.2.124

Richards, K. (in press). Circles of Support and Accountability: The role of social relations in core member desistance. *International Journal of Offender Therapy and Comparative Criminology*. doi: https://doi.org/10.1177/0306624X20964094

Richards, K., Death, J., & McCartan, K. (2020). *Community-based approaches to sexual offender reintegration*. Australia's National Research Organisation for Women's Safety. https://www.anrows.org.au/project/community-based-approaches-to-sexual-offender-reintegration/

Rocque, M., Posick, C., & Paternoster, R. (2016). Identities through time: An exploration of identity change as a cause of desistance. *Justice Quarterly*, *33*(1), 45–72. doi: https://www.tandfonline.com/doi/full/10.1080/07418825.2014.894111

Sampson, R., & Laub, J. (2016). Turning points and the future of life course criminology: Reflections on the 1986 criminal careers report. *Journal of Research in Crime and Delinquency*, *53*(3), 321–335. doi: https://journals.sagepub.com/doi/10.1177/0022427815616992

Scheirs, V. (2016). Doing reintegration? The quest for reintegration in Belgian sentence implementation. *European Journal of Probation*, *8*(2), 82–101. doi: https://journals.sagepub.com/doi/10.1177/2066220316661660

Schinkel, M. (2015). Hook for change or shaky peg? Imprisonment, narratives and desistance. *European Journal of Probation*, 7(1), 5–20. doi: https://journals.sagepub.com/doi/full/10.1177/2066220315575204

Simon, J. (1998). Managing the monstrous: Sex offenders and the new penology. *Psychology, Public Policy, and Law*, *4*(1/2), 452–467. doi: https://psycnet.apa.org/record/1998-11556-017

Stone, R. (2016). Desistance and identity repair: Redemption narratives as resistance to stigma. *British Journal of Criminology*, *56*, 956–975. doi: https://academic.oup.com/bjc/article/56/5/956/1745580

Strang, H. (2000). The future of restorative justice. In D. Chappell, & P. WIlson (Eds.), *Crime and the criminal justice system in Australia: 2000 and beyond* (pp. 22–33). Butterworths.

Sullivan, K. (2012). *Motivating and maintaining desistance from crime: Male Aboriginal serial offenders' experience of 'going good'* [PhD thesis, Australian National University]. Canberra.

Taylor, R. (2018). Foreword. In H. Elliott, K. Hocken, R. Lievesley, N. Blagden, B. Winder, & P. Banyard (Eds.), *Sexual crime and Circles of Support and Accountability* (pp. v–vii). Palgrave Macmillan. doi: https://www.palgrave.com/gp/book/9783319748221

Thompson, D. (2015). *Moving on after getting out: Support and accountability for convicted sex offenders* [PhD thesis, University of Leeds]. Leeds. https://etheses.whiterose.ac.uk/13410/1/Thompson_D_Law_PhD_2015.pdf

Thompson, D., Thomas, T., & Karstedt, S. (2017). *The resettlement of sex offenders after custody: Circles of Support and Accountability*. Routledge. doi: https://www.routledge.com/The-Resettlement-of-Sex-Offenders-after-Custody-Circles-of-Support-and/Thompson-Thomas/p/book/9780367227111

Toby, J. (1957). Social disorganization and stake in conformity: Complementary factors in the predatory behavior of hoodlums. *Journal of Criminal Law, Criminology, and Police Science, 48*(1), 12–17. doi: https://psycnet.apa.org/record/1959-01797-001

Vieira, C., Rose, R., Craissati, J., & Campbell, C. (2020). The impact of a community psychological treatment programme on desistance in personality disordered sexual offenders. *The Journal of Forensic Psychiatry & Psychology, 31*(6), 837–853. doi: https://doi.org/10.1080/14789949.2020.1807041?journalCode=rjfp20

Wagmeister, E., & Nichols, M. (2020, 24 February). Harvey Weinstein stunned by verdict: 'I'm innocent. How could this happen in America?'. *Variety*. https://variety.com/2020/biz/news/harvey-weinstein-reaction-guilty-rape-sexual-assault-1203513485/

Walker, K., Bowen, E., Brown, S., & Sleith, E. (2015). Subjective accounts of the turning points that facilitate desistance from intimate partner violence. *International Journal of Offender Therapy and Comparative Criminology, 61*(4), 371–396. doi: https://journals.sagepub.com/doi/10.1177/0306624X15597493

Ward, T. (2002a). Good lives and the rehabilitaiton of offenders: Promises and problems. *Aggression and Violent Behavior*, 7(5), 513–528. doi: https://www.sciencedirect.com/science/article/pii/S1359178901000763?via%3Dihub

Ward, T. (2002b). The management of risk and the design of good lives. *Australian Psychologist, 37*(3), 172–179. doi: https://www.tandfonline.com/doi/abs/10.1080/00050060210001706846

Ward, T., & Brown, M. (2004). The good lives model and conceptual issues in offender rehabilitation. *Psychology, Crime & Law, 10*(3), 243–257. doi: https://www.tandfonline.com/doi/full/10.1080/10683160410001662744

Ward, T., Fox, K., & Garber, M. (2014). Restorative justice, offender rehabilitation and desistance. *Restorative Justice: An International Journal, 2*(1), 24–42. doi: https://www.tandfonline.com/doi/abs/10.5235/20504721.2.1.24

Ward, T., & Gannon, T. (2006). Rehabilitation, etiology, and self-regulation: The comprehensive good lives model of treatment for sexual offenders. *Aggression and Violent Behavior, 11*(1), 77–94. doi: https://psycnet.apa.org/record/2006-00981-006

Ward, T., & Laws, R. (2010). Desistance from sex offending: Motivating change, enriching practice. *International Journal of Forensic Mental Health, 9*(1), 11–23. doi: https://www.tandfonline.com/doi/abs/10.1080/14999011003791598

Ward, T., & Stewart, C. (2003). The treatment of sex offenders: Risk management and good lives. *Professional Psychology: Research and Practice, 34*(4), 353–360. doi: https://psycnet.apa.org/record/2003-06801-003

Ward, T., Yates, P., & Willis, G. (2012). The good lives model and the risk need responsivity model: A critical response to Andrews, Bonta, and Wormith (2011). *Criminal Justice and Behavior, 39*(1), 94–110. doi: https://journals.sagepub.com/doi/10.1177/0093854811426085

Whitehead, P., Ward, T., & Collie, R. (2007). Time for a change: Applying the good lives model of rehabilitation to a high-risk violent offender. *International Journal of*

Offender Therapy and Comparative Criminology, 51(5), 578–598. doi: https://journals.sagepub.com/doi/10.1177/0306624X06296236

Willis, G., Levenson, J., & Ward, T. (2010). Desistance and attitudes towards sex offenders: Facilitation or hindrance? *Journal of Family Violence, 25*, 545–556. doi: https://psycnet.apa.org/record/2010-14059-002

Willis, G., & Ward, T. (2013). The good lives model: Evidence that it works. In L. Craig, L. Dixon, & T. Gannon (Eds.), *What works in offender rehabilitation: An evidence-based approach to assessment and treatment* (pp. 305–318). John Wiley & Sons. doi: https://onlinelibrary.wiley.com/doi/book/10.1002/9781118320655

Wilson, C. (2018). A history of the development of Circles of Support and Accountability. In H. Elliott, K. Hocken, R. Lievesley, N. Blagden, B. Winder, & P. Banyard (Eds.), *Sexual crime and Circles of Support and Accountability* (pp. 1–24). Palgrave Macmillan. doi: https://www.palgrave.com/gp/book/9783319748221

Wilson, R., & Yates, P. (2009). Effective interventions and the good lives model: Maximizing treatment gains for sexual offenders. *Aggression and Violent Behavior, 14*(3), 157–161. doi: https://www.sciencedirect.com/science/article/pii/S1359178909000184?via%3Dihub

Zehr, H. (1990). *Changing lenses: A new focus for crime and justice*. Herald Press.

Zehr, H. (2002). *The little book of restorative justice*. Good Books. doi: https://www.simonandschuster.com.au/books/The-Little-Book-of-Restorative-Justice/Howard-Zehr/Justice-and-Peacebuilding/9781680990447

Zehr, H., & Mika, H. (2003). Fundamental concepts of restorative justice. In E. McLaughlin, R. Fergusson, G. Hughes, & L. Westmarland (Eds.), *Restorative justice: Critical issues* (pp. 40–43). Sage Publications. doi: https://uk.sagepub.com/en-gb/eur/restorative-justice/book225657

Chapter 3

Researching Circles of Support and Accountability

The material contained in this book draws from a program of research on Circles of Support and Accountability (CoSA) that I have conducted since that memorable day at Wendy's in Fresno, California, with Clare Ann and Rory. Since then I have undertaken research on a range of topics relating to CoSA, including examining public opinion about CoSA (Richards, 2018; Richards & McCartan, 2018), examining Australia's first CoSA program (Richards et al., 2020) and investigating the views of victims/survivors of sexual violence about CoSA (Richards et al., in press). The material in this book references all of these projects but focuses in particular on one major piece of empirical research undertaken in 2017, when I returned to North America in an attempt to further understand and make sense of CoSA. This time I sought to examine the role of CoSA in the desistance journeys of core members. As described in the last chapter, recent scholarship had begun to position CoSA as desistance-promotion; my research in North America set out to subject this to detailed empirical investigation for the first time.

Methodological Approach

Like much of my research, this project adopted a broad phenomenological approach. In other words, it was primarily concerned with identifying and understanding participants' *own understandings* (Pompili, 2010) and *own views* of the world (Chamberlain, 2009; Skrapec, 2001) – in this case, CoSA. Following Farmer et al. (2015, p. 324), the research aimed "to gain an appreciation of participants' own understanding of their lives, and the relationship between these self-understandings and desistance from sexual crime" (see further Farmer et al., 2016). At heart, I am fundamentally interested not in "the truth" of any particular matter, but in how people understand issues, events and phenomena themselves – people's own "truths" and how they arrive at these and the stories we tell ourselves to make sense of our lives and worlds. The research project, therefore, involved examining participants' own understandings of core members' desistance from sexual offending and the role of CoSA in this. It was concerned with how CoSA participants –

DOI: 10.4324/9781003125532-4

especially core members themselves – made sense of the role of CoSA in "going straight" and "making good" (Maruna, 2001) and the role(s) that CoSA played in the men's stories in this regard.

The research was therefore also embedded, in broad terms, in the tradition of "narrative criminology" (Presser, 2009). This approach centralises the stories that individuals – in this case, individuals convicted of sexual offences – tell. Such stories are important to comprehend because, as Presser (2009) and Sandberg (2010) argue, narratives precede crime. They, therefore, might be understood to also precede desistance from crime: "Narratives are important not because they are true records of what happened, but because they influence behavior in the future" (Sandberg, 2010, p. 452; see also Victor & Waldram, 2015). A narrative criminological approach thus provides a backcloth to the current research as it invites an examination of the stories core members tell, the relationship of these stories to their current and future identities and the role of CoSA in the development of these.

Academic interest in narrative criminology has flourished over about the last decade, and scholars have begun to document and analyse the narratives of a wide range of offenders, from mass murderers to drug suppliers (see Sandberg & Ugelvik, 2016 for an overview). However, the narratives of people convicted of sexual offences pose unique challenges. The stories of offenders generally may be dismissed as lies, since it is often assumed that offenders are inherently untruthful or that their stories are "strategically pitched" (Presser, 2009, p. 181) towards some instrumental end such as early release on parole (see Sandberg, 2010 for a discussion). This is more so the case for people with sexual offence convictions, who are often deemed manipulative (Richards & McCartan, 2018). As Victor and Waldram (2015) pointed out, the often rigid legal prescriptions and social stigmatisation to which those with sexual offence convictions are subject makes the construction of an authentic (let alone positive) self-narrative a virtual impossibility. In particular, individuals with convictions for sexual offending are usually required to disclose their convictions to prospective friends and partners, all but disallowing the development of a coherent positive identity (Victor & Waldram, 2015).

The research reported here abandoned any positivist notion of "the truth" (see Renzetti, 1997), as foreshadowed above. I did not set out to seek "the truth" from or about core members. Rather, I approached the research from a constructivist epistemological standpoint, assuming that "knowledge and truth are created, not discovered" (Schwandt, 1998, p. 236), and that realities are both plastic and plural. As Schwandt (1998, p. 236) explains, according to a constructivist viewpoint, realities are "stretched and shaped to fit purposeful acts of intentional human agents". I, therefore, worked from the assumption that core members' narratives would reveal *a* truth – *their* truth – and that these would provide a rich source of information in and of themselves. As Sandberg (2010, p. 448) argued, whether a participant is telling the "truth" is less important than interrogating what a participant's stories reveal about their perceptions, and what these, in turn, indicate about the events and/or experiences upon which they are reflecting: "…the "truth" is not always important. Whether true or false, the multitude of stories people tell reflect, and help us understand, the complex nature of values, identities, cultures, and communities".

Does this mean that the core members I interviewed simply told me what they thought I "wanted to hear"? The short answer is: I certainly hope not. By this I don't mean I hope they didn't lie to me, but rather that I hope what they told me was not what they thought I "wanted to hear". As discussed in detail later in this book, a number of the core members denied the offences for which they had been convicted. Others minimised or justified their offending. Bryce continually insisted that he had not done anything really wrong, claiming moral equivalence with his victims (as discussed further below). When I asked core members about making amends or giving back, many enthusiastically described their plans to give back – to others with sexual offence convictions. Needless to say, to the extent that I wanted or expected to hear anything in particular, this was not it. Indeed, the content of many of the interviews was deeply discomforting. On these grounds, it seems reasonable to assume that the men were simply telling me their versions of the truth. It is also worth noting that I had met four of the core members seven years previously, in an informal capacity, when I had visited their CoSA programs as part of my Churchill Fellowship. In all these cases, the men recounted the same stories in their interviews that they had shared with me seven years prior. This does not necessarily mean that the stories are "true", but it does not indicate that the men's truths are consistent.

A qualitative approach was adopted to explore in detail the rich layers of participants' experiences with and understandings of CoSA in this regard. Qualitative research involves exploring the opinions, beliefs, experiences and knowledge (Bayens & Roberson, 2011, p. 24) of participants, rather than seeking to quantify these. It is often considered the "poor cousin" of quantitative research (Richards & Bartels, 2011, p. 1) and seen as "soft and subjective, an anecdotal supplement to the real science" (Winchester cited in Richards & Bartels, 2011, p. 1). This is, of course, utter nonsense: qualitative research sets out to achieve something entirely different from quantitative research, and should be judged on its own merits, not those belonging to the quantitative paradigm. Only qualitative research can capture the in-depth, complex and nuanced experiences and understandings of people's lives. It is therefore the only suitable methodological approach for phenomenological research (Bevan, 2014; Chamberlain, 2009; Paley, 2017). Granted, qualitative projects cannot be deemed representative of whole populations, or generalisable to whole populations (Higgins, 2009; Tewkesbury, 2009), but this is not the point. The point, rather, is to elicit and describe the rich layers and vicissitudes of people's life worlds – a task that simply cannot be accomplished by collecting official statistics or conducting a large-scale survey.

Participant Sampling and Recruitment

I recruited participants into the study with the help of existing contacts from my Churchill Fellowship, with whom I had remained in contact. They came from six CoSA programs based in and around three locations in Canada and the United States: four programs from Toronto, Canada, and the surrounding areas; one from Fresno, California, USA and one from St John's, Newfoundland and Labrador, Canada. These programs vary in a number of key ways. Perhaps most significantly, Toronto is a major metropolitan centre and the fourth most populated city in North America, with a population of nearly three million (nearly six million in the Greater Toronto Area), and a sprawling suburbia that bleeds into smaller towns on its outskirts, including Hamilton and Kitchener-Waterloo. Fresno, as noted earlier in this book, is comparatively small, with a population of about half a million, while St John's is comparatively both remote and tiny, with a population of just 100,000 or so. These differences are important to note given CoSA's reliance on the community; the "communities" included in my research vary substantially in size and makeup. Another important difference is that Toronto and its surrounds are the birthplace of CoSA (as described in Chapter 1), although other CoSA sites proliferated across Canada soon afterwards. CoSA programs right across Canada have been subject to funding instability since their inception – even effectively losing all federal funding under the Harper Government (Kay, 2014) and later having it reinstated in 2017 under Prime Minister Trudeau (Hong, 2017). The Toronto-based programs included in the research have, however, long been key players in a national network of Canadian CoSA programs and are currently the site of evaluation activity under a federally funded research project. Neither the Fresno nor the St John's programs are embedded in a broader network in this way. Indeed, the St John's program has always maintained an identity and presence separate from the national network of CoSA programs in Canada that come under the auspices of national umbrella organisation CoSA Canada (see www.cosacanada.com). No national network of this nature exists in the United States. Both the Fresno and St John's programs thus operate without the benefit (or otherwise) of shared practice wisdom from allied programs.

To recruit participants for the research, I used a combined purposive and convenience sampling strategy (see generally Gray, 2009). Purposive sampling focuses on recruiting those individuals who may be most affected by a specific issue (Valerio et al., 2016, p. 148). Convenience sampling often "uses existing relationships to identify participants" (Valerio et al., 2016, p. 148); it involves including in the research those individuals who are available, easy to recruit and willing to participate (Bachmann & Schutt, 2012). I contacted program staff in each location and provided them with a written copy of a participant information and consent form and list of indicative interview questions for each of four participant groups: core members; volunteers;

program staff and key stakeholders. Program staff then circulated this information to prospective participants from their programs and related networks, in-person and/or via email, and either arranged interview times for those willing to take part or encouraged prospective participants to make contact with me to discuss the research and/or make a time to meet for an interview. In my discussions with program staff, I stressed the importance of informing as diverse a group of potential interviewees as possible about the research. This was critical in order to capture varied core member experiences. I did not only want to hear from the "success stories" of CoSA – those core members whose CoSA had transpired without incident, who had existing supports in the community, and whose desistance had been relatively straightforward. To this end, program staff made deliberate efforts to recruit core members of varying ages and cognitive capacities, and with varying offending histories and experiences of CoSA (e.g., differing lengths of time involved in CoSA).

Using this strategy, I was able to recruit 65 participants from across the six CoSA programs from four participant groups:

1 Core members (n = 31);
2 CoSA volunteers (n = 17);
3 CoSA program staff (n = 14) and
4 Key stakeholders (n = 3).

Data Collection

I asked each participant questions from a pre-determined list specifically designed for each of the four participant groups. The interviews were semi-structured; in other words, they were guided by the pre-determined list of questions rather than dictated by it (Chan et al., 2018). In interviews of a semi-structured nature, "the researcher follows the cues of the participants.... the interviewer is free to probe interesting areas that arise from participants' interests or concerns....[and].... must ask focusing but not leading questions" (Chan et al., 2018, pp. 4–5). The interview questions were open-ended in order to capture rich, detailed narratives from participants in their own words, rather than according to a pre-determined range of potential responses. Open-ended questions are designed to elucidate what is of principal importance to the participant (Weller et al., 2018) and to enable participants to make sense of their own experiences without constraints; they are thus integral in research of a phenomenological nature (Bevan, 2014; Chan et al., 2018).

This was the case in theory at least. In practice, interviewing people with sexual offence convictions can sometimes involve simply listening to their version of their life story, or the story(ies) they want to share, with the list of pre-determined questions being thrown out the proverbial window. This was by no means always the case. Indeed, some core members I interviewed were exceptionally bright and extremely articulate; they gave genuine thought to each of my questions, carefully checking their understanding of questions and thoughtfully responding as helpfully and fulsomely as they could. Others, however, seemed almost immune to my questioning, and seemingly wanted to offload their life story to a sympathetic ear rather than contribute towards an understanding of CoSA. This is to be expected on some level. People with sexual offence convictions are used to telling "their story". They have little choice but to recount it, *ad nauseam*, to a veritable army of therapists, clinicians, correctional professionals and other offenders in group therapy sessions in prison, in civil commitment facilities and in the community. This is often exacerbated by high staff turnover in some of these fields. A probation officer is transferred to another office, and the offender must, once again, recount his story to a new professional. Core members, of course, must also relate their stories to members of their CoSA.

It is also the case, in my experience, that people subject to the very harsh, rigid and often permanent measures of the sex offender management industry (Wacquant, 2009) often feel hard done by, and relish the opportunity to vent their woes to a sympathetic stranger, even when this is clearly not the intended focus of the interview. This was apparent in a number of the interviews, but came into sharp relief in late 2019, when I returned to Fresno for a whirlwind visit and had the opportunity to present some of my preliminary findings to a community circle comprised of about 15 or so CoSA staff, core members and volunteers. I seized excitedly on this opportunity to present my emerging thinking about the project back to some of the men I had interviewed and drew up a two-page flyer outlining a couple of key points I wanted to share. I had little notice about this forum, but in the short time I had, I thought carefully about presenting the material in a manner that was comprehensible to a group with extremely varied educational backgrounds without being patronising, all the while maintaining strict confidentiality. I believed I accomplished this with aplomb – particularly given the handicap of my funny Australian accent, to which most Americans are not accustomed – but was immediately disabused of this notion by one of the core members present. This core member cared little for my theoretical insights about the role of CoSA in desistance from sexual offending. Instead, he was incensed that my flyer had not detailed the profound difficulties, derogations, denigrations and indignities to which those convicted of sexual offences are subject on release from prison. Holding the flyer aloft, and gesticulating heartily, he launched into a very public peer review of my research, highlighting its deficiencies and failure to capture the sheer awfulness of his, and other core members', predicament. Humbled in the face of the core member's ire, I meekly mumbled something about the purpose of the research, before being rescued by the organiser of the meeting. I tell this story not to make fun of the core member, but to underscore my point here, that interviews with people who have sexually offended can sometimes occur on their, rather than the interviewer's, terms.

Such interviews are somewhat more frustrating, but no less valuable, than the "ideal" interview in which the participant responds carefully and articulately to the interviewer's questions. Importantly, these rather more unwieldy interviews highlight what is of primary significance to the interviewee themselves, often providing essential background and context that would have been missed if the researcher's narrower concerns were strictly adhered to.

The interviews were conducted at a variety of locations – mostly at CoSA program offices, but also at the facilities used for individual Circles, such as church basements and community centres, as well as the occasional café or in one case, on the steps of an unopened church building in the early hours of the morning, before the core member's work for the day commenced. On average they took approximately one hour, with some lasting far longer, and a small number conducted with core members requiring support to take part, lasting a much shorter time. In terms of the content of the interviews, core members were asked questions about their experiences of CoSA and whether and how these had shaped their sense of identity in the context of desistance. The interview questions had been developed to elucidate *how CoSA contribute to core members' narratives of identity transformation in the context of their desistance from sexual offending*. In addition to a number of demographic and introductory questions (e.g., "How did you first come to participate in CoSA?"), they were asked questions that sought to explore this question, such as: "Has being in a CoSA changed the way you see yourself? How?", "What do you make of the term 'core member'?", "Looking back on your offending, how to you make sense of it now?" and "Does being in a CoSA encourage you to want to give back? How do you go about this?". All other participants were asked questions along the same lines but in relation to the core members with whom they had been involved as a CoSA volunteer or staff member. For example, they were asked: "Do you think being in a CoSA changes the way core members see themselves? How?", "How do CoSA help core members desist?" and "Are core members encouraged to give back to the community and/or make amends? How?".

All interviews except one were conducted in person by me. One core member was unavailable at the time of data collection but wanted to take part in the research, and as a result, I arranged to interview him by telephone at a later date. Interviews were mainly conducted one-on-one, but in a few cases, small groups of staff or volunteers were interviewed together for practical reasons. This proved fortunate since group interviews provoke rich layers of detail and debate that may not arise in interviews with individuals, as participants tend to consider one another's comments and thus reflect more critically on their own (Coggan et al., 1997). This was emphatically the case with the group interviews I conducted, with volunteers, in particular, taking the opportunity to challenge and be challenged by other volunteers' understandings of CoSA and their impact on core members.

The Participants

Table 3.1 provides an overview of participants in the study (n = 65). All core members (n = 31) were male, as is typically the case. Almost all identified as Caucasian (one identified as Mexican-American and another as First Nations Canadian). Their average age was 55 years (range = 24–76). Most (n = 19; 61%) had been incarcerated in relation to contact sexual offences against minors. A smaller number (n = 6; 19%) had been incarcerated for non-contact offences (such as possessing child exploitation material, exhibitionism or meeting a minor for the purposes of sexual contact) and contact offences against adult women (n = 2; 6%). Three did not reveal their index offence. One core member, Seamus, had not been convicted of a sexual offence but participated

Table 3.1 Research participants by location and category

	Core members (n = 31)	*Volunteers (n = 17)*	*Staff (n = 14)*	*Stakeholders (n = 3)*
Fresno, California, USA	Brian	Volunteer 1	Staff member 1	Stakeholder 1
	Daniel	Volunteer 2	Staff member 2	Stakeholder 2
	Damien	Volunteer 3	Staff member 3	
	Alan	Volunteer 4	Staff member 4	
	Richard	Volunteer 5	Staff member 5	
	Sean	Volunteer 6	Staff member 6	
	Terry		Staff member 7	
	Rory			
	Mathias			
	Gerald			
	Wayne			
Greater Toronto area, Ottawa, Canada	Ewan	Volunteer 7	Staff member 8	
	Seamus	Volunteer 8	Staff member 9	
	Kevin	Volunteer 9	Staff member 10	
	James	Volunteer 10	Staff member 11	
	Bryce	Volunteer 11	Staff member 12	
	Todd	Volunteer 12		
	Adam	Volunteer 13		
	Peter	Volunteer 14		
	Don	Volunteer 15		
	Kaleb			
	Dean			
	Leon			
	Joshua			
	Stan			
	Zack			
	Lachlan			
	Morgan			
St John's, Newfoundland and Labrador, Canada	Keith	Volunteer 16	Staff member 13	Stakeholder 3
	Donny	Volunteer 17	Staff member 14	
	Frank			

in a CoSA in a preventative capacity as a result of his diagnosed pedophilia. Core members had served between 14 and 612 months in prison (and/or in civil commitment facilities), with an average time served of 110 months (just over 9 years) and a median of 48 months (4 years). As a small number from the Fresno sample had served very long periods in prison and then in civil commitment facilities, this average is skewed and the median is a better measure of time served. While most core members in the sample had been incarcerated for the first time for this index offence, six had been incarcerated previously for a sexual offence (two of these on multiple occasions) and three had been incarcerated previously for non-sexual offences. This is not surprising, since most individuals charged with sexual offences are previously unknown to criminal justice authorities (Sandler et al., 2008).

Twelve core members were not currently participating in a CoSA but had effectively completed a CoSA; some of these had remained in touch with the program in a variety of ways (e.g., by remaining in contact with volunteers and/or participating in organised social events). For those currently participating in a CoSA, the average time in the Circle was 58 months (4 years and 8 months; median = 36 months (3 years)), suggesting that the recruitment strategy outlined above may have favoured core members with long histories of involvement in CoSA.

Seventeen CoSA volunteers (8 males and 9 females) were interviewed. Most (n = 11) had participated or were currently participating in more than one CoSA. In the St John's program, volunteer involvement in CoSA is somewhat less structured than elsewhere, and volunteers may engage with core members across multiple Circles at any given time (i.e., the membership of the Circle is more fluid). Volunteer involvement with CoSA ranged from six weeks to many years, with some very long-term volunteers unable to recall exactly how long they had been involved in Circles.

CoSA staff interviewed for the research (8 males and 6 females) held a range of roles, from board member to program coordinator to more specific roles such as volunteer coordinator. Staff had been involved with CoSA for an average of approximately seven years (range = 3 months to approximately 20 years).

Stakeholders (1 male and 2 females) had been involved with CoSA in some capacity for an average of approximately four years (range = 3 months to approximately 6 years). These interviewees worked with the same population of core members as the local CoSA program in therapeutic or correctional roles.

Making Sense of the Data

Most of the interviews were audio-recorded with the participant's consent. However, in a small number of interviews, the participant expressed a preference for handwritten notes to be taken, and this request was honoured in all cases. All transcripts and handwritten notes were imported into the qualitative data analysis software program NVivo (Jackson & Bazeley, 2019). I read through the transcripts multiple times in order to familiarise myself with them and become immersed in the interview data (Caulfield & Hill, 2014; Grbich, 2013). This is critical in qualitative research, especially because participants' meanings must be understood and presented in the context of their broader narratives, rather than being broken apart to the point of becoming decontextualised. This was especially important to enable the narrative analysis to be undertaken, as described below.

Following this period of familiarisation, I coded the interviews in NVivo. Coding – also called labelling and/or indexing (Elliott, 2018) – involves "analyzing qualitative text data by taking them apart to see what they yield before putting the data back together in a meaningful way" (Creswell, 2015). For Elliott (2018, p. 2851), coding is the process of "indexing or mapping data, to provide an overview of disparate data that allows the researcher to make sense of them in relation to their research questions....[in order to]... render it into something we can report". The data were primarily coded *deductively* (i.e., according to pre-determined themes (Hsieh & Shannon, 2005)). Excerpts of text were coded according to the ways in which they mirrored elements of the theoretical precepts of desistance (see Chapter 2). However, as is usually good research practice when conducting qualitative research (Creswell, 2015; Elliott, 2018), the approach to coding also allowed for themes and concepts to emerge *inductively* (i.e., not according to pre-determined themes (Hsieh & Shannon, 2005)).

Analysis of the data was conducted using both thematic and narrative analysis techniques. Thematic analysis involves exploring the views, perceptions and experiences of participants (Braun & Clarke, 2006; Caulfield & Hill, 2014) and convergences and divergences across these (Caulfield & Hill, 2014; Mason, 2018). Fundamentally, thematic analysis involves identifying patterns in the data (Braun & Clarke, 2006; Floersch et al., 2010) – "the search for and identification of common threads" (Vaismoradi et al., 2013, p. 400) – and producing descriptions of these (Floersch et al., 2010; Vaismoradi et al., 2013). Identified patterns are compared with the researcher's own experience of a topic or phenomenon and/or with the extant literature on the topic of inquiry (Floersch et al., 2010). Narrative analysis is concerned more centrally with – as the name suggests – participants' narratives, or "stories that give meaning to an experience or event" (Narendorf et al., 2015, p. 124). While thematic analysis focuses on illuminating patterns *across* the dataset, narrative analysis focuses on the overall story *within* an individual's interview responses (Narendorf et al., 2015) and on stories as representations of lives (Frank, 2016). Perhaps most salient to the current research, "narratives are the central mechanism for *meaning making*" (Floersch et al., 2010, p. 412; italics in original). Given its phenomenological grounding, this focus on the use of narratives to create meaning was critical in elucidating participants' understandings about CoSA and their role in desistance from sexual offending.

Ethical Considerations

A project of this nature requires close attention to a range of ethical issues. Chief among these is the confidentiality of participants. As some interviewees have been incarcerated for sexual offending, or volunteer/work with individuals with sexual offence convictions, it was important to ensure that participants' identities would remain confidential. As such, volunteers, staff and stakeholders are referred to throughout simply as "Volunteer 1", "Staff Member 1" and so on. I have given core members pseudonyms to bring their stories to life; however, identifying details (e.g., places of work) have been changed to provide anonymity.

To ensure all prospective participants were able to make an informed decision about whether to take part in the research, prospective interviewees were informed in writing and/or verbally about the risks associated with participating (such as becoming upset) and the confidentiality procedures in place. Participants were informed that they were free to withdraw from the research, or to not answer any question they were not comfortable answering, at the outset of each interview. This was reiterated to core members in particular as each interview progressed. Participants were provided with information about free counselling services to ensure they had a supportive follow-up contact if required. The research was approved by Queensland University of Technology's Human Research Ethics Committee.

What Was It Like?

When family, friends and colleagues hear about my research, they invariably cringe a little at the prospect of interviewing people who have sexually offended (especially if the offending was against children), before wanting to know: what is it like? This is a hard question to answer succinctly, and I usually struggle to give the pithy, punchy answer no doubt being sought on these occasions. It is many things: challenging and confronting, thought-provoking and even, at times, heartening. These people may have committed heinous acts, but they are in most instances doing their best, under trying circumstances, to do the right thing now. There are gut-wrenching stories of the sexual harm caused both by interviewees and often, against them, and of lives irrevocably altered by selfish and thoughtless acts. But there are also stories of hope, transformation and redemption in often hopeless circumstances.

What stands out to me most forcefully when I think back on the interviews is my own polarised reactions to the core members. I clearly remember pulling Rory (who I met again and interviewed for this research following our initial meeting) into a full-body embrace at the end of his interview, in what felt like the most natural conclusion to our meeting. He had been so candid with me, revealing the full, soul-shattering repercussions of his crimes. I swallowed back tears as he recalled the impacts on his then-wife, who, following a brutal divorce, had sworn she would never re-marry – only to fall in love with and marry Rory. Imagining the depths of her despair when Rory's crimes came to light – not to mention Rory's own despair and guilt at having caused this – was deeply saddening, to say the very least.

Another moment that stands out on very different grounds is my interview with Bryce. Like Rory, I had originally met Bryce during my Churchill Fellowship, and he agreed to be interviewed when I returned to Toronto seven years later. Bryce's interview endures in my memory, standing out above so many of the others, because it is the only time in a 15-year career when I have lost my composure with a research participant. I have interviewed many hundreds of individuals – from victims/survivors of sexual violence, human trafficking and online fraud to criminal justice professionals, young people in trouble with the law and perpetrators of sexual violence – without losing my cool. As researchers, we are there to listen to our participants, and to understand where they are coming from, not to judge them. I fully understand this. Even when we interview people with histories of sexual offending against children, we do so to understand their backgrounds, motives and perspectives, to build a better picture of the problem, although we may be horrified by their past actions. But Bryce's unrelenting attempts to get me to see things from his point of view – manna from heaven for a phenomenologist! – clashed violently with my staunchly held belief that children cannot consent to participate in sex work, no matter the context and however willing they may appear. Bryce's insistence on labelling as "hookers", the 11-year-old victims/survivors of his crimes prompted a visceral reaction – a mix of revulsion and sorrow – that I still feel when I read the transcript of his interview. In a way that I have never done before or since, and am not proud of, I eventually gave in to my frustration at Bryce's view of his offences:

BRYCE: Here this girl, she's 14, 15 years of age, she's out there causing trouble. "What do you mean she's causing trouble?" Well she's hooking, she's been selling her arse since she was 10 years old, she's bothering the people. These men that are trying to stay out of trouble but she's out there, she knows how to do it.

KR: It sounds like you're blaming the victim though.

BRYCE: Yes, aren't we, but what about me?

KR: But you're an adult but she's not.

BRYCE: Yes, that's it.

KR: At 10 she's still a child.

BRYCE: Yes.

KR: Yes, I mean does that come in – does that come into it?

BRYCE: Oh, yes....Now do I blame my victims – no. I blame their choices. I blame my choices. But I made a choice and they made a choice, when some girl is 14 years of age and she got her sister in the back seat and she's 11 and they're both going to do oral sex on you for $20...

KR: [Interjects] Do you accept though that an 11-year-old has limited choices?
BRYCE: Oh yes.

I grappled with these contradictory and competing emotions and responses and still wonder about them. Why did my reactions vary so greatly, from skin-crawling discomfort to warm and welcome hugging? The likeliest explanation, I am loath to admit, is that those core members who said the "right" things – expressing remorse and taking ownership of their offences – are simply easier to take. Those who minimise, deny, obfuscate or justify their misdeeds provoke a less sympathetic internal response. I am loath to confess this too, but I suspect that in addition to this, interviewees who are well-presented, well-dressed and have good personal hygiene and interpersonal skills are easier to relate to and accept. Perhaps this is why my interview with Rory ended in a hug, while my interview with Bryce ended with me physically holding the office door open and sternly "encouraging" him to leave after he attempted to reverse roles and began questioning me about my own sex life.

Conclusion

The interviews were confronting and difficult, and at other times, hopeful and heartening. Above all, however, they were enlightening. Whatever their story, or approach to being interviewed, I am grateful to all those who divulge their thoughts, experiences and beliefs with me, especially those for whom doing so is awkward, shameful and uncomfortable. Many of the core members I interviewed noted that they wanted to help with my research in the hopes that a better understanding of sexual violence could be built. In this way, their participation was framed by them as a way of "giving back" or a move towards redemption (see also Harris, 2017). In the following chapter, this notion of redemption, and the role of CoSA in facilitating it, will be explored in detail.

References

Bachmann, R., & Schutt, R. (2012). *Fundamentals of research in criminology and criminal justice* (2nd ed.). Sage. doi: https://us.sagepub.com/en-us/nam/fundamentals-of-research-in-criminology-and-criminal-justice/book248692

Bayens, G., & Roberson, C. (2011). *Criminal justice research methods: Theory and practice* (2nd ed.). Taylor & Francis. doi: https://www.routledge.com/Criminal-Justice-Research-Methods-Theory-and-Practice-Second-Edition/Bayens-Roberson/p/book/9781439836965

Bevan, M. (2014). A method of phenomenological interviewing. *Qualitative Health Research*, *24*(1), 136–144. doi: https://journals.sagepub.com/doi/10.1177/1049732313519710

Braun, V., & Clarke, V. (2006). Using thematic analysis in psychology. *Qualitative Research in Psychology*, *3*(2), 77–101. doi: https://www.tandfonline.com/doi/abs/10.1191/1478088706qp063oa

Caulfield, L., & Hill, J. (2014). *Criminological research for beginners: A student's guide*. Routledge. doi: https://www.routledge.com/Criminological-Skills-and-Research-for-Beginners-A-Students-Guide/Caulfield-Hill/p/book/9781138041431

Chamberlain, B. (2009). Phenomenology: A qualitative method. *Clinical Nurse Specialist, 23*(2), 52–53.

Chan, Z., Fung, Y. l, & Chien, W.T (2018). Bracketing in phenomenology: Only undertaken in the data collection and analysis process? *The Qualitative Report, 18*(30), 1–9. doi: https://doi.org/10.46743/2160-3715/2013.1486

Coggan, C., Patterson, P., & Fill, J. (1997). Suicide: Qualitative data from focus group interviews with youth. *Social Science & Medicine, 45*(10), 1563–1570. doi: https://psycnet.apa.org/record/1997-43357-008

Creswell, J. (2015). *30 essential skills for the qualitative researcher*. Sage. doi: https://us.sagepub.com/en-us/nam/30-essential-skills-for-the-qualitative-researcher/book237360

Elliott, V. (2018). Thinking about the coding process in qualitative data analysis. *The Qualitative Report, 23*(11), 2850–2861. doi: https://doi.org/10.46743/2160-3715/2018.3560

Farmer, M., McAlinden, A. M., & Maruna, S. (2015). Understanding desistance from sexual offending: A thematic review of research findings. *Probation Journal, 62*(4), 320–335. doi: https://journals.sagepub.com/doi/abs/10.1177/0306624X16668175

Farmer, M., McAlinden, A. M., & Maruna, S. (2016). Sex offending and situational motivation: Findings from a qualitative analysis of desistance from sexual offending. *International Journal of Offender Therapy and Comparative Criminology, 60*(15), 1756–1775. doi: https://journals.sagepub.com/doi/10.1177/0306624X16668175

Floersch, J., Longhofer, J., Kranke, D., & Townsend, L. (2010). Integrating thematic, grounded theory and narrative analysis: A case study of adolescent psychotropic treatment. *Qualitative Social Work, 9*(3), 407–425. doi: https://journals.sagepub.com/doi/10.1177/1473325010362330

Frank, A. (2016). Practicing dialogical narrative analysis. In J. Holstein & J. Gubrium (Eds.), *Varieties of narrative analysis* (pp. 33–52). Sage. doi: https://us.sagepub.com/en-us/nam/varieties-of-narrative-analysis/book234829

Gray, D. (2009). *Doing research in the real world* (2nd ed.). Sage. doi: https://us.sagepub.com/en-us/nam/doing-research-in-the-real-world/book248702

Grbich, C. (2013). *Qualitative data analysis: An introduction*. Sage. doi: https://us.sagepub.com/en-us/nam/qualitative-data-analysis/book236861

Harris, D. (2017). *Desistance from sexual offending: Narratives of retirement, regulation and recovery*. Palgrave Macmillan. doi: https://www.palgrave.com/gp/book/9783319631998

Higgins, G. (2009). Quantitative versus qualitative methods: Understanding why quantitative methods are predominant in criminology and criminal justice. *Journal of Theoretical & Philosophical Criminology, 1*, 23–37.

Hong, J. (2017, 7 May). Ottawa gives $7.48M for sex offender reintegration program. Toronto Star, np.

Hsieh, H., & Shannon, S. (2005). Three approaches to qualitative content analysis. *Qualitative Health Research, 15*(9), 1277–1288. doi: https://journals.sagepub.com/doi/10.1177/1049732305276687

Jackson, K., & Bazeley, P. (2019). *Qualitative data analysis with NVivo* (3rd ed.). Sage. https://us.sagepub.com/en-us/nam/qualitative-data-analysis-with-nvivo/book261349?page=1

Kay, B. (2014, 6 March). Ottawa's curious decision to cut funding to successful sex offender program. Postmedia Breaking News, np.

Maruna, S. (2001). *Making good: How ex-convicts reform and rebuild their lives*. American Psychological Association. https://www.apa.org/pubs/books/431645A

Mason, J. (2018). *Qualitative researching* (3rd ed.). Sage. doi: https://us.sagepub.com/en-us/nam/qualitative-researching/book244365

Narendorf, S., Munson, M., & Floersch, J. (2015). Perspectives on psychotropic medication treatment among young adults formerly served in public systems of care: A thematic and narrative analysis. *Journal of the Society for Social Work and Research*, *6*(1), 121–143. doi: https://www.journals.uchicago.edu/doi/full/10.1086/680318

Paley, J. (2017). *Phenomenology as qualitative research: A critical analysis of meaning attribution*. Routledge. doi: https://www.routledge.com/Phenomenology-as-Qualitative-Research-A-Critical-Analysis-of-Meaning-Attribution/Paley/p/book/9780815359104

Pompili, M. (2010). Exploring the phenomenology of suicide. *Suicide and life-threatening behavior*, *40*(3), 234–244. doi: https://onlinelibrary.wiley.com/doi/abs/10.1521/suli.2010.40.3.234

Presser, L. (2009). The narratives of offenders. *Theoretical Criminology*, *13*(2), 177–200. doi: https://journals.sagepub.com/doi/abs/10.1177/1362480609102878?journalCode=tcra

Renzetti, C. (1997). Confessions of a reformed positivist: Feminist participatory research as good social science. In M. Schwartz (Ed.), *Researching sexual violence against women: Methodological and personal perspectives* (pp. 131–143). Sage. doi: https://sk.sagepub.com/books/researching-sexual-violence-against-women

Richards, K. (2018). Born this way? A qualitative examination of public perceptions of the causes of pedophilia and sexual offending against children. *Deviant Behavior: An Interdisciplinary Journal*, *39*(7), 835–851. doi: https://doi.org/10.1080/01639625.2017.1335526

Richards, K., & Bartels, L. (2011). The story behind the stories: Qualitative criminology research in Australia. In L. Bartels, & K. Richards (Eds.), *Qualitative criminology: Stories from the field* (pp. 1–10). Federation Press.

Richards, K., Death, J., & McCartan, K. (2020). *Community-based approaches to sexual offender reintegration*. Australia's National Research Organisation for Women's Safety. https://www.anrows.org.au/project/community-based-approaches-to-sexual-offender-reintegration/

Richards, K., Death, J., & Ronken, C. (in press). What do victim/survivors of sexual violence think about Circles of Support and Accountability? *Victims & Offenders*. doi: https://www.tandfonline.com/doi/abs/10.1080/15564886.2020.1850578

Richards, K., & McCartan, K. (2018). Public opinion about Circles of Support and Accountability: A qualitative analysis. *Deviant Behavior. An Interdisciplinary Journal*, *39*(3), 400–416. doi: https://www.tandfonline.com/doi/abs/10.1080/01639625.2017.1304800

Sandberg, S. (2010). What can "lies" tell us about life? Notes towards a framework of narrative criminology. *Journal of Criminal Justice Education*, *21*(4), 447–465. doi: https://www.tandfonline.com/doi/abs/10.1080/10511253.2010.516564

Sandberg, S., & Ugelvik, T. (2016). The past, present, and future of narrative criminology: A review and an invitation. *Crime, Media, Culture, 12*(2), 129–136. doi: https://journals.sagepub.com/doi/10.1177/1741659016663558

Sandler, J., Freeman, N., & Socia, K. (2008). Does a watched pot boil? A time-series analysis of New York state's sex offender registration and notification law. *Psychology, Public Policy, and Law, 14*(4), 284–302. doi: https://psycnet.apa.org/record/2008-18509-003

Schwandt, T. (1998). Constructivist, interpretivist approaches to human inquiry. In N. Denzin, & Y. Lincoln (Eds.), *The landscape of qualitative research: Theories and issues* (pp. 221–259). Sage. doi: https://us.sagepub.com/en-us/nam/the-landscape-of-qualitative-research/book237869

Skrapec, C. (2001). Phenomenology and serial murder: Asking different questions. *Homicide Studies, 5*(1), 46–63. doi: https://journals.sagepub.com/doi/10.1177/1088767901005001004

Tewkesbury, R. (2009). Quantitative versus qualitative methods: Understanding why qualitative methods are superior for criminology and criminal justice. *Journal of Theoretical & Philosophical Criminology, 1*, 38–58.

Vaismoradi, M., Turunen, H., & Bondas, T. (2013). Content analysis and thematic analysis: Implications for conducting a qualitative descriptive study. *Nursing and Health Sciences, 15*(3), 398–405. doi: https://onlinelibrary.wiley.com/doi/full/10.1111/nhs.12048

Valerio, M., Rodriguez, N., Winkler, P., Lopez, J., Dennison, M., Liang, Y., & Turner, B. (2016). Comparing two sampling methods to engage hard-to-reach communities in research priority setting. *BMC Medical Research Methodology, 16*(1), 146–157. doi: https://bmcmedresmethodol.biomedcentral.com/articles/10.1186/s12874-016-0242-z

Victor, J., & Waldram, J. (2015). Moral habilitation and the new normal: Sexual offender narratives of posttreatment community integration. In L. Presser, & S. Sandberg (Eds.), *Narrative criminology: Understanding stories of crime* (pp. 96–124). York University Press. doi: https://www.jstor.org/stable/j.ctt15r3xt2

Wacquant, L. (2009). *Punishing the poor: The neoliberal government of social insecurity*. Duke University Press. doi: https://www.jstor.org/stable/j.ctv11smrv3

Weller, S., Vickers, B., Bernard, R., Blackburn, A., Borgatti, S., Gravlee, C., & Johnson, J. (2018). Open-ended interview questions and saturation. *PLoS One, 13*(6), 1–18. doi: https://journals.plos.org/plosone/article?id=10.1371/journal.pone.0198606

Chapter 4

A Shot at Redemption

Circles of Support and Accountability, Desistance and Redemption Scripts

This chapter argues that Circles of Support and Accountability (CoSA) provide an avenue for people who have sexually offended to develop, enact, practise, refine and maintain "redemption scripts", or narratives that ex-offenders adopt to make sense of their criminal past and subsequent shift away from crime. It argues that this function of CoSA has been overlooked previously, but that the crafting of redemption scripts should form a focus of CoSA practice. The chapter begins by outlining the sparse body of literature on desistance from sexual offending. It then plots the narrative arc of the redemption scripts of core members interviewed for the study to demonstrate the key argument.

Redemption and Condemnation Scripts

As noted in Chapter 2, doing "narrative repair" work (Stone, 2016) is increasingly recognised as an important aspect of the process of desistance (Bullock et al., 2019; Presser, 2008; Rocque et al., 2016; Thompson, 2015) (see Chapter 2 for an overview of desistance and its related concepts). Seminal research studies have identified that individuals who desist from crime engage in a process of "rebiographing" (Maruna, 2001) in which they develop believable self-stories about why they are leaving crime and "going straight" (Maruna, 2001; Presser, 2008). These narratives put forth a coherent identity, which is believable to others and accounts for the offending past of the individual (Vieira et al., 2020). Such recovery stories or "redemption scripts" (Maruna, 2001; see also Farmer et al., 2015) typically include a number of "key plot devices" (Maruna, 2001; Stone, 2016). First, the individual establishes a set of core beliefs that characterise their "true self" or the "real me". This is accomplished via foreshadowing episodes in which the individual demonstrated, even at the height of their criminal behaviour, that they were essentially a good person, at least "deep down" (Maruna, 2001). Thus "instead of discovering a 'new me', the desisting ex-offender reaches back into early experiences to find and reestablish an 'old me' in order to desist" (Maruna, 2001, p. 89). In such narratives, crime

DOI: 10.4324/9781003125532-5

is not demonstrative of the individual's character but is instead cast as an aberration: "the self is *not* himself for only as long as the harmful action lasts" (Presser, 2008, p. 82; italics in original).

Second, the desister categorises poor past behaviours as separate from the "real me" and characterises these not as a reflection of their true self but as a product of the environment: "The offending came from out there, not inside" (Maruna, 2001, p. 93). Desisters commonly make reference to an external "It" – some alien source of action distinct from the narrator (Maruna, 2001). As Stone (2016) saw it, desisters distinguish the "bad It" from the "good me". In constructing a narrative of desistance, individuals must then free the true self from this environment, positioning themselves as a "diamond in the rough" (Maruna, 2001, p. 95). Usually, desisters make reference to an external force that has given rise to this: "If it weren't for X (organization, new philosophy or religion, some special individual, God, etc.), I would still be involved with crime" (Maruna, 2001, p. 96).

Third, the narratives of those individuals who desist are characterised by a sense of "tragic optimism", with desisters recasting their lives in such a way that positive emerges from the negative: "If it weren't for X (me going to jail, my life of crime, etc.), I never would have realized Y (that there are more important things in life than money, that I was good at helping others, etc.)" (Maruna, 2001, p. 98). Crime is thus positioned as a necessary precursor to the desister's current, law-abiding self.

Fourth, desisters' narratives are characterised by an optimistic sense of control over the future (Maruna, 2001). Research has shown that those who desist from crime maintain an optimistic sense of control over their future coupled with strong beliefs about their own self-worth (Anderson et al., 2020). Desisters rewrite the script "from a hopeless one to an optimistic one" (Ansbro, 2008, p. 232).

Finally, desisters' self-stories involve the discovery of a higher purpose, the desire to be productive and "give something back to society", particularly to the next generation (Maruna, 2001; McNeill & Maruna, 2007; Shover, 1996). Such desires are described in the literature as "generativity" (McAdams & de St Aubin, 1998). This concept is discussed in detail in Chapter 6.

Conversely, those who persist in offending develop "condemnation scripts" (or "contamination scripts") or narratives that portray the offender as "doomed to deviance" (Maruna, 2001, p. 74). Rather than conveying a sense of control over their ability to desist, condemnation scripts highlight offenders' sense of themselves as passive "pawns" or victims of circumstance who do not exercise agency over the future (Maruna, 2001, pp. 76–83). Often, condemnation scripts point to criminal justice measures – such as prison or other stigmatising responses to crime – as impeding the individual's opportunities to exit a life of crime (Kras, 2014; Maruna, 2001).

Desistance and People Who Have Sexually Offended

Most desistance research excludes individuals who have offended sexually (Harris, 2017; Milner, 2017) and there is only limited research on desistance from sexual offending specifically (Farmer et al., 2015; Harris, 2014, 2017; Milner, 2017). This is likely because it is commonly assumed that people who have sexually offended are fundamentally "different" as a population from non-sexual offenders, or simply that sexual offenders do not desist (Harris, 2017; Kras, 2014; Laws & Ward, 2011). However, statistically speaking, desistance is the norm for people who have sexually offended (Cooley & Sample, 2018; Harris, 2017) – at least if we define desistance as a lack of recidivism (Cooley & Sample, 2018). Indeed, as a cohort, people who have sexually offended have a much lower rate of reoffending (typically found to be 7–15% over a 5–6 year follow-up period (Hanson et al., 2014; Kruttschnitt et al., 2000)) than other groups of offenders such as violent, drug and/or property offenders (Gelb, 2007; Kras, 2014). As I have argued elsewhere (Richards, 2011), criminologists often latch onto this "truth" about sexual recidivism, wielding it as a type of weapon against legislators, policy-makers and members of the public who favour very punitive responses to prevent sexual recidivism. While it is "true" that people who have sexually offended have a comparatively low rate of reoffence, this truth obfuscates important details. Specifically, certain groups of people who have sexually offended recidivate at much higher levels than others. For example, rapists of adults reoffend more frequently than people who sexually abuse children (Hanson & Bussiere, 1998). Those deemed to be "high risk" offenders – in other words, those whose offending reflects particular patterns, such as the targeting of children outside of the family as victims – have very high rates of recidivism indeed, at 56–70% over a 10-year follow-up period (Doren, 1998; Hanson et al., 2014). As such, presenting aggregated statistics about the recidivism risk of all people who have sexually offended can be highly misleading.

In terms of making a commitment to a prosocial lifestyle and adopting a redemption script to make sense of this – rather than simply stopping offending, as per Cooley and Sample's (2018) conceptualisation of desistance (see Chapter 2) – the sparse literature reveals conflicting findings. For most of the desisters in Harris's (2017, pp. 219–222) study of 73 men desisting from sexual offending, redemption scripts were unattainable: "Redemption was simply not an option….no one mentioned successfully turning over a new leaf, being able to honestly start anew, or to have truly righted their wrongs… Men convicted of sexual offences do not have this luxury" (for a broader discussion see Kras, 2014). Elsewhere, Harris et al. (2017, p. 105) stated that:

> …in the current political and social landscape (especially in the United States), such a process [the creation of a redemption script] is largely impossible for those who have been labeled as "sexually dangerous

> persons" or "sexually violent predators."...While redemption and forgiveness are of value, we acknowledge that it is unlikely that individuals who have been labeled as "sex offenders" or "sexually violent predators" will ever be able to attain such transformation.

Maruna (2016) has likewise argued that public perceptions of sex offenders are so negative that narratives of redemption for this group might be impossible. In a presentation to the American Society of Criminology annual conference in 2016 in New Orleans, Maruna asked: for people who have sexually offended, "where are the redemption scripts?" (Maruna, 2016).

A nascent body of research, however, suggests that people convicted of sexual offences can and do develop redemption scripts, although often in ways that differ from the script as originally conceptualised by Maruna (2001). Harris (2014) acknowledged that a small number of men in her sample – those who had been free from prison the longest – did articulate a type of redemption narrative. This finding suggests that rather than redemption scripts always being unavailable to all people who have sexually offended, such narratives may emerge over time. Farmer et al.'s (2012) study of men who had desisted from sexual offending against children (n = 5), and men who were potentially still active offenders (n = 5) found that broadly, the narratives of the desisters followed the contours of a traditional redemption script (see further Geiger & Fischer, 2017). In particular, the desisters in the study more consistently framed their life stories in terms of having found redemption and expressed a higher degree of optimism and self-efficacy than the (potential) persisters. Interestingly, Farmer et al. (2012) noted that members of the desisting group were more likely than members of the persisting group to report having experienced adversity during childhood. While we might assume that those who experience abuse, neglect, poverty and so on as children will be more likely to persist in offending, Farmer et al. (2012) argued that such experiences were positioned by the desisting men in their study as precursors to redemption. In other words, adverse childhood experiences enable the men to make sense of their offending by providing a "bad It" in which to locate the (external) cause of their later offending behaviour.

Other researchers, however, have found that people who sexually offend construct redemption narratives in ways distinct from the traditional redemption script. For example, Kras (2014) conducted qualitative interviews with 73 men convicted of sexual offending after their release from prison in Missouri, and followed up with 29 of these men three years later. Kras (2014) found that in telling their stories, the men adhered to the plot contours of both redemption and condemnation scripts, with redemption scripts often "wrapped within condemnation scripts" (Kras, 2014, p. 75). Like Farmer et al. (2012) she found that desisters pointed to external rationales such as mental health conditions and adverse childhood experiences for their offending (see also Kras & Blasko, 2016). Conversely, persisters pointed to internal causes of their offending, seeing their deviant sexual preferences as a fixed trait. (This echoes the findings of Farmer et al. (2015), whose interviews with 25 people desisting from and seven persisting in sexual offending revealed that desisters typically view their offending as situational and anomalous; in contrast, persisters did not separate their offending from their "true selves" in this way). There were, however, some key differences between the scripts in Kras's (2014) sample and the traditional redemption script identified by Maruna (2001) (based on a sample of non-sexual offenders). Most significantly, while Maruna's (2001) non-sexual offenders commonly reported feeling "doomed to deviance" (see further Maruna & Mann, 2006), the individuals in Kras' (2014, p. 56; italics in original) research "did not feel condemned to reoffend, but rather felt condemned by society's *perception* that they would reoffend".

Although Thompson (2015) does not characterise his findings in these terms, a small number of the core members in his UK CoSA study articulated a true good self as per the notion of a redemption script, positioning themselves as "good guys", "deep down". For example, core member Fred (in Thompson, 2015, p. 257) claimed that "Underneath … there is quite a nice person you know, it's just hard to see through the big bad monster", and Phil claimed that "I'm not an evil person, basically all I want is to find a partner which is what everyone else wants". Core member Maurice (in Thompson, 2015, p. 257) similarly stated that:

> I'm not a bad person, if I'm walking down the street and see an old person being beaten up by a group of youths then I'm gonna help that old person if I know 'em. If I don't then I will call the police, if they don't come I will help. I've been the same practically all my live, a big softie until they get on the wrong side of me and then they get slashed!

Interestingly, the examples that Thompson (2015) provided suggest that in some cases at least, the core members were not harking back to a consistent, underlying good self, as per Maruna (2001), but were instead casting recent good deeds (such as pleading guilty at trial to avoid further traumatising the victim or making good progress in treatment) as evidence of a current good self. This is an important distinction, as it departs from the redemption script as articulated by Maruna (2001), which involved the identification of an *enduring* good self, rather than a *new* good self. This tension is explored later in this chapter.

My own recent work (Richards et al., 2020b) involved analysing the desistance narratives of Aboriginal and/or Torres Strait Islander men who had been formerly incarcerated in relation to serious sexual offending. The 11 men in the study had been released from prison subject to the requirements of Queensland's *Dangerous Prisoners (Sexual Offenders) Act*, which meant they were electronically monitored and subject to intensive therapeutic and correctional interventions and police surveillance (see Richards et al., 2020a;

Richards, Death, et al., 2020 for more detail). The study found that the men did craft "redemption scripts" but that these were culturally informed. While they articulated a version of the "true self" as per Maruna (2001), this involved crafting an abstract, cultural good self rather than an individual good self. For example, the men in the study positioned their ancestors, families and/or cultures as unspoiled, and constructed their true, non-offending selves as connected to them (Howell, 2008). In line with the contours of the redemption script as articulated by Maruna (2001), the men for the most part expressed a sense of optimism about the future and took credit for their own desistance. Many also described wanting to help members of the younger generation in line with the concept of generativity, and for some, the generative projects they described were explicitly cultural. For example, one explained that it is his job to teach the younger generation about culture, claiming: "Some boys have lost their culture. I have to teach them the didgeridoo" (Hundleby et al., 2007).

Taken together, this scant literature suggests that redemption scripts may be utilised by people convicted of sexual offences in varying ways across a range of contexts. This variation may be due to varying sociogeographic and policy contexts. In any case, as Kras (2014, p. 93) argued, the redemption script "may need to be refined when considering the circumstances of sex offenders".

This chapter argues, however, that CoSA enable core members to craft redemption scripts that follow the traditional format articulated by Maruna (2001). Alan's self-story (below) follows the narrative arc typical of the redemption narrative. As set out in the remainder of this chapter, CoSA promote the development of redemption scripts among core members, a cohort for whom redemption scripts have previously been considered off-limits.

Alan's Story

When we meet, Alan is in his early 60s. He is a large man with a loud voice and a great willingness to share his story. He is currently completing a home study course and enjoys reading – mainly self-help books. Alan doesn't work anymore for reasons that will become obvious, but had supported himself most of his adult life doing seasonal work in sport and leisure and had maintained stable employment in that field for 25 years. He played baseball and "was real good at it", something he took pride in revealing during his interview. Alan also had what he described as "about 30 years' worth of addiction" to pornography:

> I was addicted to porn for over 30 years. When I was…[arrested]…I had approximately 550 VHS tapes that were all gay, about 200 to 250 DVDs, and anywhere from 11[00] to 1500 books and magazines that were all gay. I would get a catalogue in the mail, thumb through it, pick out a bunch of stuff, call an 800 number, give them the debit card, and spent $375.

> Two days later I got another catalogue from another company, I spent another 200-and-something dollars. I spent a whole lot. I spent enough money in that 30 years' time to buy a nice house, a nice car, and live comfortably....The addiction was just running my life. I would get paid on a Friday from work, go to the bank, drive 20 miles to the porn store and spend anywhere from $85 to $150 in magazines and DVDs.

Although his description of his addiction suggests a high degree of active engagement and commitment, Alan downplays the role of agency in his offending. Some he characterises as almost accidental: "I used to pick up all kinds of books and magazines without looking at them". By his own admission, Alan also blamed others, at least in part, for his offending. He recounted that the owner of a store from which he purchased pornography would allow him to purchase material on credit, thus "feeding my addiction":

> The guy would - I'd have a stack of magazines probably 10 inches high and he'd add them up and he'd say, "well what can you get me"? I'd give him part of it and he'd put the rest of it on paper.

Alan explained that his consumption of pornography "progressed from legal porn to gay porn to twinks [young, slim and typically hairless males]". It also "progressed" to child sexual abuse material. Alan explained that his age range of interest – or "addiction" as he frames it – is 7–14-year-old boys and that this obsession was "just running my life". After importing child sexual abuse material across state lines, Alan was arrested, convicted and sentenced to nearly three years in a Federal prison. He was 52 years old at the time and had never been in trouble with the law previously. He described his arrest and incarceration as "scary" and went into some detail about the treatment of "chomos" – child molesters – in prison, and the location of this group of prisoners at the bottom of the prison hierarchy. Despite these experiences, Alan subsequently returned to prison twice for breaching the conditions of his probation.

Alan learned about CoSA from his probation officer – he'd been sentenced to 12 years probation to follow his prison sentence – and became a core member shortly after his final release from prison. He describes his CoSA as a "tremendous help", but not an easy path to tread, due to his volunteers challenging his behaviours: "when I got into my CoSA Circle group, there was myself, [male volunteer] and two ladies. One of them [exhales], wow [noise of exclamation] - she used to read me the riot act when I would come in and say, 'well this happened'". As a result, Alan explained that he has changed his thinking and turned over a new leaf. In fact, "I would say, if it wasn't for CoSA I would probably still be in Federal prison. I would".

At the time of our meeting, Alan had been out of prison and living in the community for about five years. He now feels "really, really good about myself" and mentions several times over the course of my visit that he has "never been happier". This is reflected back to him by members of his CoSA and other, allied, supporters: "I'm doing a lot better. My therapist says I'm doing a lot better; my probation officer says I'm doing a lot better. [Name], who's my mentor from S[ex] A[ddicts] A[nonymous], he says I'm doing a lot better. [CoSA volunteer], when I talk to him, he's like 'okay....you're doing the right thing'". Alan is confident that he will not reoffend. As he puts it: "the thing is, I have come too far; I have worked too hard and too long to even think about going there".

Alan has taken on the role of a cleaner for his local CoSA program premises, a role of which he is exceptionally proud. Alan raises it a number of times during my visit and is even known to introduce himself as "Alan, the CoSA cleaner". Alan is optimistic about the future and looks forward to mentoring new core members and drawing on his life experiences to support them in their own journeys to reintegrate after prison and desist from sexual offending. In fact, Alan now sees himself as something of a model ex-sex-offender. He describes, for example, a bus trip home from his court-ordered group therapy session as follows:

> I was on the bus and we stopped at a bus stop and about eight to 10 young boys got on the bus. At that time - I didn't feel comfortable because the age of the boys....So, I didn't feel comfortable; I went down the road a couple of stops and I got off the bus. At my next [treatment] group, I brought it up and they [the other participants] said, "well why didn't you just ignore [it]?" No. It was just too much of a trigger. I felt I did the right thing. Some people in my [treatment] group didn't agree with me, but they....don't have the triggers that I have, so I made the decision.

In his interview, Alan recounted a number of similar incidents. In another example:

> I was at [NAME] Park, which is an area where the local courthouse is here....There was a lady at the bus stop and she was changing a male child. I saw his genitals and I looked and I'm like, "okay" and I moved out of the area. So my bus came and I got on my bus. I also told my [treatment] group that day about it and they said, "well you seem like you're too critical about certain things". I got mad; I mean I really got mad. I blew up and I told them, "you don't walk in my shoes; you don't have the same triggers that I have; you don't have the same conditions that I have".

Alan reports any incidents of this nature to his CoSA volunteers: "Anytime something happens, where there's an incident happens, I'll call them and say 'okay, this is what happened'". His volunteers reinforce to Alan that he has done the right thing in these situations:

> [Male volunteer], when I talk to him, he's like "okay, you know what to do. You're doing the right thing"….I was on the bus and three youngsters got on and one of them was real cute looking. It just made me a little uncomfortable, so I went down a couple of stops and I got off and I waited for the next bus. [Male volunteer said] "okay you did the right thing".

Alan has also become quite evangelical in his interactions with others who have been incarcerated in relation to sexual offending. He describes completing a 12-step program in his Sex Addicts Anonymous (SAA) group and then revising the course manual: "They have a book; I went through all 12 steps and then went through the tools and then read some of the stories. I actually re-wrote a couple of the stories in the SAA book that I could relate to myself, of things that happened to me. [CoSA volunteer] was like 'wow….you're so open'. Well that's the only way to be. If you're going to help yourself you have to be 100 – 110 per cent – open or else you can't get ahead. You cannot get ahead if you have skeletons in the closet. You have to bring everything out; no matter how hard it hurts. If you don't do that, then you're not going to succeed; you're going to fall".

Alan now looks forward to mentoring and supporting others who have similar life experiences to himself: "I want to help people that are being released from the Federal system so they don't make the same mistake I did. I don't want them to fall through the cracks and get - and reoffend and go back". Apart from his cleaning role and supporting other people who have sexual offence convictions, Alan seeks to be useful, and construes his participation in his interview with me in these terms. Indeed, when I thank him for taking part, he states that one of the volunteers recommended that he participate as he is known as an open and honest person.

Establishing a True, Good Self

Like Alan, many of the core members interviewed for this project went to some lengths to establish a true good self. This took a number of forms. Some made declarative statements about their character. Adam, for example, asserted: "I'm not a bad person. I'm not out to get blood". Others declared:

> Even with the issues I was going through [after prison], constantly I'd be sitting back saying "I should help that person". You don't have to, but you do. I did that. *I always did it; I think it got bred into me from my mum*. I always helped out no matter what. It's probably more now than back in my past but *it's always been part of my make-up*.
>
> (Peter)

> Me losing my mom and dad when I was in prison - that was real hard. Coming out here without them, without their support is really hard, but I'm going to fight. *I'm a fighter.* I'm going to fight on.
>
> (Damien)

Others positioned recent good deeds as illustrative of enduring character traits. For example, Rory described helping at a charity banquet event, going into detail about the importance of physically helping rather than making a cash donation to the charity, which he considered something of an easy way out. When I asked, "is this atonement, like you're working something off?" He responded, "no, no, it's something I just desire to do. I really do. I just enjoy it". In doing so, Rory emphasises his fundamentally good nature; his charitable acts are not a means to an end – they are an end in themselves. Similarly, Wayne described repaying a CoSA volunteer who had repaired his bicycle at his own expense: "I paid him back. I did that as soon as I got my disability [payment]. *That's the way I am*". Frank, reflecting on his difficult relationship with his father, described an incident in which he became so angry that he felt the urge to punch his father, but instead held back, because "I'm not that type of person". Mathias recounted a story about his release, after 10 years in prison and 20 in a civil commitment facility. In order to be released, inmates required two independent evaluators to provide a professional opinion that they would not pose a risk to community safety if released. In the current risk-obsessed climate, evaluations of this nature are difficult to come by. Mathias was receiving assistance from a paralegal with this process, and recalls that "He sent me a release plan to try to flip [ie fool] an evaluator. I don't use that term, because I never wanted to flip them. *I wanted them to see me for who I was* and just come to that conclusion".

Moreover, those who had committed violent acts were eager to highlight these as particularly uncharacteristic and driven by circumstance. Lachlan recalled having to assault a fellow prisoner in order to avoid being raped, but noted: "I'm not a violent person....he had a shank". Richard's story is also instructive here. Richard had been convicted in relation to using the internet to recruit minors for sexual purposes. In his interview, I gently tried to tease out his motivation for doing so, asking "Would you say that you were attracted to younger girls or was it more that you kind of thought you might get along better with a 13-year-old?" Richard responded that "I always seem to get along better with the younger kids" but immediately used this as an entry point to a lengthy description of his experience as a volunteer sporting coach for young people. The focal point of Richard's narrative positioned him as a champion of child-safe practise. He described in detail that as a volunteer coach, he was only to allow children to leave sporting practice with approved adults, and that he adhered to this role with singular fervour:

> I had a situation a couple of times where the relative of one of the kids came to pick up the kid but say they weren't being allowed to because I

> wasn't letting them go. Because they weren't on my [approved] contact list. I had no information from the kid's parents. They would say "well they know us. They're calling out my name, calling out saying 'uncle'.... I'm like: 'it doesn't matter'"....So I'm like - I have to have it verified by myself before I can do it. So we all walked back up to the office and the secretary is there going "what are you doing"? "Well they're telling me that they're here to pick up the kid but they say they're on the school's emergency contacts but they're not on mine". They go "oh that's why you're being so hard-nosed about it".

In telling this story, Richard seeks to portray himself as fundamentally good and concerned in particular about children's welfare. In doing so, he draws on a true, good self and thus locates his offending behaviour as an aberration from – rather than a reflection of – his true character or disposition. As Farmer et al. (2016) argued, this type of self-story enables individuals who have sexually offended "to construct their sexual crimes as aberrations, unrelated to their true self-identities, and, hence, maintain a positive self-image in their own and others' eyes".

Core members were thus able to articulate a good self – the building block of a redemption script – at the behest of their Circle. Both Morgan and Daniel described their CoSA as helping them to rediscover their true selves. As Daniel put it, his CoSA helped him to see that "this is who I am. I am a sex offender, but this is who I *really* am". Morgan likewise claimed that "meeting with CoSA, meeting with these members has helped me shape who I really am and find out who I really am". In other words, CoSA had helped these core members to articulate a good self that always existed "deep down" (Maruna, 2001), independently of their offending. In some cases, this articulation of a good self appeared to be a deliberate act of resistance against both what staff member 13 called "the big S" – the stigma that core members face from the public – and the imposition of a subjectivity defined as permanently risky by correctional and therapeutic authorities who "drive it into you that you are a bad person" (James). As Sean sees it: "that's not who I am [a sex offender]; but society, that's who they see you as pretty much permanently". Daniel even described putting on what he called "an act of sorts" with his parole officer, while in contrast, he viewed CoSA as helping him to excavate his real self.

In many ways, it is hardly surprising that CoSA foster the identification and articulation of a true good self among core members since a key tenet of CoSA philosophy is the separation of the *actor* from their *acts* (Hannem & Petrunik, 2007). CoSA explicitly support the core member as a person while renouncing their sexually violent past behaviours (Höing, 2015). This was well-understood and noted repeatedly by both CoSA staff and volunteers and core members themselves in this project. Volunteers interviewed for the project went to some lengths to emphasise that while they rejected the offending behaviour of core members, they accepted the core members as human beings, mirroring the CoSA philosophy that "no one is disposable". Volunteer 17 declared that "everyone makes mistakes", and volunteer 13, drawing on his Christian faith, which underpinned his participation in CoSA, simply stated that "everyone is inherently good". Others commented:

> I think you're a good guy. What you did is not okay, and I want to make sure you don't do that again.
>
> (Volunteer 9)

> You're not your mistakes. You're a person and you made mistakes. Very serious mistakes, but you're not your mistakes.
>
> (Volunteer 7)

> ...you can tell your story and be honest and people still value you as the person that you are.
>
> (Staff member 1)

Core members clearly heeded this message from their volunteers: "There's ownership [over the offending] absolutely, but they don't see me as the offence" (Joshua); "They don't look at you as an offender; they look at you as a person" (James); "They've asked me to not let it define me by any means, and that's what I do" (Morgan). Sean explained that as a result of his participation in CoSA:

> you sit there and you think back now on what you did and you go, "that's not me, that's not who I am"; and to let that define you for the rest of your life, to me, is a big waste and it's not who I am.

Of course, separating acts from actors may be easier said than done given the serious nature of many core members' sexual offending, as well as the influence of therapeutic and correctional narratives that insist that individuals who have sexually offended consider themselves permanently risky. In his interview, Donny vacillated between these competing constructions of his self: "I still look at myself as a sex offender. I did this. But they're [CoSA volunteers] like 'it's not who you are. It's what you've done, it's not who you are'. It's just - it does help. Still, it's always in the back of my mind, especially when I get upset or depressed".

Indeed, a tension emerged in the interviews around the desirability of core members articulating an enduring good self. For some, both a core member's often serious sexual offending and the lifestyle and life circumstances that gave rise to it ought to be eschewed entirely and a new self-created. As volunteer 17 argued, "preferably we want to hear them say that 'I'm not that person....I'm not that person who committed that crime, I'm no longer that person'". Other volunteers agreed: "I think it's more important just to help them discover their new self. So help them discover that that might have been who they were but...this is your new self and we're here to support that (Volunteer 6). For others, however, it would not be desirable to renounce a core member's offending self altogether. Reflecting the correcto-therapeutic narrative that people who sexually offend pose a permanent risk, and that downplaying that risk could lead to reoffence, some staff members and volunteers were of the view that a core member's offending past would and should always form a part of their self-narrative. As one interviewee persuasively argued: "why erect statues that commemorate the Holocaust? Because history needs constant reminders that very normal human beings do very, very terrible things" (staff member 11). Others were likewise in favour of core members holding on to the metaphorical albatross (Harris, 2017, p. 216) of their past offending behaviour:

> I think to separate it is probably not achievable and may actually not be the right thing either. The past identity is going to carry forward. Hopefully, the learnings of the ramifications of what happened also carry forward. I think you want that.
>
> (Volunteer 11)

For one volunteer, preserving the past was a moral imperative. She stated that "one of the [other] volunteers said [to the core member] 'can you remember the victim's name?'. He was like, 'no, I can't even remember'. It was almost like: how can you forget that?" (volunteer 17). Unsurprisingly, given the many treatment programs in which the core members had participated, most adhered to the notion that their offending could never be altogether renounced, but would always form some part of their identity. For Dean, "Those charges are always going to be there, regardless, no matter what I do. There's nothing I can change - do to change that", and likewise for Keith, "it's always at the back of my mind". Joshua eloquently described this situation as follows:

> It's still me, still part of me. It's not a part that I enjoy or like or certainly not proud of....but it's part of me now. There's a metaphor that I like to use. When I try to explain it to my mom it's like, "imagine you've never had chocolate in your life and then one day you have chocolate. Now you know what chocolate is like". Now I know it's there and it will never be gone.

Brian, who was an active participant in both CoSA and SAA, was able to reflect on the different imagined subjectivities that these two measures engender in participants in this regard:

> [In SAA] we introduced ourselves as, "I am Brian, I'm a sex addict". So, that kind of defines us there right from the start. From their [SAA] side of

> it, well, you're always - you've got the potential [to reoffend]. One click of a [computer] mouse and you could be back. So, you want to maintain that you have a sex addiction but you're managing it and controlling it. Whereas with CoSA, it's like, well that shouldn't define you, who you are. You're more than your addiction. So, there was a difference between the two.

Importantly, core members sometimes adopted a more fluid conceptualisation of selfhood than is usually considered in relation to the development of redemption scripts. Rather than constructing their current self as either an enduring or entirely new self, core members sometimes described their offending selves as either a *part* of their overall self or a different *version* of themselves. For example, James explained that he does not see himself as a different person now as such, but rather a different version of himself. Joshua likewise described his offending self as an "unrestrained version of myself, uncontrolled, hyper-stimulated", and Mathias conceptualised his selfhood as being in parts: a past offending part, alongside an enduring "healthy part". An uneasy mix thus emerged in which core members' offending and the narrative of permanent risk became incorporated into core members' senses of self but did not entirely foreclose the possibility of the articulation of a true good self. Volunteer 3 noted that many core members acknowledge their past offending but are adamant that they do not now, upon release from prison, want to continue to rehash this aspect of their past, preferring to "move on and start a new life". Volunteer 3 acknowledged that navigating this tension could be challenging: "it's a tight rope we walk there as to...when it's time to move on".

A key point here is that while a new identity may be more desirable for core members, rekindling an enduring good self is likely more powerful and therefore ought to be encouraged in Circles. That is, it may be tempting to present oneself as entirely disconnected from one's past, particularly given the stigma faced by people who have sexually offended, but being able to identify and articulate enduring, fixed facets of one's identity is likely a more powerful tool for constructing a non-offending identity and leading a desistant life.

Identifying a "Bad It"

Core members identified a variety of external factors or influences that in their minds at least, gave rise to or contributed in large part towards their sexual offending. These external factors are the "bad It" (Stone, 2016) in the core members' redemption scripts. The "bad It" took a number of forms in this study, including pornography use, overwork, general "life circumstances" (Damien) and mental illness ("I'm not mentally unstable. When I offended I was but I'm not mentally unstable" (Rory)). However, three explications of the bad It were particularly prominent among core member narratives: experiencing sexual abuse themselves; being in the throes of an addiction and being enabled by others.

Core members commonly raised the sexual abuse that they had suffered as children in their interviews, and posited this as the bad It. While most victims/survivors of child sexual abuse do not subsequently become perpetrators, and most perpetrators were not abused themselves as children, male victims/survivors of child sexual abuse are overrepresented among perpetrators (Cossins & Plummer, 2016; Plummer & Cossins, 2018). While the relationship between being victimised and becoming a victimiser remains unclear (for a discussion see Cossins & Plummer, 2016; Plummer & Cossins, 2018; Richards, 2011), for some core members, victimisation and subsequent perpetration of child sexual abuse were inextricably linked. As staff member 14 put it, "these people come from, sometimes horrendous backgrounds. Not every family is the Brady Bunch. Some of these people have been seriously abused and used and taken advantage of". Bryce had spent some of his childhood in a now-infamous orphanage, with a documented history of widespread sexual abuse of boys under its care. Bryce was sexually abused as a child in the orphanage – in his words, "forced to do things that I didn't want to do" and "abused viciously". Kevin explained that between the ages of 4 and 21 he was sexually abused by numerous men as part of an organised child sexual abuse ring, including being bound to a tree and raped by 24 men in one evening. He described not knowing any different and assuming that his experiences were normal. Indeed, Kevin was eager for me to understand that as an adolescent, he was at times at least a willing participant in the network: "you also have to understand, at the age of 14 I remember lying back and going, 'I really like this. This is awesome'".

Such experiences are silenced in the course of traditional justice procedures, and there was little natural justice for core members in this regard. While they experienced the full force of the law in relation to the abuse that they perpetrated, the abuse that they themselves suffered as children was rarely recognised or responded to. Bryce is clear on this point:

> ...nobody helped me. Why didn't they? I don't know. We all get on the bus, we went down to the police station, we told [the police] what the Brothers were doing to us, they said, "fine, thank you very much", and they gave us a pizza....Then they put us back on the bus and took us right back to where we were and nothing was done until 25 and 35 years later. Now we find out what happened at [NAME] Orphanage.... So where's your justice? I'm paying and I've been paying for it all my life.

While CoSA are not therapy (Dwerryhouse et al., 2020), they may provide an audience for perpetrators' accounts of their own childhood sexual abuse and an avenue via which some form of recognition might be accomplished: "[CoSA helped with] being more - identifying with what happened to me, at the same what I have done. So it was difficult to put all this in a big ball and try to flatten it out" (Kevin). (As staff member 3 argued, however, recognising core members' own experiences of childhood abuse should not diminish the role of accountability: "I think it's really important to recognise people's stories and histories, but not to say, "oh, like they're a victim". They continue to make victims, and those are important distinctions") (see further discussion in Chapter 8).

Addiction was another common external factor to which core members attributed their offending behaviour. Terry, for example, identified as both an alcoholic and sex addict, and noted that for him this means "it's a lot harder for me to stop than a lot of other people that aren't [addicts]....it gives me that perspective". Brian and Alan were likewise both active participants in SAA, attributing their offending to sex addiction. As Brian explained, his Circle fostered this understanding and framing of his offending. Brian's Circle members had encouraged him to write an autobiography, which was then analysed by the group:

> So, we would go through all of that line by line, going all the way back to childhood. The things that may have contributed or led up to [the offending to] get an understanding. Not to make that an excuse but being able to understand why I made the decisions that I made. CoSA helped me see that. My family origin. There was a loving family in all, but [there was] not a lot of accountability. Then they got me in and taught me the work ethic [i.e. overwork and the accompanying stress] that helped to lead up to it and all. Then I made some bad choices that allowed me to get into the [online child sexual abuse material] addiction. Then it was downhill from there.

Both addiction and the cycle-of-abuse explanation of child sexual abuse perpetration are culturally accepted narratives in the contemporary historical moment. As I have argued elsewhere (Richards, 2019), there is widespread public adherence to the victim-becomes-victimiser narrative despite this not being entirely consistent with the empirical evidence. As Salter (2003, p. 74) claimed, the cycle-of-abuse narrative is "strangely comforting" for the public (see also Hindman & Peters, 2001). Similarly, the discourse of addiction-as-disease has become increasingly accepted in recent years, and the public has become increasingly willing to view a vast array of behaviours as stemming from addiction rather than an inability or unwillingness to exercise self-restraint (Reinarman, 2005). In other words, it has become increasingly palatable to understand a host of behaviours as the result of addiction (Reinarman, 2005).

Finally, core members pointed to others who they perceived as having enabled or supported their sexual offending. In Alan's story, detailed above, some blame is apportioned to the store owner who allowed Alan to purchase pornographic material on credit. Joshua pointed to both stimulant drugs, which "erased any inhibition that I had" and his girlfriend at the time of his arrest in relation to online child sexual abuse material: "I was in a relationship that was supportive of my habits and my proclivities. I had a girlfriend that was into the same things". For Terry, a permissive military official played the role of enabler:

> When I was in the military I got caught downloading pornography and putting it on a computer, on a government computer. I got investigated and they sent me to see a therapist, actually a psychiatrist. It was one of my resentments later, had that guy sent me to S[exaholics] A[nonymous], maybe my life would be different....He treated me for "well that's just stress, that's normal, everybody surfs porn".

Importantly, these examples of the bad It or external cause of offending were not typically presented by core members as excuses or justifications for their sexual offending. Rather, participants positioned these external factors as contributing in part to their offending and were often quick to accept responsibility for their own role in the offences. Whether these core members' narratives are accurate is not the point here. Instead, it is of note that Circles help foster narratives among core members that enabled them to construct their offending as at least partly *situational* rather than an expression of a fixed, immutable offending self. As Farmer et al. (2015, p. 327) have argued:

> ...this situational aspect of their offending past is a narrative frame that the individuals have retrospectively applied to past behaviours so as to separate their desired, present selves from undesirable past selves. In such cases, the framing itself might be understood as a protective cognition that helps them desist by moving away from the internal and external stigma of their past behaviours.

As (Maruna (2001); Maruna & Mann 2006, p. 164) has argued, while such cognitions might not be "real", they may help stigmatised individuals create a non-deviant future self, and in turn foster desistance from crime.

Incorporating a Sense of "Tragic Optimism"

Core members' narratives in some cases incorporated a sense of "tragic optimism" (Maruna, 2001); in other words, some participants framed their stories in such a way that some positive emerged from the overwhelming negative. Most did not directly rewrite their sexual offending into a necessary prelude to their current law-abiding selves in the same way that Maruna (2001) documented among property and/or drug offenders. In this way, their redemption narratives diverged from that identified by Maruna (2001). A number did, however, articulate a more general version of this aspect of the redemption script, identifying a positive that had emerged as a consequence of their offending and its aftermath.

For a couple of core members this "tragic optimism" took the form of a spiritual or religious awakening (see also Winder et al., 2020). Daniel framed his offending as ultimately supporting him on a journey towards spiritual growth: "God put all these things in place; I grow from each one". Rory was adamant on this point:

> [Other people] they all say that they go to jail and they all find God. No, God found me. Unfortunately, he didn't want this [the offending] but He knew this was the way I would come to Him. He knew that. I'm a firm believer of that. He didn't want me divorced. He didn't want my children out there without their Dad, but He knew this would be the way for it to be - for me to know Him. He didn't want me where my Dad died while I was incarcerated. No, He didn't want any of that but again, He knew: "Rory, this is the only way I'm going to get your attention".

In one sense, this may be unsurprising given the religious roots of CoSA. However, it is important to note that by no means do all core members participating in CoSA profess a religious affiliation or interest; nor is this a requirement for participation. While some volunteers are motivated by faith, non-faith volunteers are also heavily involved in CoSA across the globe (see Chapter 1). These core members' sense of spiritual awakening *is* surprising when we consider that prior research suggests that for people who have sexually offended, redemption via religion is a virtual impossibility. As Harris et al., (2017, p. 110; italics in original) found in their study of 71 men desisting from sexual offending, even for the men who identified as devout, the intractable nature of their offending meant that "there was nothing they could do and they had no chance for redemption. They frequently identified specific friends or family members who *hadn't* forgiven them or would *never* forgive them and, in some cases, agreed that their crimes were irredeemable". The fact that core members in the present study were able to develop a desistance narrative by laying claim to a religious awakening is therefore an important finding.

In the main, however, core members' identification of a positive emerging from the negative of their offending, conviction and incarceration, took a more general form. Morgan, for example, explained that while the public response to his offending – including community picketing and extensive media coverage – was far "worse than I expected", it "made me stronger at the same time, so I can't really [complain]". In his interview, Morgan made this point a number of times: "It's part of what I've overcome. It's made me a stronger person". To disavow the offending would also be to deny or repudiate this uncomfortable "silver lining". To this end, Morgan considered his offending very much "a part of my makeup" and "part of who I am", something that he thinks about "on a daily basis...Before I go to bed, I think about it; when I wake up, I think about it". In a similar vein, Brian framed his conviction and incarceration as helping "make me who I am today". For Brian, the incident was something of a "wakeup call": "my family is better off now, afterwards, because we're close together. It got them on the right track. They saw that they could do without me and became their own people. So, I guess that's - change happened, during all of this".

Developing a Sense of Optimistic Control and Self-Efficacy

Like Alan, who looks forward to mentoring other ex-prisoners (see Chapter 7), other core members in the current study frequently described being optimistic and hopeful about the future, in sharp contrast to what we might expect to find among a cohort of individuals convicted of often serious sexual offending in an extremely punitive and unforgiving legal and social climate. Morgan was keen for me to understand that his CoSA volunteers are optimistic about his future, and deliberately make efforts to cultivate a sense of optimism in him:

> I don't think there's anybody in my life that's more optimistic about what lies ahead [than my CoSA volunteers]. Even my own family...even they, like when I said I was opening my own business, were sceptical and are still sceptical and, so I call my Dad - because I talk to my Dad - I try and talk to him every day, but it doesn't always happen. You know when I get a call for a job and you know I think it's a little over my head but I think I can learn it....You know, my Dad's always the one that's like, "oh I don't think you should do that", right. He's always sceptical and my Mum's always sceptical, right. But, it's CoSA that really says like, "you got to go for what you think you should go for, if it's not going to put you in danger, or put you in harm, then you go for it", right.

Stakeholder 2 described what he called a "cognitive restructure" by one core member, who had determined to take carriage of his future and play an active role in his own reform – to move from "desistance by default" (Rocque et al., 2016, p. 50) to displaying "agentic moves" (Giordano et al., 2002, p. 992) or from simply not reoffending to actively desisting in Cooley and Sample's (2018) terms:

> I mean he changed his whole perspective as far as "I'm done with legalising everything. I'm done with minimising my behaviour, I'm starting to hold myself more accountable. I want to be less argumentative, I want

> to learn more in [my treatment] group"....he seems like he's had a total change in how he thinks, his thought process. So I think with that and also the fact that he's somewhat active with CoSA, I think that's been helpful.

Perhaps the strongest expression of the sense of control and self-efficacy felt by the core members was their tendency to position themselves as the architects of their own successful desistance. Core members commonly took credit for their successes and downplayed or denied altogether the help of their CoSA and the ecosystem of supports within which CoSA commonly operate:

> Oh, they had a little [influence] - but it was mainly me, because unfortunately I'd been in prison before, but this last stint that I did, it really opened my eyes and I'm just not going back. It's just not worth it. I'd rather be out here, struggling like I am, having hard times, instead of be in prison, because prison is no fun.
>
> (Damien)

When pressed about whether his CoSA had helped him to remain offence-free, Damien continued: "They had a part in it, yes, but it's mainly my choice....I'm glad that I did make that choice, because CoSA confirmed what I was already feeling and thinking. So I mean they did have a part in it, but I mean, just my experience, being in prison and stuff like that, knowing the reality if I go back to that, it's - I don't want to do that".

Peter acknowledged that his CoSA had played a key role in supporting him to develop a prosocial lifestyle and identity, but took pains to emphasise his own role and agency in that process too. He even somewhat audaciously took credit for the support he receives from his Circle by claiming that "I put people in front of me who will challenge me". In eschewing the role of their CoSA and instead emphasising their own agency in creating and maintaining a desistant identity, the core members were following a commonly trodden path. The empirical evidence clearly demonstrates that in Western countries at least, "adults make predominantly external attributions for our failures and predominantly internal attributions for our successes" (Maruna & Mann, 2006, p. 161). In other words, we all have a tendency to blame our mistakes and poor behaviours on others, while inviting recognition for our achievements and good behaviours. Whether this is an accurate estimation of events is largely irrelevant; the point is rather that this attribution style is a healthy and beneficial one in that it helps individuals combat stress and anxiety and maintain a sense of self-esteem (Maruna & Mann, 2006). It also fosters a sense of optimistic control over future events (Maruna & Mann, 2006) and is, therefore, a critical component of the development of a desistant self.

Importantly, in some instances, volunteers appeared cognisant of this, at times even stating that they deliberately imbue their communications with core members with the aim of promoting self-efficacy. As one volunteer put it:

> If there's anything that they're struggling with, any issues, we try to use our judgment and advise them on what we think they should do. *Mostly, we try to let them solve it themselves, so it gives them a feel that they're solving and helping their own,* helping themselves and we're just there to help them along.
>
> (Volunteer 17)

Volunteer 17 described this as "sow[ing] the seeds" and explained that this approach is used to support core members to "become a bit more confident in themselves. That the next time if they should have an issue that probably they can [resolve it themselves], even though I mean they still come here [for support], but probably in a way it's a little bit of an accomplishment". As I have argued elsewhere (Richards, in press), this relationship dynamic between CoSA volunteers and core members can be understood as based on Donati, (2009, 2015) notion of "subsidiarity". This term refers to relations in which an individual assists another "without making him or her passive" (Donati, 2009, p. 226), and "without replacing her/him" (Donati, 2015, p. 98). Subsidiarity involves helping another person without rendering them dependent or helpless – in other words, promoting self-efficacy.

Conclusion

This chapter has argued a modest but nonetheless important point. While redemption scripts have largely been considered an impossibility for people who have sexually offended, the findings outlined above suggest that narratives of redemption are indeed available to this group under certain circumstances. Specifically, CoSA can be a tool to enable and shape redemption scripts among those with convictions for sexual offences. CoSA both implicitly and explicitly communicate to core members that they are redeemable subjects. This is achieved through supporting narrative activity (e.g., weekly meetings) via which core members can cast about for narratives that feature a true, good self or aspects thereof, as well as external, situational causes of their offending behaviour and a sense of self-efficacy in relation to the future. Moreover, CoSA provide witnesses in the form of volunteers to reinforce and reflect these narratives back to core members. This is critical since as Maruna et al. (2004, p. 276) have argued, "desistance may be best facilitated when the desisting person's change in behavior is recognized by others and reflected back to him". The role of volunteers as witnesses to core members' desistance will be examined in detail in the following chapter.

This chapter thus demonstrates the influence of practise on the development of redemption scripts. If redemption scripts were not available to the individuals convicted of sexual offences in prior research (Harris, 2017; Harris et al., 2017), this may simply reflect the different policy and practise measures to which participants were subject. Indeed, this underscores the central tenet of my argument, which is that CoSA, unlike punitive end exclusionary measures to which people who sexually offend are more commonly subject, can support individuals to develop redemption scripts, and thus to take an important step on the path to desistance.

Although CoSA provide a vehicle through which redemption scripts can be crafted, they are currently not understood in these terms. This is a significant missed opportunity, given the link between the crafting of redemption scripts, the development of prosocial identities and reduced recidivism among individuals convicted of other types (i.e., non-sexual) offences. The practical implications of understanding CoSA as an avenue for the development of redemption narratives will be considered in Chapter 8.

References

Anderson, A., Weiss, D., & Oselin, S. (2020). When I grow up: Exploring the link between future expectations and criminal trajectories. *Journal of Developmental and Life-Course Criminology*, *6*(1), 43–66. doi: https://link.springer.com/article/10.1007/s40865-020-00136-6

Ansbro, M. (2008). Using attachment theory with offenders. *Probation Journal*, *55*(3), 231–244. doi: https://journals.sagepub.com/doi/abs/10.1177/0264550508092812

Bullock, K., Bunce, A., & McCarthy, D. (2019). Making good in unpromising places: The development and cultivation of redemption scripts among long-term prisoners. *International Journal of Offender Therapy and Comparative Criminology*, *63*(3), 406–423. doi: https://journals.sagepub.com/doi/10.1177/0306624X18800882

Cooley, B., & Sample, L. (2018). The difference between desistance from sexual offending and not reoffending. *Journal of Crime and Justice*, *41*(5), 483–503. doi: https://www.tandfonline.com/doi/full/10.1080/0735648X.2018.1479286

Cossins, A., & Plummer, M. (2016). Masculinity and sexual abuse: Explaining the transition from victim to offender. *Men and Masculinities*, *21*(2), 163–188. doi: https://doi.org/http://journals.sagepub.com/doi/abs/10.1177/1097184X16652655

Donati, P. (2009). What does "subsidiarity" mean? The relational perspective. *Journal of Markets & Morality*, *12*(2), 211–243.

Donati, P. (2015). Manifesto for a critical realist relational sociology. *International Review of Sociology*, *25*(1), 86–109. doi: https://www.tandfonline.com/doi/abs/10.1080/03906701.2014.997967

Doren, D. (1998). Recidivism base rates, predictions of sex offender recidivism and the 'sexual predator' commitment laws. *Behavioural Sciences and the Law*, *16*(1), 97–114. doi: https://psycnet.apa.org/record/1998-01652-006

Dwerryhouse, M., Winder, B., Blagden, N., & Lievesley, R. (2020). Conceptualising success and failure in circles of support and accountability. *Aggression and Violent Behavior*, *55*. doi: https://doi.org/10.1016/j.avb.2020.101492

Farmer, M., Beech, A., & Ward, T. (2012). Assessing desistance in child molesters: A qualitative analysis. *Journal of Interpersonal Violence*, *27*(5), 930–950. doi: https://journals.sagepub.com/doi/10.1177/0886260511423255

Farmer, M., McAlinden, A. M., & Maruna, S. (2015). Understanding desistance from sexual offending: A thematic review of research findings. *Probation Journal, 62*(4), 320–335. doi: https://journals.sagepub.com/doi/abs/10.1177/0306624X16668175

Farmer, M., McAlinden, A. M., & Maruna, S. (2016). Sex offending and situational motivation: Findings from a qualitative analysis of desistance from sexual offending. *International Journal of Offender Therapy and Comparative Criminology, 60*(15), 1756–1775. doi: https://journals.sagepub.com/doi/10.1177/0306624X16668175

Geiger, B., & Fischer, M. (2017). Incarcerated sex offenders in rehabilitation account their offending. *Journal of Investigative Psychology and Offender Profiling, 14*(1), 43–59. doi: https://doi.org/10.1002/jip.1460

Gelb, K. (2007). *Recidivism of sex offenders: Research paper.* Victoria Sentencing Advisory Council.

Giordano, P., Cernkovich, S., & Rudolph, J. (2002). Gender, crime, and desistance: Toward a theory of cognitive transformation. *American Journal of Sociology, 1077*, 990–1064. doi: https://www.journals.uchicago.edu/doi/10.1086/343191

Hannem, S., & Petrunik, M. (2007). Circles of Support and Accountability: A community justice initiative for the reintegration of high-risk sex offenders. *Contemporary Justice Review, 10*(2), 153–171. doi: https://doi.org/10.1080/10282580701372046

Hanson, K., & Bussiere, M. (1998). Predicting relapse: A meta-analysis of sexual offender recidivism studies. *Journal of Consulting and Clinical Psychology, 66*(2), 348–362. doi: https://psycnet.apa.org/doiLanding?doi=10.1037%2F0022-006X.66.2.348

Hanson, K., Harris, A., Helmus, L., & Thornton, D. (2014). High-risk sex offenders may not be high risk forever. *Journal of Interpersonal Violence, 29*(15), 2792–2813. doi: https://journals.sagepub.com/doi/abs/10.1177/0886260514526062?journalCode=jiva

Harris, D. (2014). Desistance from sexual offending: Findings from 21 life history narratives. *Journal of Interpersonal Violence, 29*(9), 1554–1578. doi: https://journals.sagepub.com/doi/abs/10.1177/0886260513511532?journalCode=jiva

Harris, D. (2017). *Desistance from sexual offending: Narratives of retirement, regulation and recovery.* Palgrave Macmillan. doi: https://www.palgrave.com/gp/book/9783319631998

Harris, D., Ackerman, A., & Haley, M. (2017). "Losing my religion": An exploration of religion and spirituality in men who claim to have desisted from sexual offending. *Criminal Justice Studies, 30*(2), 101–116. doi: https://www.tandfonline.com/doi/abs/10.1080/1478601X.2017.1300385?journalCode=gjup20

Hindman, J., & Peters, J. (2001). Polygraph testing leads to better understanding adult and juvenile sex offenders. *Federal Probation, 65*(3), 8–15. doi: https://psycnet.apa.org/record/2002-10215-002

Höing, M. (2015). *Empowering circles: CoSA and their contribution to a safer society* [PhD thesis, Tilburg University]. Tilburg.

Howell, T. (2008). *The point of no return: Aboriginal offenders' journey towards a crime free life* [PhD thesis, University of British Columbia]. Vancouver.

Hundleby, J., Gfellner, B., & Racine, D. (2007). Desistance and identity change among Aboriginal females. *Identity: An International Journal of Theory and Research*, 7(3), 225–253. doi: https://www.tandfonline.com/doi/abs/10.1080/15283480709336932?journalCode=hidn20

Kras, K. (2014). *Redemption or condemnation? A long-term follow-up of the desistance patterns of sex offenders* [PhD thesis, University of Missouri]. St Louis.

Kras, K., & Blasko, B. (2016). Pathways to desistance among men convicted of sexual offenses: Linking post hoc accounts of offending behavior and outcomes. *International Journal of*

Offender Therapy and Comparative Criminology, 60(15), 1738–1755. doi: https://journals.sagepub.com/doi/abs/10.1177/0306624X16668178

Kruttschnitt, C., Uggen, C., & Shelton, K. (2000). Predictors of desistance among sex offenders: The interaction of formal and informal social controls. *Justice Quarterly, 17*(1), 61–87. doi: https://www.tandfonline.com/doi/abs/10.1080/07418820000094481

Laws, D. R., & Ward, T. (2011). *Desistance from sex offending: Alternatives to throwing away the keys*. The Guilford Press.

Maruna, S. (2001). *Making good: How ex-convicts reform and rebuild their lives*. American Psychological Association. doi: https://www.apa.org/pubs/books/431645A

Maruna, S. (2016, November). *Self-narratives of desisting sex offenders: Where are the redemption scripts?* American Society of Criminology annual meeting New Orleans.

Maruna, S., Le Bel, T., Mitchell, N., & Naples, M. (2004). Pygmalion in the reintegration process: Desistance from crime through the looking glass. *Psychology, Crime & Law, 10*(3), 271–281. doi: https://www.tandfonline.com/doi/full/10.1080/10683160410001662762

Maruna, S., & Mann, R. (2006). A fundamental attribution error? Rethinking cognitive distortions. *Legal and Criminological Psychology, 11*(2), 155–177. doi: https://bpspsychub.onlinelibrary.wiley.com/doi/abs/10.1348/135532506X114608

McAdams, D., & de St Aubin, E. (1998). *Generativity and adult development: How and why we care for the next generation*. American Psychological Association. doi: https://www.apa.org/pubs/books/431601A

McNeill, F., & Maruna, S. (2007). Giving up and giving back: Desistance, generativity and social work with offenders. In G. McIvor, & P. Raynor (Eds.), *Developments in social work with offenders* (pp. 224–239). Jessica Kingsley Publishers.

Milner, R. (2017). *Desistance in men who have previously committed sexual offences: An exploration of the early processes* [PhD thesis, University of York]. York.

Plummer, M., & Cossins, A. (2018). The cycle of abuse: When victims become offenders. *Trauma, Violence, & Abuse, 19*(3), 286–305. doi: https://doi.org/10.1177/1524838016659487

Presser, L. (2008). *Been a heavy life: Stories of violent men*. University of Illinois Press. doi: https://www.jstor.org/stable/10.5406/j.ctt1xcj9k

Reinarman, C. (2005). Addiction as accomplishment: The discursive construction of disease. *Addiction Research and Theory, 13*(4), 307–320. doi: https://www.tandfonline.com/doi/abs/10.1080/16066350500077728

Richards, K. (2011). *Trends & issues in crime and criminal justice no. 429: Misperceptions about child sex offenders*. Canberra: Australian Institute of Criminology. https://aic.gov.au/publications/tandi/tandi429

Richards, K. (2019). Sympathy for the devil? Child sexual abuse, public opinion and the cycle-of-abuse theory. In K. Gleeson & C. Lumby (Eds.), *Age of consent* (pp. 87–101). University of Western Australia Press. doi: https://uwap.uwa.edu.au/products/the-age-of-consent

Richards, K. (in press). Circles of Support and Accountability: The role of social relations in core member desistance. *International Journal of Offender Therapy and Comparative Criminology*. doi: https://doi.org/10.1177/0306624X20964094

Richards, K., Death, J., & McCartan, K. (2020a). *Community-based approaches to sexual offender reintegration*. Australia's National Research Organisation for Women's Safety. https://www.anrows.org.au/project/community-based-approaches-to-sexual-offender-reintegration/

Richards, K., Death, J., & McCartan, K. (2020b). Toward redemption: Aboriginal and/or Torres Strait Islander men's narratives of desistance from sexual offending. *Victims & Offenders, 15*(6), 810–833. doi: https://www.tandfonline.com/doi/full/10.1080/15564886.2020.1754311

Richards, K., Death, J., & McCartan, K., & Australia's National Research Organisation for Women's Safety. (2020c). *Research to policy and practice issue 07: Community-based approaches to sexual offender reintegration: Key findings and future directions*. Australia's National Research Organisation for Women's Safety. https://www.anrows.org.au/project/community-based-approaches-to-sexual-offender-reintegration/

Rocque, M., Posick, C., & Paternoster, R. (2016). Identities through time: An exploration of identity change as a cause of desistance. *Justice Quarterly*, *33*(1), 45–72. doi: https://www.tandfonline.com/doi/full/10.1080/07418825.2014.894111

Salter, A. (2003). *Predators: Pedophiles, rapists & other sex offenders: Who they are, how they operate, and how we can protect ourselves and our children*. Basic Books. doi: https://psycnet.apa.org/record/2003-02239-000

Shover, N. (1996). *Great pretenders: Pursuits and careers of persistent thieves*. Westview Press. doi: https://www.routledge.com/Great-Pretenders-Pursuits-And-Careers-Of-Persistent-Thieves/Shover/p/book/9780813328119

Stone, R. (2016). Desistance and identity repair: Redemption narratives as resistance to stigma. *British Journal of Criminology*, *56*, 956–975. doi: https://academic.oup.com/bjc/article/56/5/956/1745580

Thompson, D. (2015). *Moving on after getting out: Support and accountability for convicted sex offenders* [PhD thesis, University of Leeds]. Leeds. https://etheses.whiterose.ac.uk/13410/1/Thompson_D_Law_PhD_2015.pdf

Vieira, C., Rose, R., Craissati, J., & Campbell, C. (2020). The impact of a community psychological treatment programme on desistance in personality disordered sexual offenders. *The Journal of Forensic Psychiatry & Psychology*, *31*(6), 837–853. doi: https://doi.org/10.1080/14789949.2020.1807041?journalCode=rjfp20

Winder, B., Blagden, N., Lievesley, R., Dwerryhouse, M., Kitson-Boyce, R., & Elliott, H. (2020). *UK national evaluation of big lottery funded Circles of Support and Accountability*. Nottingham Trent University Sexual Offences Crime and Misconduct Research Unit. https://www.circles-uk.org.uk/images/documents/SOCAMRU_BL_final_report_1_April_2020_v82.pdf

Chapter 5

Circles of Support and Accountability, the 110-Percenters and Witnesses to Identity Transformation

This chapter explains the key concept of the "110-percenters" and its role in desistance from sexual offending. It argues that Circles of Support and Accountability (CoSA) provide core members with a platform to demonstrate their commitment to desistance in front of an audience, and to have their new desistant identities witnessed by supportive others and reflected back to them, thereby solidifying these emerging identities. Using a thematic and narrative analysis of the interview data, the chapter demonstrates that CoSA can provide an opportunity for core members to perform the role of the 110-percenter, or super-reformed. In doing so, it also argues that a critical, yet previously unidentified, role of CoSA volunteers is as sympathetic witnesses to core members' performances of this new identity and role. As such, this chapter begins to position members of the community as key actors in offender reintegration and desistance.

Todd's Story

Todd had been living in and around the Toronto area for about ten years when we met in 2017. He had been incarcerated for five years for offences relating to non-contact sexual offences. He discovered CoSA through links with another community organisation, and claims that CoSA came along at just the right time – his case and his release from prison had attracted much media attention, and he felt under threat by both law enforcement officers and members of the general public. Todd also had little support from his family, both as a consequence of his offending and of their abuse of him as a child. The nature of Todd's offending – "I had no contact [with victims] whatsoever" – set him apart, in his mind, from other "real" perpetrators of sexual violence. But Todd feels different in other ways too. He describes the purpose of CoSA as helping core members to stay out of trouble, but this isn't an issue for Todd personally: "they asked me like questions if I was getting back into trouble. If I had any thoughts [about] getting back into trouble. The answer was the same all the time – 'no'". He considers himself "more independent than a lot of the [other] guys [core members]". Not only does Todd

DOI: 10.4324/9781003125532-6

sees himself as different from other core members but he also sees himself as different from the media and state construction of himself as a perpetrator: "even [two CoSA staff members] said to me, 'if you were anything like they'd portrayed you to be, you would have been [back] in trouble by now'".

Todd performs this difference from other "real" perpetrators – including the constructed image of himself as a "real" perpetrator – by deliberately differentiating and distancing himself from other core members. He does this by playing the role of "desistance missionary" (Harris, 2017a; Maruna, 2001), offering a type of guidance or mentorship towards other core members (see Chapter 7): "I tell them that if they get themselves back into trouble, it might be their last time. And they could be locked up for the rest of their lives. And is it worth it?" This is a theme that Todd returns to a number of times. He also draws on what he sees as his particular expertise to informally gather intelligence and inform CoSA staff about other core members who he sees as a recidivism risk: "I've helped them out a few times when I've talked to different people, I get this feeling that they're going to be back into trouble. Every time I've told these Circle people that they're going to be back into trouble, I've been proven right". By doing so, Todd performs the role of an uber-desister. He does this even when it may come at a personal cost: "If I see someone breaking the law, I'm going to give someone a [call]. Even if they call me a rat or whatever. I want my community safe. For everybody". Todd conveyed a sense of pride when his actions in this regard were witnessed by others and reflected back to him as evidence of his desistant identity: "Even when the police officer thanked me the second time, saying that because of what I'm doing they can focus on people that really need it". By implication, Todd himself does not "really need it". When I ask him a parting question about what could be done to improve CoSA, Todd takes the opportunity to situate himself in opposition to the other core members in the program, and to again distinguish himself from other, ordinary, core members: "just make sure that the guys stay out of trouble. I know it's hard sometimes because there are guys out there, like I said, [who] don't care. If you don't care about yourself or others, then you're going to continue hurting others. That's what sets me aside from everybody because I do care".

The 110-Percenters

Maruna (2001, p. 97) documented in his seminal study that desisters often adopted the role of the "110-percenter". In other words, the drive to demonstrate reform prompts desisters to want to be seen not as *ordinary* but *extraordinary* members of their families, groups and communities. As Maruna (2001, p. 97) puts it, reformed ex-offenders rarely merely "get by"; instead they "seem to always operate at 110 percent". To that end, "the fathers I talked to were not just fathers, but super-fathers. The volunteers were super-volunteers. The counselors were super-counselors".

Desistance scholars have also argued – drawing on the symbolic interactionist perspective, which posits that identities are built through interactions with others – that the development of a reformed identity is negotiated via interactions between the desister and significant others (Maruna, 2001; Richards, in press; Smith, 2021). Specifically, as Maruna et al. (2004, p. 274) have recognised, "desistance may be best facilitated when the desisting person's change in behavior is recognized by others and reflected back to him". They draw on labelling theory – i.e., the notion that once stigmatised as deviant, an individual will "live up to" this deviant label and adopt it as their "master status" (Becker, 1963) – to argue for a "looking glass" conceptualisation of desistance. In other words, positive reinforcement from witnesses should be used to reinforce desisters' identities as reformed and prosocial members of communities (Maruna et al., 2004). Importantly, this should occur at the level of an individual's *self* or *identity* rather than at the level of specific *acts* or *behaviours*; witnesses should ideally reinforce that a kind *act* reflects that the ex-offender is a kind *person* – that the act reflects an enduring good self – rather than positioning the act as singular or an aberration. Maruna et al. (2004) emphasised that they are not arguing here that desisters are passive recipients upon whom observers' positive reinforcements are bestowed, but rather that observers/reinforcers are one key element in the development of a desistant identity. Weaver's (Weaver, 2015; Weaver & McNeill, 2015) notion of desistance as being "co-created" by desisters and their supporters eloquently captures this distinction.

The work of sociologist Erving Goffman is also instructive here. Goffman (1983, 1967) argued that individuals' social lives are a dramatised performance in which individuals project an idealised, desired self through a process of "impression management" – i.e., efforts made by an individual to shape audiences' belief in their performance (or "presentation of self"). According to this perspective, *audiences* are critical to understanding social interactions and impression management (Goffman, 1983); as Birnbaum (2008, p. 72) puts it, "whenever individuals are before an audience (i.e., people are aware that others are able to observe them either directly or indirectly) they are careful about the types of impressions they want to give and actively shape their self-presentation accordingly". Crucially, a Goffmanian lens suggests that performances are successful when observers accept the presentation of the performer's self as they had intended or hoped to be perceived; they are more successful still when the individual performer is convinced by their own act (Goffman, 1967).

The core members in this study, like those with sexual offence convictions more broadly, typically had few roles available to them in which they might excel. They were unlikely, for example, to be able to perform the role of "super-father" identified by Maruna (2001, p. 97), as many were precluded from having contact with children. Instead, they became "super core members", a type of uber-desister, giving "110 percent" to CoSA. They performed the role of super core member in a number of interrelated ways, which are outlined in turn in the remainder of this chapter.

Surpassing Other Core Members' Desistance Efforts

Perhaps the primary way in which core members performed the role of the uber-desister was to position themselves as fundamentally different from, and more reformed than other, ordinary, core members. Such core members sought to be viewed by others – notably CoSA volunteers and staff – as inherently better desistant subjects than their peers. This commonly took the form of core members differentiating themselves on the grounds that, unlike their peers, they have taken responsibility for their offending pasts and non-offending futures. When I asked Morgan whether his Circle volunteers had helped him in a practical sense – with housing for example – he replied: "I would say that they would do it, but they haven't had to for me". Rory spoke with some annoyance about other core members who were content living on welfare and/or remaining uneducated when he himself had managed to accomplish so much more. Daniel likewise sought to differentiate himself from other core members by asserting that, unlike his peers, he has "taken ownership of what I have done".

Gerald is another case in point here. In the following passage from his interview, Gerald distinguishes himself from typical core members by presenting himself as more advanced in his reform and as so distinct from his peers that he can question the veracity of their narratives about their own offending and their concomitant commitment to desistance:

> When I was still on parole, I tried to work with, I think three or four others....and they were so "yeah-but, yeah-but, yeah-but". I kept telling them, I says "there's no yeah-but. You either did or you didn't do it.... it was your choice, your decision, and you can't use alcohol and drugs as an excuse, because if you hadn't already had it in your mind, in your thought process, what was going on, you wouldn't have done it. It had to have been there; you just used alcohol or drugs to weaken and make it easier. Because you're not going to be a child molester unless it's already in your head to do so".

In accentuating what he sees as the excuses of other core members, Gerald seeks to highlight his "ownership" over his own offending and thus his better performance as a desister. Gerald later returned, unprompted, to this same theme, again positioning himself as an uber-desister or 110-percenter:

GERALD: And when you get somebody that [a core member], no matter what goes on with him in his life, whether he's in the military or whether he's with a step-daughter or what, and he tries to blame everybody but himself and say he's the victim - oh boy, that was the last one I walked out on.

KR: Right. So you have walked out of a Circle?

GERALD: Oh I walked out of the room. I told - I stood up, I told him - I said "and you're telling me all the things that happened to you, that you are the victim?" and he says "yeah". And I came up [close to him] like that, and I - oh, I was - wanted to knock him out of his chair. I wanted to slap his stupid mouth. Then I thought to myself, "that's not going to do any good". So I just turned around, looked at [CoSA staff member] and I said "I've had enough, this idiot's not going to listen".

Here, Gerald not only verbally differentiates himself from his peers but also does so in a physical or material sense. As discussed further below, he deliberately positions himself as more serious about and dedicated to other core members' reform than even CoSA staff and volunteers who, in his telling, passively remain in the room and by implication, accept the excuses and justifications of the less-committed core member in question.

Rory related a strikingly similar story. He uses his role mentoring new core members (see further Chapter 7) to demonstrate his prowess as a 110-percenter and has even been in trouble with the CoSA program for being too hard on new core members. He says:

> I got ousted out from a Circle because again, at least in my case I am very blunt....When it comes to the core member, they tell me they want to change. They tell me they want – [I ask] "well how are you doing it?" I start telling them and I get in their face a little that "this is what you need to do". Then before I know it I'm hearing [from staff/volunteers] "yeah, you know Rory, we're really here just to support them and meet them at their level". I'm going "you're going to meet them at their level? Guess what, one day you're going to meet them in prison".

Kevin and Leon also told remarkably similar stories. Kevin described himself as being "ruthless when it comes to this program" and declared, despite his own convictions for sexual offences against minors:

> You understand that these [core members] are sex offenders. Don't look at that lightly. It's not lightly and you should never look at it lightly or even, don't compare, "well, I got this much time", or "I got that much time". It doesn't matter whose lawyer's better than whose....you need to come to terms with that and look at it and take full responsibility for it.

When I asked Leon about improvements he might suggest to Circles, he aligned himself with CoSA staff and volunteers rather than other core members, claiming:

> I would say that the format they have going with this since I've been in and able to observe it, it seems to be I would say more than adequate. The potential is there but the men have to be responsible. For the most part, everyone has been. But you will get the occasional rogue who no one can do anything for him, unfortunately.

Interestingly, both Leon (above) and Todd constructed in their narratives a class of core members who they considered incapable of desistance, or as lost causes: "like I tell the Circle people, 'You can help some people, but some people, no matter what you do, it won't do any good'" (Todd). This is a novel narrative device. Rather than accepting that all core members are on a journey – however unsteady – towards desistance, Leon and Todd insist on a cohort of lost causes who will never be capable of reform, thus differentiating themselves not only *in degree* but also *in kind* from this cohort and bringing into sharp relief their exceptionalism as desistant subjects. Leon and Todd present themselves not merely as better at or more advanced in their desistance from these lost causes, but as categorically distinct. In defining desistance as a categorical rather than continuous variable, these core members deliberately position themselves as more like their Circle volunteers than other core members – or strive for "we-ness" in Weaver's (Weaver, 2015; Weaver & McNeill, 2015) terms (see further below).

In some cases, core members who positioned themselves as uber-desisters did so by eclipsing not only the commitment of other core members but also the commitment of criminal justice professionals, including CoSA program staff and volunteers. Recall Gerald's comment, that in response to his frustration with another core member he "turned around, looked at [CoSA staff member] and I said 'I've had enough, this idiot's not going to listen'". Consider also Terry's discussion of the group therapy in which he participated:

> When I go to therapy....I participate to the point where I will challenge what people say because it's not true and it's easy to see. Or [I] ask a few questions to get to that. Sometimes the therapists don't like it because it's almost taking over the group.

Kevin narrated a similar incident involving the Circle of his foster son (see further discussion below):

> I finally got fed up and I had to confront his group. I came in and I said, "look, no more of this, this, this and this. I want you to be confronting him on this, this and this. I even want you to even ask him, every time you see him every week, how many times did he masturbate within that week. If he did, what the hell was he masturbating to? Those are issues, the key issues that I want to know about, that he should know about, that you should know about, because if they're images of this, or are they

> images of this and in what positions? That's what's important. You guys are sitting here talking about the fucking football game".

In these examples, core members use Circles to demonstrate that they are super-committed to their own and others' desistance – more so even than the volunteers and professionals specifically appointed for this purpose.

Ratting Out Other Core Members

As Todd's story (above) demonstrates, another way in which core members aim to be recognised as super core members, whose reform outshines that of their ordinary peers, is through calling the attention of criminal justice professionals to the behaviour of these less successful desistant subjects. To put it bluntly, super core members seek to distance themselves from their ordinary peers by "ratting them out". By not only demonstrating commitment to their own desistance but also recognising the failings of others to do so, super core members "give 110 percent". In doing so, they implicitly align themselves with criminal justice authorities and highlight their superiority over their ordinary peers. For example, Frank claimed that during his time in prison, "If a prisoner said he was going to commit a serious crime, I told the warden I would let him know". Todd revelled in ratting out other individuals with sexual offence convictions, not for instrumental but demonstrative purposes: "every time I've told these Circle people that they're going to be back into trouble, I've been proven right". The point for Todd appears to be the fact of being "proven right" – that is, in the emotion, he attaches to the good opinion of his Circle members.

Bryce took a slightly different approach to ratting out a peer as part of his project of becoming a super core member. He described knowing another core member from external group therapy sessions and therefore feeling that he understood his "triggers" and "track record" and "what he was like". He described warning a CoSA staff member (and was implicitly warning me as a researcher) about the other man:

> I was always leery because [staff member] when we first met used to meet me by myself…and I didn't want [her] being with that guy alone. Because he'll gain your confidence and all of a sudden, you'll let your guard down and you're in trouble.
>
> (Bryce)

Lachlan similarly informed his Circle about another perpetrator with whom he had spent time in prison, warning them that "this guy's going to do something". Morgan participated in a somewhat gentler form of this behaviour. Rather than reporting others to criminal justice authorities, Morgan regularly advocated on behalf of other individuals with sexual offence convictions with whom he shared accommodation. He recounted repeatedly telephoning his CoSA coordinator, to say "this person needs a Circle", and upon hearing the news that CoSA in Canada had secured significant funding, "list[ing] off a list of people" who in his view needed the support of a Circle and asking "so can they all get Circles [now]"? In fact, in his telling of this event, the CoSA program coordinator contacted Morgan to let him know the good news about the renewed funding. This is an important aspect of Morgan's narrative because it highlights the importance to Morgan of having CoSA staff view him as different from other (prospective) core members. It also highlights the staff member's acceptance of Morgan's reform. In his narrative, he is not the beneficiary of the funding, but a trusted ally from whom they seek input about who else might be a beneficiary. Morgan identifies others who are risky and in need of a Circle and casts himself as not risky by implication.

Kevin narrated a similar story, claiming to have "personally put two guys back into the prison with the information that they've given me". Kevin elaborated:

> This was a guy in my group at [treatment facility]. He said, "well, what all can I tell you?" I said, "you can tell me whatever the hell you want. Just know that I'm into no more victims and I'm not your friend". He told me. I laid low with it for a couple of weeks 'til I went out to [town] and then saw the evidence and then came back, informed my Circle. He was arrested and [put] back in prison.

Putting two individuals back in prison was not, however, Kevin's most dramatic attempt to be perceived as a super desister by ratting out another person. He claimed also to have been instrumental in the return of his own foster son to prison. While it is unclear whether the individual in question was Kevin's foster son in formal legal terms (this seems unlikely given Kevin's own convictions for sexual offences), Kevin claimed responsibility for returning a young man over whom he had exercised some form of guardianship to prison. Kevin explained that the young man had spent much of his youth in detention facilities and had later been in prison in relation to online child sexual exploitation material offences and had joined a Circle following his release. To Kevin's mind, the young man was "not honest with his Circle" about his sexual thoughts and urges. As a result, "even my own foster son, who I put back in the jail, who I can look in the eye and say, 'I love you, but no, no'".

Other core members also recounted making great personal sacrifices in the process of ratting others out. Lachlan, for example, discussed his role in ensuring that a fellow former prisoner was returned to prison in relation to a planned violent attack, before declaring that the incident "pushed me beyond the point of [reason]. I think it's why I've got some of the injuries I have". Lachlan thereby paradoxically demonstrates his own success at reform by coming to bear physical markers of his commitment to it. While not an example of snitching on others, Peter narrated an incident at his workplace, in which a staff member complained of chest pains. When Peter's supervisor did not take the complaint seriously, Peter advocated on behalf of the man, resulting in him getting into an altercation with his supervisor and ultimately losing his job. Like Lachlan and Kevin, Peter thus created material evidence of his status as hyper-moral super-desister. While these evidentiary markers – a lost job, a foster son in prison and wounds from physical fights – appear self-defeating or in counter position to desistance, they might equally be read as powerful reinforcers of it. In other words, the very fact of the personal loss suffered by the core members emphasises their devotion to reform).

The Judge Judy Effect: Adopting Hyper-Conservative Criminal Justice Values

Core members also played the role of super-desister by adhering to very conservative criminal justice values. CoSA staff seemed bemused by this, as the following exchange from a Toronto focus group illustrates:

STAFF MEMBER 12: [Core members] tend to be the hardest people, very unforgiving of each other, as if the need to be a reconciled and full member of the community actually stops with them. They fail to recognise that need or that desire in another, right, and instead want to be particularly harsh. One interesting phenomenon I think at one of our [supported accommodation] houses is that every day at one of our previous houses they would watch [reality television show] *Judge Judy* and always take the militant, conservative standpoint. "That jerk should be in jail". Oh, really? Like, what about the context? What about his life story? It's like, "forget about it".

STAFF MEMBER 11: I just had a really, really interesting conversation with one of our core members who has a friend who was in a physical domestic [violence] situation and the man that had assaulted her was arrested. He was adamant that this guy should get more time…[that the judge should] really throw the book at him.

Some core members interviewed for the study similarly adhered to this ethos. For example, Todd made the following comment in his interview:

> I like met guys that were in my group at vacation halfway house and they're back inside. That's because, I could tell that they weren't telling the truth. And sure, there's guys that should be locked up and kept locked up. I agree with that.

Later in his interview, Todd discussed a local stranger assault, declaring that the perpetrator is now "locked up as a dangerous offender and will never get out, and it's a fitting sentence for him". Todd distinguishes himself, however, from these perpetrators, who he sees as appropriate targets of the punitive state response. He went on to state: "But there are guys that you give them half the chance, they'll stay out of trouble forever". Todd is thus (at least outwardly) supportive of highly punitive and risk-obsessed criminal justice responses but does not believe – or rather does not want us as audience members to believe – that it is warranted in his own case. In doing so, he positions himself not as a "real" perpetrator of sexual violence but as a reformed individual. Kevin's disparaging comments (see above) about CoSA volunteers discussing the "fucking football game" with a core member similarly demonstrates his adherence to a confrontational correcto-therapeutic approach supported by the state and repudiation of the social support aspects of CoSA.

While some staff seemed perplexed about why core members, of all people, would adopt very conservative criminal justice values, this makes sense when considered in light of the notion of the 110-percenter. Paradoxically, to profess allegiance to the punitive stance of the state allows core members to refute the notion that they are deserving targets of it. Obversely, to advocate for leniency towards people with sexual offence convictions involves conceding that they themselves would benefit from this leniency, and as a corollary, that they are really a sexual offender. The identity repair work of this cohort of core members thus involves being so radically opposed to sexual violence that taking umbrage with the state's response to sexual offending – no matter how extreme – would significantly undermine this stance. Thompson (2015) has argued that Circles allow core members to begin to claim "a more acceptable and conventional set of values akin to the 'normal' citizen". As such, we might also read core members' adoption of very punitive values as simply an attempt to fit in with conventional society and to feel and be perceived as "normal".

If Desistance Occurs in the Woods and There Is No One There to See It…

Core members in this study yearned for their desistance to be witnessed. Desisting from crime, in and of itself, was not enough – core members wanted others to see and be convinced of their desistance and to accept their desistant identities. Due to the stigmatisation and ostracisation, typically experienced by people with sexual offence convictions, there are usually few desistance witnesses available. Core members thus frequently spoke about wanting various criminal justice professionals to recognise their reform. Frank, for example, described helping a number of CoSA volunteers who were seeking careers in criminal justice by providing advice that included the importance of "watching their backs" and "never turning their backs" on a potential perpetrator. In doing so, Frank implicitly communicates to these prospective law enforcement officers his own reform. He revels in this experience of being accepted by criminal justice authorities: "every time I see one of the officers up there, [they say] 'how are you doing today? How are you doing in the Circles?' [I say] 'pretty good'. He says, 'you're looking good'. Yeah!" For Frank, the desire to have others witness his changed identity commenced in prison. He proudly recalled a prison warden commenting on his good behaviour in prison and recognising that he often helped prisoners with physical disabilities. Rory also yearned for his success as a desister from sexual crime to be witnessed by others. In his interview, he stated:

> One of the things even my lawyer said and correctional officers that would talk with me would say "Rory, you know what" – I would tell them, I said "one of these days I'll let you see. I'll write to you". He goes "no, no, no first of all we can't. Second of all if you want me to know everything is good I don't want to ever see you again. Then I'll know everything is good". He goes "because unfortunately your situation we would know if you return [to prison]. That would be disappointing". Anyway, I hope, I really do I hope they would if they're still working in the system they would look my name up and say "damn that dude's been out for nine years and he's alright". I really do. I hope they do.

Dean narrated in his interview that he was informed by a senior criminal justice officer that he had an 80% chance of reoffending. As a result, Dean is "out to prove them wrong. I'm out to prove what I did was a mistake - a very horrid mistake". In a sense, criminal justice professionals such as prison wardens and parole officers provide ideal witnesses to core members' reformed identities. Their acceptance of core members' reformed identities provides a powerful counter-narrative to the subject position imposed on people with sexual offence convictions – i.e., a permanently risky and stigmatised subjectivity (for a powerful example, see Sample et al., 2021). Acceptance by actors within the criminal justice apparatus might therefore carry significant weight for ex-offenders (for another example see Geiger & Fischer, 2017), as the narratives of core members outlined above illustrate. Drawing on the work of therapeutic jurisprudence progenitor Wexler (2002), Maruna et al. (2004, p. 275) concur:

> ...delabeling might be most potent when coming from "on high", particularly official sources like treatment professionals or teachers, rather than from family members or friends - where such acceptance can be taken for granted....In particular, if the delabeling were to be endorsed and supported by the same social control establishment involved in the "status degradation" process of conviction and sentencing (e.g. judges or peer juries), this public redemption might carry considerable social and psychological weight for participants and observers.

Such narratives are, however, probably rare, and particularly so for those with sexual offence convictions. Indeed, the correcto-therapeutic apparatus deliberately resists even the possibility of sexual offender reform and propagates instead the image of the perpetually risky sexual offender (Harris, 2017b; Wacquant, 2009). As Lofland (1969, p. 210) has argued, because it can be difficult for criminal justice authorities to distinguish between legitimate and illegitimate claims of personal reform, such authorities are likely to err on the side of interpreting such claims as phony or implausible. Correcto-therapeutic professionals otherwise risk not only being proven wrong and thus looking foolish (Lofland, 1969; Maruna et al., 2004) but also making decisions with potentially catastrophic consequences. As stakeholder 2 argued in his interview for this research, less-experienced correctional supervisors in particular tend to be extremely cautious in this regard. Thus, opportunities for people with sexual offence convictions to experience delabelling from official actors may be scarce. They may also be impracticable. In the excerpt above, while Rory considers the prison warden as a potential witness to his reform, he acknowledges that the warden will not be able to see Rory thriving in the community. Instead, he will "see" Rory's success only in his *absence* from prison. For Rory, this is clearly not a potent enough form of witness-bearing to his desistance.

CoSA thus have a potentially powerful role to play in providing witnesses to core members' reform. Having one's desistance accepted by CoSA volunteers will likely be both more practical and more powerful given that volunteers both have closer (as well as more regular and possibly longer-lasting) contact with core members and represent the general community. To be believed by members of ordinary society may be particularly potent, especially in the context of the extreme stigma that people with sexual offence convictions currently face (Jahnke et al., 2015; Spencer, 2009; Ten Bensel & Sample, 2017; Wacquant, 2009). In this way, CoSA volunteers may become the "personal voucher" – "a person of good moral standing who will act as a witness to their reformed character" (Maruna, 2001) upon whom successful desisters often rely (Maruna et al., 2004, p. 275). CoSA volunteers are far better placed than members of the judiciary or other criminal justice authorities to play this vital role. Moreover, as staff member 3 explained, a key limitation of state correctional authorities is that "what parole does is tell you what you *can't* do but not really what you *can* do". Staff member 2 concurred, arguing that correctional officials are bound by strict practice guidelines; in contrast, "CoSA provides all of the moral support that the policies and directives that your parole and probation officer [must adhere to precludes]". Unlike state correctional officials, CoSA staff and volunteers can bear witness not only to core members' lack of recidivism but also to their active development of desistant selves; in staff member 14's words, CoSA support core members "to get to the point where they, voluntarily, are respecting these things [their conditions of release] anyway. As opposed to, 'I'd better do this, or I'm going back to prison'".

This chapter argues that Circles can and should play the crucial role of bearing witness to core members' identity repair work. CoSA volunteers are a specifically constructed audience that can strengthen core members' desistant identities by accepting (where appropriate) the veracity of these. As outlined above, a number of theoretical tenets suggest that a powerful reinforcement of a reformed identity is others' acceptance of it.

The potential of Circle volunteers as witnesses to core member reform has yet, however, to be afforded detailed attention by researchers, despite the vital role that such witnesses may play in promoting identity repair and thereby promoting desistance. In addition to providing direct witnesses, CoSA also often connect core members to other potential desistance witnesses and/or create opportunities for core members to rehearse desistant identities in other supportive contexts. They do this through working with core members to develop appropriate relationships with individuals and organisations beyond the Circle, such as through employment, education, hobby or church groups. This was powerfully demonstrated in many of the interviews I undertook for this research; in Don's case – to use just one example – his CoSA had connected him with a range of other relevant service provisions and social avenues, including a local Native centre. Thus, while CoSA are by no means the sole source of such desistance witnesses, volunteers have often taken carriage of the groundwork involved in discovering, building and maintaining other potential sources, as well as supporting the core member to successfully navigate these.

The role of volunteers as sympathetic desistance witnesses is powerfully demonstrated in the following excerpt from my interview with volunteer 2:

> One of the Circle members had a trucking business and said [to the core member], "if you're able to get a trucking license I'd be glad to hire you". And so, over the course of several weeks we arranged for him to have a loan from a group of church members....And actually, it was a gift to him but when he started working, he paid that back. And the feeling of responsibility I think is one way that people get feeling the good about themselves – "I can be trusted. I fulfilled my obligation".

In this example, Circle volunteers clearly accept the core member's reformed self; their faith in this regard is keenly demonstrated by their act of sourcing a loan on his behalf[1]. In theoretical terms, this underscores the symbolic interactionist perspective, which posits that identities – in this case, desistant identities – are built through interactions with others. As volunteer 12 put it: "to feel that there is something, that they are worthwhile and that they have something to contribute is new to them and it's sort of an honour because somebody thinks...'I can manage to do that, I'm capable'. I think that's very valuable".

In some cases, Circle volunteers' acceptance of core members' reform was demonstrated through a type of "reintegration ritual" or process for delabelling and destigmatisation (Maruna, 2011, 2014). Kevin and Adam had both received material honours in recognition of their successful desistance efforts:

> I've been now 16 years. They gave me an amazing statue on Saturday and it was like, "wow, this is a shocker" [laughs]. Yeah, 16 years, and you look at it and you think, "yeah. I've seen guys come and I've seen guys go and I've bonded very much with really wonderful people, and [I'm] accepted", which is good.
>
> (Kevin)

> I went to a thing [event] last weekend and I got an award. I'm so thankful for it. But it was for being courageous to getting back into the community. I never looked at it that way. That makes me feel good that they're saying, "look, you did good. Look, this is what you got".... I'm proud of it, yeah. Right, so I'm happy about it. It hasn't even been a year [that I've been involved in CoSA].
>
> (Adam)

Previously, CoSA researchers have stressed the important role that volunteers play in creating a sense of belonging for core members (Blagden et al., 2018; Fox, 2015; Höing et al., 2013; Richards et al., 2020). This narrative was also reflected in the current study, with staff members and volunteers talking at length about the work that CoSA do in reducing core members' isolation and creating a sense of community for them. To use just a couple of examples, staff member 6 understood CoSA's capacity to reduce reoffending to stem from their focus on "giving the offender a place to belong", and staff member 14 extolled the virtues of "that whole feeling of belonging" that Circles can provide. This is no doubt the case; however, the findings presented above advance our understanding in this regard by suggesting that the relationships between CoSA staff and volunteers not only provide a sense of belonging to core members but also (perhaps more potently) witnesses to their desistance.

Adam's Story

Adam has been involved in his current CoSA for about six months when we meet in Toronto. (He had previously been involved in CoSA in another jurisdiction). Adam had spent about four years incarcerated in relation to contact offences against minors. He originally connected with CoSA while still incarcerated; after deciding that "I want to be able to put a lot of this behind me [when I am released]", he met with CoSA representatives during their visit to his prison. Participating in CoSA was crucial for Adam as he was released from prison with "absolutely no-one, no-one. No support whatsoever". The main benefit of CoSA as Adam sees it is his volunteers' assistance with decision-making:

> In this CoSA, we talk about the emotional impact of the decision [ie any decision about his life]. "Are you sure you want to go down that road? If you want to go down that road, these are the consequences da-da-da-da". "Oh, yeah, you're right". But the decision's still mine, whether I want to go that road or not.

One of the main difficulties experienced by Adam is building new relationships in the community given his offending past: "when you're out of prison, you already have that stigma that, 'oh, you're a criminal. Oh, well, what did you do'? The prying starts. You've got to think, 'should I tell them'? No, because if you tell them, boom, you're dead meat". This is particularly challenging for Adam as it means that "sometimes you have to lie". This goes against Adam's sense of his true, good self: "that's not good, especially when you have a moral standing. Even though you may break your moral standing [when you offend], you still have moral standings".

Despite articulating this enduring moral self, Adam spoke in terms that suggest he has "knifed off" his former offending self:

> They [my CoSA volunteers] don't bring up, "well, you were incarcerated because of da-da-da-da". They don't bring that back up to me. That's gone. It's a new start for me, so why brand me under that umbrella? I'm an individual who's trying to make a new life. They're helping me do that....They already know my situation. I've been right upfront with them on sexual stuff, on anything. They don't throw it back in my face.

Adam views his desistance very much as being co-created with his volunteers, or in Weaver's (2015, p. 212) terms, "co-produced by individuals-in-relation". As he sees it, "whatever they give me is a reflection of them". If a core member reoffends, "that's a reflection on you guys, because you really didn't help this guy". It isn't only up to the volunteers, however: "CoSA is offering help. You can accept the help or not accept it. I accept it".

Adam is the quintessential super-desister. Like a number of other core members interviewed for this study, rather than railing against the strict conditions of his release, Adam takes his reform so seriously that he has internalised these conditions and plans to adhere to them for the rest of his life:

ADAM: I know what my conditions are. Even after warrant, those conditions still apply. I don't care how you look at it. They are going to be there for the rest of your life.

KR: Are you technically still on an Order?

....

ADAM: No, I'm done. I'm done on my Warrant. But because of what my Warrant - what my conditions were, I'm going to carry that with me, because those are things, if I wouldn't follow them, they'd allow me to get back into trouble. I don't want that, so I'm going to follow even the conditions long after it's over and done with....Yeah, it's life or death. That's how I look at it.

Throughout his interview, he repeatedly contrasts his own success in this regard with other core members' lacklustre efforts at reform. For example:

ADAM: I'm putting myself in somebody else's position at this point and comparing myself to them. I see how long they've been in [CoSA] and the progress they've made. Even though I don't know their story, I just kind of [think] 'wow....you should be a little bit more advanced than I am. How come you're not?'...

KR: Yeah. No, I get it. Some people have higher needs. Some people have cognitive [limitations] - I mean, as we discussed.

ADAM: I don't know if it's called higher needs or if it's just called lackadaisy.

KR: Or maybe some combination of the two.

ADAM: Well....I look at it as being lackadaisy.

In comparison, Adam is a highly motivated: "I want to get into the community. I want to be accepted. I want to do what they want me - whatever their expectations are".

Adam positions himself as a better therapeutic subject than his peers. In relation to his Alcoholics Anonymous group, in which he was heavily involved, he bemoaned "the lies that I would hear from older men and even younger people!" Similarly, Adam constructs himself as a more devout and devoted therapeutic subject than his fellow core members:

> We just had an incident not long ago with one of our fellows. When I heard that he was back in prison, tears come to my eyes. What happened? Why didn't you talk? Why didn't you share? But that was him. He would get involved, but he wouldn't say much. "Well, how are you doing today"? "Mm, okay". "Are you sure"? The actions and the words you said don't match....No. If I'm hurting, I let them know. If I'm mad, I let them know.

Here, Adam distinguishes himself from his less successful peers not merely in behavioural terms, but in terms of character: his peer reoffended because "that was him". Adam also constructs himself as a superior spiritual subject: "I do have that belief of God. I know most of these men here probably don't. I can't say for sure, but that's how - I think a lot of them [don't] - if you're really going to be honest with God, you got to be honest with yourself".

Importantly, while many other 110-percenters appear to rely on their CoSA volunteers to bear witness to their desistance, for Adam, involvement in CoSA is a marker of a still-reforming self and is therefore at odds with his self-image: "I like CoSA, but I don't want it to be there for the rest of my life.... [I know] it's going to end eventually. I don't look at it as being 10 years down the road or 20 years down the road. I look at it as being soon". To Adam's mind, being involved in CoSA for an extended period is evidence of a poor effort at reform:

> When I see these people that are...five years [in a CoSA] or whatever, it's like, "wow, you've been there that long and you're still doing or saying what you're not supposed to be doing and saying. What's wrong? Are you not working on yourself"?

Conclusion

While CoSA are often characterised as aligned with the Good Lives Model (see Chapter 2) – and certainly appear to support core members to build and sustain the elements of a Good Life (Blagden et al., 2018; Chouinard & Riddick, 2014; McCartan et al., 2014; Richards et al., 2020) – this chapter argues that CoSA play an important role beyond this. Specifically, CoSA provide *witnesses* to a core member's attempts to create and maintain a Good Life, and an *audience* for the new role he plays as a law-abiding, trustworthy citizen, with a meaningful life and character beyond that of stigmatised "sex offender". CoSA volunteers play an important role in this regard, especially as agents of the state (e.g., parole officers) must resist displaying trust (Lofland, 1969) in an individual's reform (as discussed above). This highlights the importance of CoSA being delivered at arm's length from state authorities (see further McCartan et al., 2014; Richards, in press).

It has been documented a number of times in descriptive studies (Richards, 2011; Thomas et al., 2014; Thompson et al., 2017) that core members value the voluntary nature of the support they receive from their Circles. Elsewhere (Richards, in press), I have argued that core members value the voluntary nature of CoSA due to the "we-ness" (Weaver, 2015; Weaver & McNeill, 2015) that this creates; it eschews the "us and them" flavour of core members' relationships with state authorities (e.g., mandated treatment providers) and instead, creates a sense that core members and volunteers not only share the "same moral space" (Fox, 2015, p. 83; see also Hannem & Petrunik, 2007) but also are similar moral subjects (Richards, in press). As this chapter emphasises, further to this, the creation of we-ness implicitly demonstrates an acceptance of desistance and the believability of a core member's performance of desistance. No identity transformation – no matter how profound – will successfully diminish the distance between an agent of a statutory correctional authority and a person with a sexual offence conviction. CoSA then fill a critical gap in this context: unlike agents of the state, they enable core members to undertake identity transformation work in front of an audience willing to accept (indeed, actively invested in) their identity transformation.

CoSA thus provide an excellent, and rare, opportunity for core members to perform the role of the 110-percenter. This is critical in and of itself since we know that these are precisely the identities that desisters adopt (Maruna, 2001). Opportunities to rehearse these identities in a safe space, in front of an encouraging audience, are vital. In performing this role, core members implicitly seek to minimise the distance between themselves and "us" as represented by CoSA volunteers. Their actions say, "I am less like that offender, and more like you, the non-offender". In other words, they are attempting to develop a sense of "we-ness" (Richards, in press; Weaver, 2015; Weaver & McNeill, 2015).

A final point of note is that uber-desisters may be overrepresented among core members, and certainly among core members who formed the sample for the current study. Indeed, given that CoSA are voluntary, it is unsurprising perhaps to find so many of those very committed to reform. That said, as I have argued elsewhere (Richards, 2011), voluntariness exists on a spectrum, with some core members participating in CoSA with more enthusiasm than others. For example, some core members may participate in CoSA at the encouragement of their parole officer rather than being fully committed to this measure (Richards, 2011). Furthermore, it is important to note that by no means all the core members in this study could be characterised as 110-percenters. Farrall and Calverley (in Burnett, 2009, p. 523) raise an important question in this regard: "do they always...develop into 'desistance missionaries', spreading the gospel of 'reform', or are some of them 'ordinary people' now worrying about getting to work on time, paying bills and getting dinner ready?" The answer in relation to my own study is that the lives of people with convictions relating to serious sexual offending – at least in the current criminal justice climate – may never approach ordinariness, again potentially explaining the overrepresentation of desistance missionaries among core members.

Note

1. Lending money to a core member would not be permissible in many CoSA programs (see https://www.edmontoncosa.org/volunteering-with-cosa/volunteer-code-of-conduct/) and is not a common occurrence.

References

Becker, H. (1963). *Outsiders: Studies in the sociology of deviance.* Free Press. doi: https://psycnet.apa.org/record/1965-08393-000

Birnbaum, M. (2008). *Taking Goffman on a tour of Facebook: College students and the presentation of self in a mediated digital environment* [PhD thesis, University of Arizona, USA].

Blagden, N., Elliott, H., & Lievesley, R. (2018). Circles of Support and Accountability, assisted desistance and community transition. In H. Elliott, K. Hocken, R. Lievesley,

N. Blagden, B. Winder, & P. Banyard (Eds.), *Sexual crime and Circles of Support and Accountability* (pp. 25–42). Palgrave Macmillan. doi: https://www.palgrave.com/gp/book/9783319748221

Burnett, R. (2009). Post-corrections reintegration: Prisoner resettlement and desistance from crime. In J. Adler & J. Gray (Eds.), *Forensic psychology: Concepts, debates and practice* (2nd ed., pp. 508–528). Willan. doi: https://www.routledge.com/Forensic-Psychology-Concepts-Debates-and-Practice/Adler-Gray/p/book/9781843924142

Chouinard, J., & Riddick, C. (2014). *An evaluation of the Circles of Support and Accountability demonstration project: Final report.* Collaborative Centre for Justice and Safety. https://www.justiceandsafety.ca/rsu_docs/cosa-final-report-with-cover.pdf

Fox, K. (2015). Theorizing community integration as desistance-promotion. *Criminal Justice and Behavior, 42*(1), 82–94. doi: https://doi.org/10.1177/0093854814550028

Geiger, B., & Fischer, M. (2017). Incarcerated sex offenders in rehabilitation account their offending. *Journal of Investigative Psychology and Offender Profiling, 14*(1), 43–59. doi: https://doi.org/10.1002/jip.1460

Goffman, E. (1967). *The presentation of self in everyday life.* Doubleday.

Goffman, E. (1983). The interaction order: American Sociological association, 1982 presidential address. *American Sociological Review, 48*(1), 1–17.

Hannem, S., & Petrunik, M. (2007). Circles of Support and Accountability: A community justice initiative for the reintegration of high-risk sex offenders. *Contemporary Justice Review, 10*(2), 153–171. doi: https://doi.org/10.1080/10282580701372046

Harris, D. (2017a). Desistance from sexual offending: Behavioral change without cognitive transformation. *Journal of Interpersonal Violence, 32*(20), 3049–3070. doi: https://journals.sagepub.com/doi/abs/10.1177/0886260515596537

Harris, D. (2017b). *Desistance from sexual offending: Narratives of retirement, regulation and recovery.* Palgrave Macmillan. doi: https://www.palgrave.com/gp/book/9783319631998

Höing, M., Bogaerts, S., & Vogelvang, B. (2013). Circles of Support and Accountability: How and why they work for sex offenders. *Journal of Forensic Psychology Practice, 13*(4), 267–295. doi: https://www.tandfonline.com/doi/abs/10.1080/15228932.2013.808526

Jahnke, S., Imhoff, R., & Hoyer, J. (2015). Stigmatization of people with pedophilia: Two comparative surveys. *Archives of Sexual Behavior, 44*(1), 21–34. doi: https://link.springer.com/article/10.1007%2Fs10508-014-0312-4

Lofland, J. (1969). *Deviance and identity.* Prentice-Hall.

Maruna, S. (2001). *Making good: How ex-convicts reform and rebuild their lives.* American Psychological Association. doi: https://www.apa.org/pubs/books/431645A

Maruna, S. (2011). Reentry as a rite of passage. *Theoretical Criminology, 13*(1), 3–28. doi: https://journals.sagepub.com/doi/10.1177/1462474510385641

Maruna, S. (2014). Reintegration as a right and the rites of reintegration: A comparative review of de-stigmatization practices. In J. Humphrey, & P. Cordella (Eds.), *Effective interventions in the lives of criminal offenders* (pp. 121–138). Springer. doi: https://www.springer.com/gp/book/9781461489290

Maruna, S., Le Bel, T., Mitchell, N., & Naples, M. (2004). Pygmalion in the reintegration process: Desistance from crime through the looking glass. *Psychology, Crime & Law, 10*(3), 271–281. doi: https://www.tandfonline.com/doi/full/10.1080/10683160410001662762

McCartan, K., Kemshall, H., Westwood, S., Solle, J., MacKenzie, G., Cattel, J., & Pollard, A. (2014). *Circles of Support and Accountability (CoSA): A case file review of two pilots.* Ministry of Justice. https://assets.publishing.service.gov.uk/government/uploads/system/uploads/attachment_data/file/293400/cosa-research-summary.pdf

Richards, K. (2011). *The potential of Circles of Support and Accountability (COSA) to reduce child sexual abuse in Australia*. Winston Churchill Memorial Trust. https://www.churchilltrust.com.au/media/fellows/Richards_Kelly_2010.pdf

Richards, K. (in press). Circles of Support and Accountability: The role of social relations in core member desistance. *International Journal of Offender Therapy and Comparative Criminology*. doi: https://doi.org/10.1177/0306624X20964094

Richards, K., Death, J., & McCartan, K. (2020). *Community-based approaches to sexual offender reintegration*. Australia's National Research Organisation for Women's Safety. https://www.anrows.org.au/project/community-based-approaches-to-sexual-offender-reintegration/

Sample, L., Cooley, B., Ten Bensel, T., Hyter, C., & Hurley, B. (2021). Forced interactions with sheriff deputies over time and their influence on stigma and self-identities among individuals convicted of sex crimes. *Qualitative Criminology*, *10*(1). doi: https://doi.org/10.21428/88de04a1.dcb307ab

Smith, J. (2021). The formerly incarcerated, advocacy, activism, and community reintegration. *Contemporary Justice Review*, *24*(1), 43–63. doi: https://www.tandfonline.com/doi/full/10.1080/10282580.2020.1755846

Spencer, D. (2009). Sex offender as homo sacer. *Punishment and Society*, *11*(2), 219–240. doi: https://journals.sagepub.com/doi/10.1177/1462474508101493

Ten Bensel, T., & Sample, L. (2017). The influence of sex offender registration and notification laws on fostering collective identity among offenders. *Journal of Crime and Justice*, *40*(4), 497–511. doi: https://www.tandfonline. full/10.1080/0735648X.2015.1131184

Thomas, T., Thompson, D., & Karstedt, S. (2014). *Assessing the impact of Circles of Support and Accountability on the reintegration of adults convicted of sexual offences in the community*. University of Leeds Centre for Criminal Justice Studies

Thompson, D. (2015). *Moving on after getting out: Support and accountability for convicted sex offenders* [PhD thesis, University of Leeds]. Leeds. https://etheses.whiterose.ac.uk/13410/1/Thompson_D_Law_PhD_2015.pdf

Thompson, D., Thomas, T., & Karstedt, S. (2017). *The resettlement of sex offenders after custody: Circles of Support and Accountability*. Routledge. doi: https://www.routledge.com/The-Resettlement-of-Sex-Offenders-after-Custody-Circles-of-Support-and/Thompson-Thomas/p/book/9780367227111

Wacquant, L. (2009). *Punishing the poor: The neoliberal government of social insecurity*. Duke University Press. doi: https://www.jstor.org/stable/j.ctv11smrv3

Weaver, B. (2015). *Offending and desistance: The importance of social relations*. Routledge. doi: https://www.routledge.com/Offending-and-Desistance-The-importance-of-social-relations/Weaver/p/book/9781138062610

Weaver, B., & McNeill, F. (2015). Lifelines: Desistance, social relations, and reciprocity. *Criminal Justice and Behavior*, *42*(1), 95–107. doi: https://journals.sagepub.com/doi/10.1177/0093854814550031

Wexler, D. (2002). Robes and rehabilitation: How judges can help offenders "make good". *Victorian Bar News*, *123*, 27–31.

Chapter 6

Giving Back from a Hopeless Place

Circles of Support and Accountability and Generativity

This chapter argues that in a sociolegal and sociopolitical context in which the notion of people with convictions for sexual offending giving back to others is almost unimaginable, Circles of Support and Accountability (CoSA) offer a rare avenue that enables exactly that. The chapter begins by fleshing out the key concept of "generativity" and its relationship to desistance. While generativity has been identified as an important feature of most offenders' redemption scripts, it has become virtually impossible for sexual offenders to give back or make amends. Against this backdrop, this chapter uses the interview data collected for the project to demonstrate that CoSA provide a unique opportunity for generative projects to be imagined and realised by core members.

Rory's Story

We met Rory earlier in this book (see introduction). Rory served 11 years in prison for sexually abusing two children who had been enrolled in the school at which he was employed but had never previously been in trouble with the law. As I noted earlier, Rory is a genial, articulate and warm character; he presents well and is an excellent and insightful communicator. At the time of his interview, Rory was in his early 60s and had been living back in the community for about nine years. He recalled feeling very worried about his impending release from prison. In particular, he was concerned about "[it] just being splattered all over internets and everything. That's a little nerve-wracking. Coming back into an area where the crime was committed, is somebody waiting around the corner to cause bodily harm?...Where am I going to live? What kind of job can I find? If I can be - if I'm able to get hired and working again". Rory had a few supports to help him navigate this transition, in the form of a couple of remaining friends and nearby family members, as well as some links with local churches formed during his incarceration and preparation for release into the community. While Rory intended to join a CoSA immediately following his release, this did not transpire for about two months. He proudly recalled

DOI: 10.4324/9781003125532-7

that during this two-month period, he had managed to find employment, housing and transportation:

> There was no [CoSA] team. There was no opportunity for me to discuss anything with anyone….it was two months later that they finally developed the team and I had already found a job. I had already found living [accommodation]. I already had a vehicle. When I got together with CoSA it was "okay, hello, what are we doing"?

Rory's CoSA volunteers, who fluctuated in number between four and six over the life of his Circle, were nonetheless extremely helpful, in emotional if not practical terms: "It was more emotional. It was psychological. Mentally, where am I when I'm alone? What are my thoughts? Am I tempted? Am I doing things that I shouldn't be doing? They were just really good at helping me through those things". Moreover, "they definitely encouraged me in letting me know 'you're worth something Rory'". Despite this support, and again somewhat proudly, Rory explained that he is no longer in contact with his original volunteers: "When my Circle ended it was like 'okay, if you want to get a cup of coffee give me a call but I'll be working over here and I'll be going to church and I'm off and running'". Like Adam (see Chapter 5), he conceptualised CoSA as being for the still-reforming rather than the fully reformed, like himself. Many of his connections in the community, however, came about through his involvement in CoSA.

Rory is, in his own estimation, now doing really well, predominantly due to his religious awakening and involvement with a church community. As he explains, he is now "a firm believer of giving back more than taking", especially because in the course of his offending, "I abused. I hurt. I took". Rory enacts generativity in a number of ways. He views his involvement in his church and Christian community as a form of giving back. This network provides him an informal avenue via which to mentor others:

> I had already made up my mind before I came out [of prison] that meeting so many young men when I was incarcerated. They had no fathers, or their fathers were drug addict dealers and so forth with their gang buddies. They just had no direction, no mentoring….They have a whole life to go….What's going to happen with them? If society doesn't welcome them, if there's no restoration of any kind they're going to go back to what they know. That's when I started thinking "somehow I've got to start a business". That's what I kept thinking. Wouldn't it be wonderful to start a business and say "look, we need to know where you've been. We need to know how bad it's been but you're not going to get cut [out of work opportunities] because of it".

Through his connections, Rory has indeed developed a social enterprise that employs formerly incarcerated individuals. The enterprise does far more than offer employment, however: "all we're looking for is people who want to change. You want something different in your life; you don't want to go the way you've been going". The business is auspiced by the church community within which Rory is heavily involved, and is part of a broader mentoring program, which Rory helps to facilitate. Through this avenue, Rory appears to have discovered (or rather created) a role that provides him with both a sense of meaning and an avenue via which he is able to give back to the community, especially to the younger generation.

What Is Generativity?

In Chapter 4, the notion of a "redemption script" was introduced. By way of a brief recap, redemption scripts are believable self-narratives developed by desisters about why they are leaving a life of crime and now "going straight" (Maruna, 2001). "Generativity" is typically the final component of the desister's redemption story. This final element or "act" of the redemption narrative involves the desister discovering a higher purpose, desire to be productive and/or "give something back to society", particularly to the next generation (Maruna, 2001; McNeill & Maruna, 2007; Shover, 1996). McAdams and de St Aubin (1998, p. xx) define generativity as: "[a] commitment to promoting the next generation, manifested through parenting, teaching, mentoring, and generating products and outcomes that aim to benefit youth and foster the development and well-being of individuals and social systems that will outlive the self".

It has been well documented in the criminological literature that individuals who desist from *non-sexual* crime often enact generative projects, incorporate these into redemption narratives, and as a corollary, adopt prosocial identities that both give rise to and reinforce desistance. Importantly, giving back through generative activities can be a marker of secondary desistance (McNeill & Maruna, 2007) – i.e., the shift from a temporary cessation of offending towards a sustained adoption of a non-offending identity (McNeill & Maruna, 2007; see generally Bullock et al., 2019). Indeed, the benefits to the ex-offender of giving back and/or helping others have long been recognised. Giving back and/or helping others has been found to assist former offenders to manage or resist stigmatisation and undertake identity repair (Perrin et al., 2018; Smith, 2021); as Lebel (2007: p. 1) succinctly summarise, "helping helps the helper" (see further Perrin et al., 2018).

How generative actions benefit former offenders has, however, been the subject of some debate, and a number of mechanisms have been suggested. Bazemore (1998) developed the concept of "earned redemption", which asserts that efforts to repair harm (whether directly to victims/survivors or to communities more broadly, and whether symbolically or materially) can promote identity repair among (ex-)offenders. According to this perspective, providing opportunities for ex-offenders to give back or make amends enables them to earn their way back into the trust of the community, and thus promotes desistance (Bazemore, 1998). Others posit generativity through "reintegration advocacy" – that is, participating in social and political advocacy and activism aimed at resisting stigmatisation and improving the human rights of (ex-)prisoners at the collective level (Smith, 2021) – as a key mechanism that contributes to the development of a non-offending identity (Flores & Cossyleon, 2017; LeBel, 2013; Smith, 2021). Donati (2009, p. 227) pointed to the importance of "reestablish[ing] the circuit of reciprocity" – that is, creating opportunities for ex-offenders to develop relationships with others in which they both receive and give support – as critical for the development of common goods (in this case, desistant identities (see Richards, in press)). Finally, the concept of the "professional ex" or "wounded healer" (White, 2000a,b) suggests that by reframing their offending history into a source of wisdom to help others as mentors, volunteers or mutual-help group members, ex-offenders fashion an identity inconsistent with continued offending (Halsey & Deegan, 2012; Maruna, 2001). This latter explanation, and its relevance to CoSA, will be explored in detail in the following chapter. Irrespective of the exact mechanism via which "helping helps the helper", the evidence in support of this general approach is strong (see Perrin et al., 2018 for a recent overview). Fostering generativity among people convicted of sexual offences might therefore be considered an important element of their desistance – and thus of strengthening community safety – however improbable and unpalatable it may seem.

It has also, however, been well-documented that there are considerable barriers to generativity for individuals with sexual offence convictions, and that in the current risk-obsessed climate, people convicted of sexual offences are largely precluded from performing generative acts. Kras (2014) for example argued that generativity was largely absent among men convicted of sexual crimes in her study due to their fear of rejection from the community. In a similar vein, Harris's (2014) study of 21 men convicted of sexual offences in the United States found that only a small number of men in the sample – those who had been free from prison the longest – were able to articulate generative aims.

Indeed, it is difficult to imagine criminal justice professionals or the broader community welcoming attempts to give back on the part of people who have sexually offended. As a case in point, the celebrated San Francisco-based Delancey Street Foundation, a reintegration enterprise explicitly premised on the generative principle of "each one teach one" – i.e., that by guiding a newer participant, ex-offenders will themselves gain the tools necessary to desist from crime and become productive community members (Burnett & Maruna, 2006; Dwyer & Maruna, 2011) – excludes people with sexual offence convictions on the grounds that "they need professional counseling and we don't offer any" (http://www.delanceystreetfoundation.org/admission.php). This highlights that for individuals with convictions for sexual offences, barriers to generativity are not merely abstract or theoretical but material. In many cases, the release conditions to which these individuals are subject make generative acts challenging to say the least. As volunteer 1 stated:

> The parameters of [release] conditions being what they are - and they need to be what they are - but does not allow some of the atonement that some [core members] would wish they could do, because if you offended against children you'd almost want to be doing something that [helps children] – "okay, I can't directly be around them, but can I build things for them or can I do something this way"? That's the - because of the [release] conditions where do you find the roundabout way to actually help out that community that you damaged?

Joshua viewed the situation in much the same way: "I can't volunteer for these groups that help women and children. That would be highly inappropriate, as much as I'd want to". Rory, ever eloquent, concurred:

> Society says "behave, go out there, be productive" and then you put up all these walls and you're telling me to go be productive and I can't get through. It truly is, it's easier to put a camel through the eye of the needle.

There appear to be some exceptions to this rule, however. My own research on Aboriginal and/or Torres Strait Islander men convicted of serious sexual offences in Queensland, Australia (Richards et al., 2020a,b) found that this group of men was committed to generativity. Their will-to-generativity was culturally shaped, often centred on passing on cultural knowledge and practice to the younger generation (Richards et al., 2020b) and developed in spite of the extremely rigid conditions under which the men were released from prison. Most significantly in the context of the current study, Thompson (2015) found that a small number of core members in his study of CoSA in the United Kingdom were determined to make good by performing generative acts. Due to the stigma they faced, this had to be done anonymously. For example, one core member made small, anonymous donations to a local school. As Thompson (2015) highlights, generative acts such as these were recognised by CoSA volunteers and thus influenced identity transformation among core members. This chapter builds on Thompson's (2015) fleeting observation to flesh out in detail the (potential) role of CoSA in fostering generativity among core members.

Core Members and the Will-to-Generativity

Core members' descriptions of giving back or making amends were often aspirational rather than material. Many spoke of wanting to give back, of looking forward to doing so, once their parole period was finished/once they were no longer required to be listed on an offender register/once they were back on their feet. In other words, core members commonly imagined generative futures and selves. Sullivan (2012), drawing on the work of Emirbayer and Mische (1998), described this as "projectivity", which involves "an imaginative engagement with the future" and precedes generativity, which in turn can inform the development of a prosocial identity (Sullivan, 2012). Wayne spoke of the difficulties of progressing from a desire to give back to giving back in practical terms, or as Sullivan (2012, p. 318) would put it, turning projectivity into generativity or imagination into action. Although one of Wayne's CoSA volunteers had invited him to volunteer on a community housing project in another state, he was concerned about whether the organisation would "approve a 290 [i.e., a person with a sexual offence conviction who is obligated to register under section 290 of California's *Penal Code*]". Nonetheless, Wayne imagines a future in which he volunteers at a hospice for HIV patients, since his son passed away from the disease some years earlier: "since then I've felt I'd like to contribute". Wayne anticipates that his CoSA volunteers will both support and assist in practical terms with this endeavour: "I'm pretty sure if I ask them to find me a place, a hospice some place, they'd have the connections to do that". But for Wayne, this is "down the line". He has discussed the idea with his CoSA volunteers but wants to be in a more stable state before undertaking this emotionally taxing type of activity: "I'm not ready to do that yet.... But I say down the road".

In addition to being infeasible, promoting generativity among core members may not be desirable in all circumstances. As one stakeholder pointed out, furthermore, pressuring core members towards generative ends may backfire:

> They might feel pressure then to be supportive to others when some of them can barely manage what they have. Any support that they get from CoSA is to help themselves. So, then to turn around and then expect them [to give back]....I don't know how some of them will respond to that. I know some would not respond at all and would probably not come [back to CoSA]. It depends on the person.
>
> (Stakeholder 3)

Volunteer 6 echoed this concern: "They might not feel they have those skills. They might not have the insight or maybe they just don't want to actually voice the 'I'm not good at anything. What do I have to offer?'" While this is a sound point, this chapter argues that a focus on generativity is optimal (rather than required) in CoSA practice. Encouraging and supporting core members towards generative ends will enhance the development of core members' prosocial identities, and ultimately reduce the likelihood of recidivism. The issue raised by stakeholder 3 and volunteer 6 is nonetheless an important one to consider and presents a valuable reminder that while giving back ought to be of goal of (some) CoSA core members, it may be a longer-term rather than immediate one.

Paying It Forward: From Projectivity to Generativity

Many core members had, however, managed to turn imagination into action. Richard spoke at length and with some pride about his involvement in a local charitable food pantry:

> Once a month we do like a food ministry give-away....Usually it's like the second Saturday of the month....the pastor and his business partner will come....Then they take it to the church downtown which is a Baptist church and they put it in there. Then we come over like around 9:45, 10 o'clock. Ten o'clock is when they start handing out the food until about 12 o'clock. I tell them [when] we have no more food to give out. So it's like we do that once a month and then every now and then in the holidays [or] whatever, we might do like a barbeque for them. Or make them like a hot meal in the morning.

Volunteers and core members themselves reported core members' involvement in a vast array of other generative activities. Don, for example, despite numerous limitations, including cognitive impairment, was supported to volunteer at a local social enterprise café. Others described: participating in paid employment (particularly when this involves working in contexts that seek to create social or environmental benefit) or formal education; volunteering to upgrade a local church's audio system; volunteering in a range of other capacities at churches and with church-sponsored activities; adopting an abandoned cat; donating board games to the organisation within which CoSA is situated; helping with bookkeeping for the organisation; participating in community restorative justice groups; volunteering at a community housing mission; visiting patients in hospital and volunteering at community business events.

Core members in some instances demonstrated impressive ingenuity in pursuing generative ends. Adam, for example, described becoming involved in a community garden project, which he has taken carriage of documenting with photography. Adam is also engaged in a writing project on restorative justice, which he hopes to turn into a book to help others. Similarly, Frank described undertaking a writing project about the organisation within which his CoSA program is situated, with the aim of "help[ing] the community [be free] from all violence". Alan's self-initiated cleaning project (see Chapter 4) reflects another creative attempt at generativity.

Of course, in some cases at least, encouraging generativity among core members may not be feasible. Some core members may lack the cognitive, social and/or emotional skills to engage in formal avenues of generativity, and as noted above, such avenues simply may not be available to individuals with convictions for sexual violence. Again, however, the core members in this study demonstrated considerable creativity in both their pursuit of generativity and their willingness and ability to conceptualise actions as generative. As was the case in Harris' (2017) research, men in this study characterised their involvement in the research as generative:

> When they ask me for stuff like this, I'm all for it (Mathias).
> I hope it helps (Gerald).
> Thank you for doing the research. I will always help with research (Joshua).
> I'm actually giving a lot of research to people who could come here, like yourself, right? I don't mind telling my story (Frank).

Ewan likewise offered his participation in research as an example of giving back. For Ewan, this is emblematic of his true self: "I am a giving person, not a taking person". Even Zack, who struggled to envisage enacting any form of generativity – "I don't know how I would really contribute" – positioned his participation in the research as a type of giving back: "even doing this interview is a way of helping or a way to give back".

Other core members characterised seemingly quotidian actions as a form of giving back. Kevin described interacting with people experiencing homelessness as a way of contributing constructively to the community: "I have a major relationship with our homeless right here in downtown Toronto, amazing relationship with my - with them. Yeah, I just love it". Gerald likewise saw interacting with a lonely person on public transport as a type of service:

> I'm sitting on the bus or sitting at the bus stop, somebody starts chatting at me and I'm looking at them and I'm watching and I listen to them, and half the things are going through one ear, out the other, but they need somebody to talk to.

When asked about giving back in his interview, Peter simply stated: "If I see someone drop something, I'm like 'here you go' [and hand it to them]". This moment from the interviews stands out to me very distinctively. I clearly remember it because at the time it felt like a longbow, as though Peter had had to cast about desperately for an example of giving back. This was by no means the case, however, as Peter also discussed volunteering at his church, including making coffee and serving cookies during coffee hour, helping his CoSA volunteers (as discussed further below) and engaging in conversation with elderly people, including an elderly woman at his church: "it gets a smile on her face...I'm always sitting and talking to one of the older community". On reflection, I see Peter's initial response not as a longbow at all, but rather as an attempt on his part to illustrate that in addition to undertaking generative *acts*, he possesses a generative *character*. In other words, Peter sought to be considered the type of person who helps others as a matter of course, rather than the type of person who might give back only at predetermined times and in structured, formal contexts.

Volunteer 12 described a core member who "wasn't a joiner" and thus had restricted opportunities for generative action, but nonetheless "developed concern for a number of indigent people; one was a woman and the other two or three were men. He used to take them for coffee…on a regular basis". Importantly for this volunteer, the core member himself instigated this: "we supported him, but he was the one who chose to do that". We might again read this as suggesting that the core member's action was perceived by the volunteer as indicative of his true character, rather than as something that transpired only at the behest of CoSA volunteers.

In some cases, core members who were restricted from giving back in more meaningful ways (such as participating in a restorative justice process and from most forms of volunteering or community work due to the nature of their offending) opted to "give back" in ways that seem oblique at first blush, but which may be as direct and meaningful as possible under the circumstances. Oftentimes, they imbued seemingly mundane activities with generative purpose. For example, one of Richard's volunteers believed that he performs his work in a commercial laundry with generative care:

> We have a core member that works in a factory type setting that's a washing laundry. The guy can fold 2,000 sheets a day and do all the pressing and all this other stuff, so his whole thought is that all that work that he does goes out to hospitals…they go out to the children's hospital, they do all this other stuff, so there's actual feeling of atonement in him that "I'm readying things for those in the hospitals and also for those just going out for dinner with a nice tablecloth or something - I'm changing the experience for people out there".
>
> (Volunteer 1)

Crucially, these varied expressions of generativity support the identity transformation required for desistance and enhance core members' sense of themselves as good people and law-abiding citizens. Sean compellingly explained that as a result of his volunteer role at a local church, "You feel a lot better. If you feel that you're accomplishing something, giving back to the community, doing something worthwhile, that can't help but change how you look at yourself and the world". Dean expressed similar sentiments about his volunteer bookkeeping role: "It makes me feel good that I'm able to. I love helping people out either doing a budget for them or helping them out with their finances, stuff like that. I love helping people out that way". As Perrin et al. (2018) have argued, promoting identity shifts along these lines encourages ex-offenders towards desistance by allowing them to distance themselves from a past offending identity and supporting them to act in accordance with the narratives they are now able to present about themselves.

Zack's Story

Zack's story could not be more different from Rory's. When I meet Zack, he has been living in the community for about five months after serving a three-and-a-half-year prison sentence. He is new to CoSA, having been a core member for only three or four months. Zack is currently unemployed but supports his mother, with whom he lives, with her health issues. Zack was convicted of contact sexual offences against a minor. However, Zack denies the offences. In contrast with some other core members who I interviewed for this research, Zack does not merely contest some of his charges or the specifics of some of his charges but denies the offending outright. Zack speaks in the present tense, and does not present his life story in two halves, as is common among desisters (Harris, 2017). He makes declarative statements about his character and portrays these as immutable: "I'm not one of those people that likes to talk to too many people at once. I can barely talk to one person"; "I am a car guy and I have a lead foot. So I don't think anything's going to change"; "I have trust issues, period"; "I'm always down on myself"; "It's me. I've always been like that".

As these statements illustrate, Zack presents as very passive and pessimistic in his interview. Zack feels doomed – not "doomed to deviance" in Maruna's (2001) terms, but by society's expectation that he will "reoffend" (as per Kras, 2014) (or as he saw it, that he will be reconvicted of more offences that he did not commit). Zack stated that he feels unable to give back to the community, predominantly due to being unemployed. He sees his former work as a builder as a role that enabled him to contribute to the community: "I used to be a builder. I built subdivisions for - so I felt like I was helping - I felt like I was part of the community because I was building the community. I was building people's homes". Zack now feels unable to make a contribution to the community or give back in any way – "I don't know how I would really contribute" – despite the support that he provides to his mother. It seems that Zack's volunteers have made attempts at encouraging generativity on Zack's part by creating situations in which he might reciprocate the support and advice that they provide to him; however, while Zack recognises these opportunities, "I am [not] really good with advice". As Zack acknowledges, his Circle is newly formed and there is much further progress to be made.

Helping Out a Brother: Core Members and Reintegration Advocacy

Numerous core members, when asked about giving back, recounted a strong desire to help other ex-prisoners, particularly those who, like themselves, had been convicted of sexual offences (see also Harris, 2017). This often stemmed from the core members' sense of having experienced injustice at the hands of an extremely unforgiving criminal justice apparatus. To be clear, core members usually readily acknowledged that they were deserving of punishment and correctional supervision. Their sense of having been dealt with unfairly resulted from two primary factors: (1) being treated in a uniform way irrespective of the nature of their offending (that is, the perception that all people convicted of sexual offences are treated with the same degree of punitiveness regardless of the extent or seriousness of their offending); and (2) the permanent nature of many of the measures to which core members are subject (that is, that while a core member may turn over a new leaf and become a prosocial, contributing member of the community, he may always be required to appear on a publicly available register of offenders and/or submit to correctional supervision, thus rendering futile any positive changes he may make).

Despite this, I found responses such as these in interviews with core members somewhat troubling (see Chapter 3). I suppose I had expected core members to describe wanting to give back to victims/survivors, or community welfare groups and organisations. Without acknowledging as much, I had perhaps expected core members to at least pay lip service to wanting to give back to the groups and communities harmed by their actions, even if this would not be feasible and even if this was not their genuine intention. Core members often did not, however, feel the need to do so. Rather, many recounted their plans to assist others in positions similar to themselves with considerable enthusiasm. In fairness, this often involved wanting to repay the CoSA program that that core members viewed as integral to their own successful reintegration and re-entry into the community. As Ewan explained, although he feels "I can't repay them", he wants to support CoSA "because of what they done for me". Daniel supports the CoSA program in which he was originally a core member because "someone gave me a chance". Terry expressed similar sentiments:

> Parole in California is set up for sex offenders to isolate them….when you have someone that has nothing but his parents he might be living with, or in a group home or something, he has nobody and so CoSA, that's where I see it's huge for especially those. That's why I like giving back to them.

Others, however, wanted to give back to others in their situation beyond the confines of the CoSA environment. For Brian, this involved not only supporting the CoSA program with which he had been a core member (see Chapter 7), but sponsoring newer members of Sex Addicts Anonymous, an organisation he saw as integral to his own desistance journey. Taken together, these roles provided Brian with the sense that "I am not just a drain on society, but I contribute". Todd reported "trying to help others stay out of jail", and Sean was adamant that for him, giving back would take the form of assisting others who had been incarcerated in relation to sexual violence:

> I wanted to do this back when I got out of prison; I said, if I ever had the financial resources, I would like to start a home for sex offenders that get out of prison so that they have a place to live; can help them with jobs but at least they have a place to live when they get out and don't have to worry about, where am I going to live? Because I figure that's the core. A job is great but living is paramount and so I thought, and just have a safe home where - of course they have to be accountable but where they aren't fearful of living.

Leon had used his experience in halfway house accommodation as an opportunity to provide emotional support to others in his situation:

> ...when I was in the halfway house and other ex-federal prisoners, of course, they like to put others down. I know that game and I just ignored them. Which of course upset them [laughs] if you don't respond they have the wind blown out of their sails so to speak. But there were times some things did trouble me because it impacted on other individuals that were going through and they didn't know what to do. But that provided me when the opportunity arose to just talk with them about how some of these other guys will want to feel superior because they're miserable with their own life. They just want to make themselves feel better by putting others down.

Terry similarly described wanting to support other individuals incarcerated in relation to sexual offending: "that's why I bought the house I have, I want to turn it into a sober home and I want to start an inpatient sex addiction program".

I was initially taken aback by core members identifying other perpetrators of sexual violence as the group most deserving of their generative actions (a phenomenon also documented by Harris, 2017). However, we might simply understand this form of "reintegration advocacy" (Flores & Cossyleon, 2017; LeBel, 2013; Smith, 2021) as a combination of the limited alternative avenues for giving back that core members have at their disposal and a response to the heavy-handed nature of the criminal justice measures to which they are subject. As volunteer 1 argued:

> ...going through the prison setting, you don't make it through without feeling a war buddyship with everybody else in there. You're all trying to get through. When you come back - when you come out - it's the same environment. You're ready to help your fellow guys that you know are going through a lot, the same you are, or, as a lot of people say, down on their luck.

Smiley (as cited in Smith, 2021, p. 17) found that advocacy efforts on the part of a group of male African-American ex-prisoners were stymied by their fear of rearrest. Such fears no doubt apply potently in relation to individuals with convictions for sexual violence. Joshua's story amply demonstrates that for an individual convicted of sexual offences, another individual in similar circumstances may simply be the only available potential beneficiary of generative activity. As noted above, Joshua identified women's and children's services as more deserving recipients but acknowledged that this would be neither appropriate nor feasible: "there's not much I can do". In light of this, Joshua describes wanting to volunteer to help others in a similar situation as himself:

> One of the things that I had intended on doing was going back to [volunteer at an ex-offender support service], because they did have volunteers come in to speak with people such as myself and I had a great volunteer when I was in to talk to once or twice a week about just getting through the mess when you get out.

Joshua argued that while such a role would not involve "repaying the victim", it could be broadly understood as such since it aimed to avoid the creation of new victims. To this end, core members' interest in mentoring other (potential, actual or ex-) offenders might be considered the purest interpretation and expression of generativity. It speaks directly to the desire to prevent (usually younger) others from making the mistakes that core members themselves have made. In any event, as LeBel (2013) has documented, reintegration advocacy by ex-prisoners can have positive psychological and behavioural outcomes and is positively associated with successful reintegration and desistance from crime.

An important consideration that emerges here is whether extremely punitive and stigmatising criminal justice measures applied exclusively to those who have sexually offended – a system of "criminal apartheid" (Soothill et al. in Roach & Pease, 2014) – has inadvertently created a population that has been subjected to punishment that they experience as so disproportionate that they now – without irony – class *themselves* as victims. As Matza (1964, p. 102) has argued, "the subculture of delinquency is, among other things, a memory file that collects injustices"; this is particularly so when those in trouble with the law are treated in ways they perceive as unjust or unnecessarily oppressive (Braithwaite, 1989, p. 24). There is a tension here: promoting generativity among ex-offenders is an important element of fostering desistance, and as argued in this chapter, CoSA can provide a potent avenue for generativity to flourish. Other ex-offenders may be the only available (or most suitable) targets of a budding desister's generative efforts. However, this might be problematic if and when it requires a desister to position himself as the "real" victim in the situation. It is important for CoSA staff and volunteers to understand and navigate this tension to best promote community safety (see further Chapter 8).

Generativity and Managing the Risky Self

Another common way in which core members conceptualised their generative attempts was to situate the perpetual management of their own risk and their cultivation of a non-offending self as a form of giving back. When I asked about ways of giving back, Donny immediately responded that he does this "by not reoffending. That really gives back to the community, following conditions, not causing trouble". Damien likewise constructed his own desistance as a method of giving back:

> Well, I'm trying to stop sex abuse. I'm trying to stop that. I don't want - I already contributed to that and I don't want that no more - I'm trying to do my part myself as well. I'm trying to - it's a hard situation. I mean, it's - it happens every day - every minute, every second, probably. I'm just - I want to be a little part. I don't want to be the bad statistic. I want to be the positive one.

Some CoSA volunteers argued that "not re-offending, not creating any new victims" (volunteer 11) is the most fitting and feasible expression of generativity:

> the best that we may ask, for the most part, is this broader feeling of good citizenship, contribution, which other people will be assisted as a result of the core member getting back into a good space in society....To live life in a healthy way. Right? To be as best they possibly can under the circumstances.
>
> (Volunteer 11)

In response to my question about how core members can make good or give back when there is no possibility of providing direct reparations to victims/survivors, Volunteer 2 asserted that "it's helping people to know the boundaries where their offences have taken place....one of the things that I really appreciated with CoSA is how seriously the core members have taken the boundaries that the state has set for them". Stakeholder 1 concurred: "knowing their triggers. Knowing maybe what your high-risk situations are, identifying those as well. Because if that person has some insight in what's going on, what happened, the chances of them doing it again [are reduced], they can be a little bit more mindful and aware".

CoSA Volunteers as the Subjects of Generativity

In some instances, CoSA support core member desistance by providing tangible targets for generative acts; volunteers provide an avenue for core members to enact generativity when other potential avenues are unavailable.

Core members recounted helping their volunteers in an impressive range of ways, from instructing a volunteer about how to play pool (Leon) to helping a volunteer with home renovations (Morgan), to using their experience of the criminal justice system to "train" volunteers with aspirations for careers in the criminal justice sector (Frank), to just generally responding to their volunteers' requests for assistance: "Sometimes if [staff member] needs help, I help. [Volunteer] phones and needs help sometimes" (see further Richards, in press). One of Sean's volunteers entrusts him with the care of his pets: "one of my volunteers he has me dog-sit when he leaves [town] so I'll go and stay at his place and dog-sit his dogs. He has me helping him do odd jobs that he picks up and needs help".

A couple of the volunteers interviewed for this study appeared to understand (implicitly at least) the importance of deliberately creating situations in which they could be the recipient of a core member's efforts to give back. Volunteer 6 described the "checking in" process that often characterises the first component of a Circle meeting, in which all members have an opportunity to relate the highs and lows they have experienced in their own lives since the last meeting (see Elliott et al., 2013, p. 19), and considered this as creating opportunities for core members to give back:

> I think in a lot of ways if I speak about a difficulty I'm having, the next week they will be like, "oh my gosh I found this resource for you". They thought about us during the week and thought about how they can help us solve a problem and they just get so excited to see you the next week and tell you, "oh I helped". So I think that is a way to give back to the community too.

Other CoSA volunteers and staff expressed similar views:

> If you're in a healthy relationship, you help each other, there is mutuality involved....this is often how it works at...Circles, that it's not a one-way relationship. It's a mutual relationship. So, if I need help, I might be asking [core member] Dean. If I've had core members who are just new in town and might be – "we're looking at the Salvation Army"....I'll say, "you know what? I'll introduce you to Dean and he could share".
>
> (Staff member 8)

> Not only does the core member share his problems during the meetings, every volunteer gets a chance to share something about their lives as well. So, what happens is, you develop some kind of a relationship.
>
> (Volunteer 3)

For volunteer 1, such mutuality was largely aspirational. He claimed that "I'd like to see it from our core members is as other people in the Circle maybe have a family loss or something, they're [core members are] giving support right back. They're part of that Circle, so we [would] see them outreach to the other members there". This is an intriguing comment in light of the oft-repeated CoSA creation story (discussed in the Introduction). To briefly recap, in this story CoSA forefather the Reverend Harry Nigh almost inadvertently created the first CoSA by recruiting members of his Mennonite congregation to form a support group around recently released prisoner Charlie Taylor. Many retellings of this origin narrative assert a type of mutuality between Taylor and his volunteers, with the Reverend Nigh turning to Charlie for emotional support when his father passed away (see Bongers, 2003). This aspect of the CoSA creation story always struck me as somewhat contrived. Of course, Charlie Taylor needed a great deal of support from Nigh and the CoSA volunteers – but would the Reverend Nigh, occupying a far more privileged social position, really need support from Charlie during a period of grieving? This seems unlikely unless we consider that perhaps Nigh – however tacitly or even unknowingly – was enacting exactly the type of mutuality that volunteer 1 identifies. In other words, is it the case that Nigh did not genuinely need Charlie's support, but sought it in order to cast himself as the beneficiary of Taylor's generativity – thereby communicating to Taylor his value as a helper of others? In any case, both Nigh's actions and the volunteers' comments in this regard acknowledge the potential for CoSA to provide avenues via which core members can enact generativity, thereby supporting their moves towards desistance.

In a more general sense, CoSA volunteers and staff also support core members to form connections with other potential beneficiaries of generativity beyond the Circle. In many of the examples discussed above, core members had been introduced to contexts in which they might enact generativity (e.g., local charities and churches) via their Circle. This highlights the broader potential of CoSA in this regard, as well as the importance of CoSA programs forging connections within communities with other groups and organisations in order to provide avenues for the development and enactment of generativity. Indeed, somewhat counterintuitively it is these avenues for generativity that are denied by risk-obsessed measures to which people with sexual offence convictions are increasingly subject.

A key point that emerges from the narratives of people who have sexually offended and that have been canvassed in this chapter is that giving back – however, conceptualised – is not considered by core members to be atonement (even though it was viewed this way by some CoSA volunteers; see comments from volunteer 1 earlier in this chapter). Core members were adamant that in the many and varied ways in which they gave back they were not atoning for their crimes or "earning redemption" in Bazemore's (1998) terms. When discussing in his interview the various ways in which he seeks to give back, Peter wanted me to understand the distinction between acts of atonement that he is *required* to perform and acts of generativity that he *desires* to perform. In particular, he highlighted the ways in which he gives back to his church community, stating "that I don't mind. If I don't feel obligated. I don't feel obligated to do it; it's my choice to help out. The church mostly [I give back to] because I feel accepted so I give back more". Like Rory, who discounted the suggestion that his efforts to give back might be a form of atonement (see Chapter 4), Peter's efforts at generativity are a way to perform a good self, to cast prior offending as an aberration not indicative of that self and weave an identity reflective of that good self: "I find with Circles helping me is find something that gives me a chance to finally put out the real me and help out.…It feels good just to give up my time". Terry felt much the same:

> When I give up an hour a week, I actually look forward to it because I desire to do it. For me, recovery, giving back is not something I do, it's something I want to live, and I hope that that's how they eventually will see it.

These narratives imply that to perform generative acts voluntarily allows core members to actively demonstrate desistance, whereas undertaking obligated acts renders core members the passive subjects of state punishment and control. As a corollary, voluntary generative act might be understood as "agentic moves" (Giordano et al., 2002, p. 992) rather than a form of "forced desistance" (Harris, 2017, p. 28).

CoSA thus might be understood as providing core members with avenues to enact generativity – and thereby forge desistant identities – both through "reintegration advocacy" (Smith, 2021) and "reestablish[ing] the circuit of reciprocity" (Donati, 2009, p. 227). They may also provide an opportunity for core members to earn redemption (Bazemore, 1998), although as noted above, some core members outwardly disavow this conceptualisation. As explored in the following chapter, CoSA may also enable core members to perform generativity via the role of the "professional ex" or "wounded healer".

Conclusion

This chapter has argued that CoSA can provide avenues for core members to perform generative acts and thereby develop desistant identities. As Smith (2021, p. 17) argued, such acts allow ex-prisoners to be recognised for what they *do* rather than for what they *do not do* – i.e., actively desist from crime rather than passively abstain from it (see Cooley & Sample, 2018 on this critical distinction). This function of CoSA has not previously been explicated, and this argument thus raises a number of implications for strengthening CoSA practice. These will be discussed in Chapter 8.

References

Bazemore, G. (1998). Restorative justice and earned redemption: Communities, victims, and offender reintegration. *American Behavioral Scientist, 41*(6), 768–813. doi: https://journals.sagepub.com/doi/abs/10.1177/0002764298041006003

Bongers, A. (2003, 9 September). Embracing lowest of the low. *The Spectator*, A.04.

Braithwaite, J. (1989). *Crime, shame and reintegration.* Cambridge University Press. doi: https://www.cambridge.org/core/books/crime-shame-and-reintegration/5F40BF6C9DFC3D5752888BC73034A1BA

Bullock, K., Bunce, A., & McCarthy, D. (2019). Making good in unpromising places: The development and cultivation of redemption scripts among long-term prisoners. *International Journal of Offender Therapy and Comparative Criminology, 63*(3), 406–423. https://doi.org/10.1177/0306624X18800882

Burnett, R., & Maruna, S. (2006). The kindness of prisoners: Strengths-based resettlement in theory and in action. *Criminology and Criminal Justice, 6*(1), 83–106. doi: https://journals.sagepub.com/doi/10.1177/1748895806060668

Cooley, B., & Sample, L. (2018). The difference between desistance from sexual offending and not reoffending. *Journal of Crime and Justice, 41*(5), 483–503. doi: https://www.tandfonline.com/doi/full/10.1080/0735648X.2018.1479286

Donati, P. (2009). What does "subsidiarity" mean? The relational perspective. *Journal of Markets & Morality, 12*(2), 211–243.

Dwyer, C., & Maruna, S. (2011). The role of self-help efforts in the reintegration of 'politically motivated' former prisoners: Implications from the Northern Irish experience. *Crime, Law and Social Change, 5*, 293–309. doi: https://link.springer.com/article/10.1007/s10611-011-9284-7

Elliott, I., Zajac, G., & Meyer, C. (2013). *Evaluability assessment of the Circles of Support and Accountability (COSA) model.* Department of Justice. https://www.ojp.gov/pdffiles1/nij/grants/243832.pdf

Emirbayer, M., & Mische, A. (1998). What is agency? *American Journal of Sociology, 103*(4), 962–1022. doi: https://www.journals.uchicago.edu/doi/abs/10.1086/231294

Flores, E., & Cossyleon, J. (2017). "I went through it so you don't have to": Faith-based community organizing for the formerly incarcerated. *Journal for the Scientific Study of Religion, 55*(4), 662–676. doi: https://onlinelibrary.wiley.com/doi/abs/10.1111/jssr.12294

Giordano, P., Cernkovich, S., & Rudolph, J. (2002). Gender, crime, and desistance: Toward a theory of cognitive transformation. *American Journal of Sociology, 1077*, 990–1064. doi: https://www.journals.uchicago.edu/doi/10.1086/343191

Halsey, M., & Deegan, S. (2012). Father and son: Two generations through prison. *Theoretical Criminology, 14*(3), 338–367.

Harris, D. (2017). *Desistance from sexual offending: Narratives of retirement, regulation and recovery.* Palgrave Macmillan. doi: https://www.palgrave.com/gp/book/9783319631998

Harris, D. (2014). Desistance from sexual offending: Findings from 21 life history narratives. *Journal of Interpersonal Violence*, 29(9), 1554–1578.

Kras, K. (2014). *Redemption or condemnation? A long-term follow-up of the desistance patterns of sex offenders* [PhD thesis, University of Missouri]. St Louis.

Lebel, T. (2007). An examination of the impact of formerly incarcerated persons helping others. *Journal of Offender Rehabilitation*, 46, 1–24.

LeBel, T. (2013). Formerly incarcerated persons' use of advocacy/activism as a coping orientation in the reintegration process. In B. Veyesy, J. Christian, & D. Martinez (Eds.), *How offenders transform their lives* (pp. 165–187). Willan. doi: https://doi.org/10.4324/9781843927310

Maruna, S. (2001). *Making good: How ex-convicts reform and rebuild their lives.* American Psychological Association. doi: https://www.apa.org/pubs/books/431645A

Matza, D. (1964). *Delinquency and drift.* Routledge.

McAdams, D., & de St Aubin, E. (1998). *Generativity and adult development: How and why we care for the next generation.* American Psychological Association.

McNeill, F., & Maruna, S. (2007). Giving up and giving back: Desistance, generativity and social work with offenders. In G. McIvor, & P. Raynor (Eds.), *Developments in social work with offenders* (pp. 224–239). Jessica Kingsley Publishers.

Perrin, C., Blagden, N., Winder, B., & Dillon, G. (2018). "It's sort of reaffirmed to me that I'm not a monster, I'm not a terrible person": Sex offenders' movements toward desistance via peer-support roles in prison. *Sexual Abuse, 30*(7), 759–780. doi: https://journals.sagepub.com/doi/10.1177/1079063217697133

Richards, K. (in press). Circles of Ssupport and Accountability: The role of social relations in core member desistance. *International Journal of Offender Therapy and Comparative Criminology.* doi: https://doi.org/10.1177/0306624X20964094

Richards, K., Death, J., & McCartan, K. (2020a). *Community-based approaches to sexual offender reintegration.* Australia's National Research Organisation for Women's Safety. https://www.anrows.org.au/project/community-based-approaches-to-sexual-offender-reintegration/

Richards, K., Death, J., & McCartan, K. (2020b). Toward redemption: Aboriginal and/or Torres Strait Islander men's narratives of desistance from sexual offending. *Victims & Offenders, 15*(6), 810–833. doi: https://www.tandfonline.com/doi/full/10.1080/15564886.2020.1754311

Roach, J., & Pease, K. (2014). Police overestimation of criminal career homogeneity. *Journal of Investigative Psychology and Offender Profiling, 11*(2), 164–178. doi: https://doi.org/10.1002/jip.1405

Shover, N. (1996). *Great pretenders: Pursuits and careers of persistent thieves.* Westview Press. doi: https://www.routledge.com/Great-Pretenders-Pursuits-And-Careers-Of-Persistent-Thieves/Shover/p/book/9780813328119

Smith, J. (2021). The formerly incarcerated, advocacy, activism, and community reintegration. *Contemporary Justice Review, 24*(1), 43–63. doi: https://www.tandfonline.com/doi/full/10.1080/10282580.2020.1755846

Sullivan, K. (2012). *Motivating and maintaining desistance from crime: Male Aboriginal serial offenders' experience of 'going good'* [PhD thesis, Australian National University]. Canberra.

Thompson, D. (2015). *Moving on after getting out: Support and accountability for convicted sex offenders* [PhD thesis, University of Leeds]. Leeds. https://etheses.whiterose.ac.uk/13410/1/Thompson_D_Law_PhD_2015.pdf

White, W. (2000a). The history of recovered people as wounded healers i: From native America to the rise of the modern alcoholism movement. *Alcoholism Treatment Quarterly, 18*(1), 1–23. doi: https://www.tandfonline.com/doi/abs/10.1300/J020v18n01_01

White, W. (2000b). The history of recovered people as wounded healers II: The era of professionalization and specialization. *Alcoholism Treatment Quarterly, 18*(2), 1–25. doi: https://www.tandfonline.com/doi/abs/10.1300/J020v18n02_01

Chapter 7

Circles of Support and Accountability and Core Members as Wounded Healers

Generativity – the final act in the redemption script – commonly involves an ex-offender assuming the role of the "professional ex" (Brown, 1991; Le Bel et al., 2015) or "wounded healer" (Halsey & Deegan, 2012; Maruna, 2001; White, 2000a,b). This chapter argues that empowering former core members to act as volunteers facilitates the "wounded healer" role and can thus make a substantial contribution in shaping the desistant identities of people who have sexually offended. It presents the first theoretical and empirical examination of what Hocken et al. (2018, p. 174) call a "bold move" – the utilisation of former core members as Circles of Support and Accountability (CoSA) volunteers.

Wounded Healers in the Criminal Justice Context

The concept of the wounded healer was developed by Henri Nouwen (1972), a Roman Catholic priest and psychologist, who drew on both Christian tradition and secular psychology to make sense of his own experience of depression (Scrutton, 2015), although it has much deeper historical roots (Nolte & Dreyer, 2010; White, 2000a; Zerubavel & O'Dougherty Wright, 2012). It is premised on the theological notion that suffering can be redemptive and on the Jungian psychological prescript that "only the wounded physician heals" (Nolte & Dreyer, 2010; Scrutton, 2015). Popularised more recently by White (2000a,b), who documented both its secularisation and application to recovery from alcohol and drug addiction, it refers to the idea that people who have experienced and overcome various adversities may possess a unique understanding of and therefore skills that may help others now facing, these same adversities (White, 2000a, p. 2). In short, "the more healers can understand their own wounds and journey of recovery, the better position they are in to guide others through such a process" (Zerubavel & O'Dougherty Wright, 2012, p. 482). The idea of the wounded healer is no doubt familiar to readers; it is embedded in Twelve-Step programs, which require participants to help others as part of their own journeys of healing (Scrutton, 2015).

DOI: 10.4324/9781003125532-8

White (2000b) summarised the unique assets that wounded healers might draw on in assisting others experiencing the same adversities they themselves have faced:

- Unique knowledge that stems from their own direct experience;
- A capacity for emotional identification with those experiencing adversity;
- A lack of condescension or contempt towards those experiencing adversity, stemming from their shared experience;
- A zeal to help others that derives from their sense of gratitude for their own recovery;
- An ability to use their own experiences to foster hope for recovery;
- A willingness to be more directive than trained professionals when engaging with those experiencing adversity;
- A capacity to act as a role model and
- An ability to offer those experiencing adversity with a detailed and personal orientation to the programs and practices with which they are now engaged (see also Morrison et al., 2006).

As Le Bel et al. (2015) explained, in the criminal justice context, wounded healers are those former offenders who craft a legitimate career (whether paid or voluntary) that capitalises on their own deviant past. Maruna (2001, p. 117) argued that "the desisting self-narrative frequently involves reworking a delinquent history into a source of wisdom to be drawn from while acting as a drug counselor, youth worker, community volunteer, or mutual-help group member" (see also Brown, 1991; Corcoran & Grotz, 2016). It has long been recognised that utilising these assets in the service of others may benefit former offenders themselves (Le Bel et al., 2015; Maruna & LeBel, 2015). As Smith (2021, p. 14) argued, a personal history of imprisonment paradoxically involves being subject to dehumanising stereotypes at the same time that it carries authenticity and legitimacy that can never be possessed by those without this history. Again somewhat paradoxically, adopting the role of the wounded healer involves *embracing* rather than *rejecting* one's deviant or criminal past (Brown, 1991).

Halsey and Deegan (2012, p. 340) identify "unaffiliated" or "hidden" (i.e., informal) wounded healers – those who do not or cannot adopt an institutionalised or formal role as a wounded healer but who nonetheless evince similar desires to help other similarly stigmatised people. While the terms "wounded healer" and "professional ex" are used interchangeably (Maruna, 2001), we might make a useful distinction based on professionalisation. In other words, some wounded healers will have the opportunity to adopt paid professional positions but others – including people who have sexually offended – will usually not be afforded this luxury and might therefore be better understood as "unaffiliated" or "hidden" wounded healers. Those with convictions for sexual offences cannot "credentialise" to use Brown's (1991) terminology, in the same way that recovered drug addicts, sex workers or anorexics might.

There is emerging evidence that adopting the role of the wounded healer can motivate desistance among former offenders. Maruna's (2001) seminal research placed particular emphasis upon generative pursuits that involve ex-offenders working with offenders and potential offenders to encourage their reform (Sullivan, 2012, p. 310). He found in the Liverpool Desistance Study that numerous ex-offenders sought formal and informal mentoring roles and that even where such roles were not available, "the impulse toward volunteerism and mentoring could be found in almost every narrative" (Maruna, 2001, p. 103). In becoming a professional ex, individuals fortify their own desistant identities: "The construction or reconstruction of one's life story into a moral tale might...be an important element of sustaining significant behavioral reform".

More recently, Le Bel et al. (2015) undertook research comparing formally incarcerated men and women who had adopted professional ex roles in drug counselling, employment support, accommodation support and other education and counselling roles, with formerly incarcerated men and women who were clients of these services. They found that those who had adopted the role of the wounded healer underwent significant transformations in both their self-identities and their worldviews. Wounded healers were better able than the comparison group to navigate stigma, develop prosocial attitudes and beliefs and active coping strategies and thus had better psychological well-being and satisfaction with life (Le Bel et al., 2015). They argued, therefore, that criminal justice policies that disallow former prisoners from associating with one another are likely to be counterproductive and that more opportunities should be created that allow former prisoners to mentor their peers (or prospective peers) (Le Bel et al., 2015).

Few studies have examined the adoption of the wounded healer role among people who have sexually offended, perhaps because few such opportunities may exist. The small number of existing studies show, however, that those with sexual offence convictions strongly desire such opportunities and can benefit immensely from them. For example, Perrin et al. (2018) conducted interviews with 13 people incarcerated for sexual offences who were involved in a range of peer support programs in a UK prison. The research found that the men in the study were able to build desistant identities through their wounded healer roles, which enabled them to earn the trust of others in the prison, to begin to see themselves in a more positive light, to have something constructive into which to channel their time and energy, to dissociate from stigmatising labels and to develop self-esteem. Acting as wounded healers also gave the prisoners "stakes in conformity" (Toby, 1957) – in other words, "something to lose" if they were to "slip up" (Perrin et al., 2018, p. 16). Perrin et al. (2018) thus concluded that such roles can encourage movements towards desistance and therefore that we ought to increase opportunities for ex-offenders to adopt roles characterised by reciprocal helping (Perrin et al., 2018, p. 26). Harris (2017, p. 245) likewise found – at least among a particular group of the men with sexual offence convictions in her study – a strong desire to give back by adopting the role of the wounded healer:

> Whether it was a motivation to help others in their treatment group, their homeless shelter, or their rooming house, this service was often described as a calling, as a way to give back, and as the most fulfilling thing they had ever done. Their mentoring of others was a source of considerable pride and was sometimes described as a path by which they might achieve some measure of atonement and true reintegration.

My own work on desistance narratives among Aboriginal and/or Torres Strait Islander men convicted of serious sexual offending in Queensland, Australia (Richards et al., 2020), which involved 14 qualitative interviews with this cohort of men after their release from prison, found that the men's access to a peer support group provided them with a critical opportunity to perform the role of the wounded healer. The men in that study revelled in mentoring members of the peer support group (which catered to both offending and non-offending men in the community), suggesting that they had reframed their offending pasts into a source of wisdom and authority on which they are now able to draw in order to help others (as per Le Bel et al., 2015; Maruna, 2001). The group provided the men an opportunity to practise generativity, thereby "legitimising the person's claim to having changed" (McNeill & Maruna, 2007, p. 231). This occurred despite the very strict limitations imposed on the men under the conditions of their release and the very limited opportunities to enact generative projects (see further Richards et al., 2020). Taken together, this sparse body of research suggests that people with convictions relating to sexual offending will take enthusiastically to opportunities to enact the role of the wounded healer and may benefit greatly from doing so.

Wounded Healers and CoSA

It may seem inconceivable in the current climate (see Ashenden, 2002; Wacquant, 2009) that any avenue would exist for people with convictions for sexual offending to coach or mentor others. Indeed, Hocken et al. (2018, p. 174) recently stated that within CoSA programs, this "is not a model that has ever been reported…and represents a bold move". Wilson and McWhinnie's (2017, pp. 48–50) "how to" guide for implementing CoSA programs does, however, acknowledge the possibility that individuals with criminal justice histories – including those with histories of sexual violence perpetration – might serve as CoSA volunteers. They urge caution in this regard, arguing that any such prospective volunteer should be carefully screened (through an interview process and reference checks) before being accepted as a CoSA volunteer. Wilson and McWhinnie (2017) acknowledge that accepting individuals with sexual offence histories as volunteers may be controversial, but ask: if we are truly committed to the notion that no one is disposable, "how can we not include in our midst those who have walked the walk to redemption and are restored as contributing citizens"? They counsel that any volunteer with an offending past – sexual or otherwise – should be prepared to make a full and voluntary disclosure to others involved in the program and that such a past should not be discovered inadvertently through a screening process. They also recommend only accepting as volunteers those who have completed all supervision requirements and who have been living offence-free in the community for a number of years. They conclude that creating opportunities for those with offence histories to volunteer in CoSA not only demonstrates commitment to the tenet that no one is disposable, but might also lead to the building of social capital and act as a protective factor against reoffending (Wilson & McWhinnie, 2017).

One of the six CoSA programs included in the current study (located in Fresno, California) operates on the premise that former core members can make helpful CoSA volunteers for new core members. This chapter presents the first theoretical and empirical examination of the utilisation of former core members as volunteers, focusing specifically on the data collected in Fresno, California. It argues that empowering former core members to act as volunteers facilitates the wounded healer role and can thus make a substantial contribution in shaping the desistant identities of people who have sexually offended. Indeed, perhaps the strongest demonstration of a commitment to and genuine belief in a core member's desistance is enabling that individual to act as a volunteer in another (newer) core member's Circle.

Morgan's Story

Morgan grew up in a small town. His early life experiences were characterised by rejection and loneliness accompanied by substance misuse; he was later diagnosed with borderline personality disorder. This diagnosis came after his arrest in relation to contact offences against a minor, for which he served four years in prison. When we spoke, he had been involved in a CoSA for about three years. The idea of CoSA appealed to Morgan on the grounds that it involved "a group of people who are always going to be there, and if one's not there then someone else is going to be there if you need to call someone and you need to talk to someone". This resonated with Morgan because of the loneliness and rejection he had previously experienced. He now describes CoSA as "probably one of the best things that's ever happened to me".

When I asked Morgan what could be improved about CoSA, he responded instantaneously and in considerable detail that he would like to move from being a core member to being a volunteer in another core member's Circle. He believes that this would have significant benefits:

> I think one of the things too is, like I know I'm still like a core member of a Circle, but I would always love to be on a Circle for someone new.

> Being able to say you know, "this is my experience and this is my walk of life and now I'm going to put it towards helping someone else"....I would like to see more core members who have been out of the program for a number of years or whatever, be able to come in and help people as well.

I asked Morgan whether having a reformed core member on his own Circle would have helped him, and he responded enthusiastically:

> Yeah....I think that would have been a big help for someone who went through everything that I've been through, being incarcerated, and then went through everything I've been through being released and can say, "you know what, this is where I am now". I think that would help a lot of people, but I think it would have helped [me] for sure.

Morgan viewed himself as bringing a particular expertise to CoSA that other volunteers simply don't possess:

> I've had that sort of debate with my...[Circle volunteers]...of saying, you know, "there's certain things that you guys may never understand". They want to understand them [other core members] and they want to try and rationalise certain things to their way of thinking, but I have to step in and say, "this is how I'm going to view it because of the way that I have lived my life and the things that I've gotten through".

By way of example, Morgan described his strong preference, since his release from prison, to sit with his back to the wall in public places such as restaurants. He explained that this stems from his experience in prison "where if you had your back to somebody, you were vulnerable". For Morgan, such experiences provide invaluable insight into the experiences of other core members: "those are just things that - they come with the territory of where you've been and what you've gone through".

"Cheeseburgers Are on Wednesday": CoSA and Wounded Healers' Unique Expertise

In line with Maruna's (2001) findings about property and drug offenders, core members' narratives often reflected the impulse towards becoming a wounded healer of some sort, even in contexts in which this was not available to them. Donny, for example, did not have access to any formal channel in which to enact such an identity, but nonetheless sought creative avenues via which to impart his wisdom to other, newer core members:

> I know another gentleman that comes here, we're friends, and he felt like he was being judged, so he didn't want somebody [a particular volunteer]

in the Circle. I got there and I was talking and I said "what did she say"? I said, "that's not judging you". I said "that's really good advice"....Now, he talks highly of her: [he says] "oh she's the best one".

Alan was "waiting for the CoSA training to start [so I can] become a volunteer", and Damien likewise aspired to adopt the role of wounded healer in the not-too-distant future. When I asked him about giving back to the community, he responded enthusiastically: "Oh yeah. I'm thinking about being a [CoSA] volunteer myself, after I discharge parole". Staff members 11 and 12 noted in their interview that this impulse is not uncommon among core members:

STAFF MEMBER 12: We have one [core member] that keeps offering to be a volunteer. I think you're not in a position where you can help somebody. But in his mind...he just wants to help people. He's here to help people.

STAFF MEMBER 11: Yeah, me too. I mean, that's interesting enough in itself, right. That need to want to help.

Core members and volunteers alike espoused the view that core-members-turned-volunteers (hereafter "wounded healers"), having experienced being incarcerated in relation to sexual offending and being a core member themselves, possess unique knowledge and expertise – "epistemic advantage" in Wylie's (2003, p. 26) terms – that other volunteers cannot. Volunteers conceded their own limitations in this regard and were firm of the belief that including wounded healers into Circles addressed this limitation. As volunteer 2 argued of wounded healers, "they've been through the journey and so they can say, 'I've been there, I know'. And sometimes they can be very helpful". Volunteers 4, 5 and 6 put forward a similar argument:

> Half the groups I was in anyway had a former core member now as a volunteer and I find it extremely valuable. They know so much more that I don't know.
>
> (Volunteer 5)

> Plus they are like an example of what you can become. I think the current core member would be - it's a thrill [for them] to have them there every week, they are so much help, and the rest of us don't really know, so I think it's so valuable to have them there.
>
> (Volunteer 4)

> I think it helps having past core members; [it] really not only gives that kind of mentorship piece, but it helps blur that line between us versus them because I think institutionalised offenders come out like, "what do you [volunteers] know about being prison?".
>
> (Volunteer 6)

Core members who have participated in Circles that included wounded healers effusively endorsed their inclusion on similar grounds:

> That helped me quite a bit because we could talk on the same level. I could help him through some things and he could help me through some things that were - you know - a different way of looking at it; a different way of approaching it; a different way of handling it.
>
> (Alan)

> They have insight, they've been through it, they can tell about their experience and different things. If you have a problem they can say, "oh yeah, I went through that when I got out..." and they can understand and empathise better, having walked that path.
>
> (Sean)

> He's been a help. In fact, one of the first things he did was...gave me $50. He said, "when I got out, one of the guys gave me 100 [dollars]. I can't afford to give you that much but here's $50 to help you out". He's been a help ever since....he's established. And it worked for him, it's going to work for me.
>
> (Wayne)

Wounded healers themselves made a similar argument – that incorporating former core members into Circles is beneficial as these individuals possess unique knowledge:

> I feel it's been beneficial, having a person who has gone through it before in a Circle. A person who has been a sex offender, dealing with it, been to prison, is a sex offender. Because the core members now in the Circles - oh, man. There's somebody that understands....I think it's been beneficial.
>
> (Brian)

> I know the loss they've experienced. I know the shame they've experienced....There's certain inside jokes that, yeah, give that credibility, of "cheeseburgers are on Wednesdays" kind of thing, that we know that you've been in.
>
> (Volunteer 1[1])

CoSA, Wounded Healers and Identity Transformation

This chapter argues, however, that the value of incorporating wounded healers into Circles is far more profound than this characterisation allows. Somewhat paradoxically, wounded healers' authenticity actually serves not to align them with current core members but with the other CoSA volunteers, since the utilisation of this expertise highlights their own successful reform. While core members who adopted the role of the wounded healer often described their decision to do so as a form of giving back (see for example Daniel's story below), its primary benefit might be better understood as reinforcing the wounded healer's own identity transformation. Consider, for example, the following extract from Leon's interview in which he describes not a formal mentoring role but informal interactions with other core members:

> I'm a positive support for others. A couple of the newcomers that came in the past few years, they thought I was one of the volunteers. Then I'd stand up and make some kind of commentary on this and this coming from my past [as a core member], and how I'm dealing with things.... This one guy - you should have seen his jaw drop! – he says, "I'm glad you said that because that shows that this group works".

This was recognised by volunteer 6, who acknowledged that acting as a wounded healer reaffirms former core members' own commitment to a non-offending identity:

> I think in a lot of ways it supports them as well. It's a never-ending process so I think even past core offenders, 15 years later that are in the Circle, that's a supportive hour for them as well; just giving back and checking in and always having – "I remember when I was there. I don't want to be there again".

This has previously been recognised as a key benefit of taking on the role of the wounded healer or professional ex (e.g., Harris, 2017; Perrin et al., 2018); my argument here is that in utilising core members as volunteers, the Fresno CoSA program provide an explicit opportunity for core members to adopt the role of wounded healer and thereby to demonstrate desistance. Becoming a wounded healer also offers former core members a rare opportunity to perform their revised law-abiding selves in front of supportive witnesses and thus to have these prosocial selves mirrored back to them (see Chapter 5 on the importance of desistance witnesses).

Moreover, empowering former core members to serve as wounded healers simultaneously allows wounded healers to distance themselves from current core members and instead powerfully assert that their moral subjectivity is similar to CoSA volunteers'. Terry, for example, uses his position as a wounded healer both to demonstrate his own reform – "I don't hesitate to point out distorted thinking, rationalisations, justification, lies" – and to align himself in moral terms with the other CoSA volunteers: "you've either got to tell the truth or we're wasting our time" (see further Chapter 5). When I pressed Damien on what it is that appeals about volunteering with other core members rather than in the broader community, he responded: "Being able to help another core member, in a similar situation like I was. I can adapt them. I can tell them, 'hey, I'm not in your shoes, but I have understanding about being there, how many months or years ago'". In doing so, both Damien and Terry use narrative devices designed to distance themselves from current core members and thus underscore their own successful reform: "wasting *our* time"; "I'm not in *your* shoes". Mathias was far more explicit about distancing himself from current core members and instead aligning himself with other CoSA volunteers:

> I don't trust a lot of the guys here. A lot of them are fake and a lot of them aren't even fake, they're just upfront about it. That's who they are. They're going to stay that way and I don't want to be round people like that....they're a bunch of criminals, sex offenders, whatever. A lot of them are just criminals still and I said "I don't want to be around people like that", so I tend to stay by myself a lot or the people I hang around with, they're few and far between. I'm pretty selective about that.

Facilitating opportunities via which core members can act as wounded healers might therefore be understood as a powerful avenue for the creation of "we-ness". Enacting the role of wounded healer allows core members to communicate that they are not (or at least are no longer) like other ("real") "sex offenders" but more akin in character to CoSA volunteers. Importantly, in this context, we-ness does not merely refer to a "sense of belonging" (as Blagden et al. (2018, p. 31) and Höing et al. (2013, p. 283) conceptualise it), since one could conceivably gain a "sense of belonging" from, for example, a sex offender treatment program or even a pro-paedophile chatroom. Rather, and crucially, the role of wounded healer provides a pathway for the expression of we-ness in the form of *like moral subjectivity*. As volunteer 4 compellingly argued, incorporating reformed core members into CoSA as volunteers powerfully demonstrate others' acceptance of these wounded healers' successful desistance: "It just seems like such a testament to what we're doing. People do come out the other end and become better people". This again emphasises the profound difference between what CoSA can provide people with convictions for sexual offending and the approach taken by the risk-focused correctional system. As wounded healer Terry beautifully articulated in his interview, while the message he receives through correctional supervision is that, "we don't trust you, we're going to isolate you and we're not going to let you integrate", in CoSA, belief in and acceptance of his reform is so strong that he is supported to mentor others.

Daniel's Story

Daniel is in his 50s when we meet in Fresno. He had served 14 months in prison following a conviction for a non-contact offence against a teenager. He is currently on parole after his release from prison over eight years ago. Unlike many of his peers, Daniel had a number of supports in the community at the time of his release, including supportive family members and members of his church. He came to be a core member after learning about CoSA through these existing networks and participated in CoSA as a core member for two years. Daniel views his time in CoSA as immensely helpful. His volunteers helped him make sense of his offending and its causation and gave advice and encouragement aimed at helping him develop a healthier lifestyle. His CoSA also helped him to reconcile his own childhood sexual victimisation as well as what he described as his "porn addiction", connecting him with services and programs to address these issues. For Daniel, CoSA provided "a good safe place to go"; nonetheless, addressing both his victimisation and his offending in this forum was highly emotional and he reported crying at every CoSA meeting he attended during the first few months of his involvement.

CoSA helped Daniel see himself as separable from his offence: "I made a bad choice, a bad decision". This was reinforced to him by his volunteers, who shared personal insights into their own lives, including discussing actions of which they were not proud. Daniel's volunteers also reinforced their belief in his desistance by asking him to do things such as mow lawns for church members. For Daniel, this was "a real positive thing". This helped him shape a new identity: "This is who I am. I am a sex offender but this is who I *really* am".

While Daniel acknowledges that his offending means "carrying that stigmatisation around", he has sought to resist this by adopting the role of a wounded healer. He does this through a number of informal channels, demonstrating both his commitment to the role and his creativity in seeking outlets for it. He has volunteered in other core members' Circles for six years. He explained that having a former core member act as a volunteer can be highly valuable since only former core members can truly understand what a current core member is experiencing. However, Daniel recognises that he also benefits from supporting others. He construes his volunteer role as giving back; as he sees it, "someone gave me a chance" and he wants to repay that generosity. Importantly, Daniel does not believe that all core members would be suitable as volunteers. Daniel sees himself as different from other core members because he has "taken ownership of what I had done".

Conclusion

This chapter has argued that CoSA can provide a forum in which successful desisters adopt the role of the wounded healer, enabling them to undertake generative activity and, in doing so, fortify their self-narratives of reform. Enabling former core members to act as CoSA volunteers delivers perhaps the most powerful message to them about others' acceptance of and faith in their reform. Given the important role that having one's desistance recognised by others plays in reinforcing reform, it is perhaps timely for CoSA programs around the globe to consider this "bold move" (Hocken et al., 2018, p. 174).

It is important to note that this practice is not widespread and is not typical of CoSA programs across the globe. Indeed, it is my understanding that it only exists – at least in a formalised way – in the Fresno, California program. Such a practice is likely to be somewhat controversial among members of the public. My previous research on public opinion about CoSA, which analysed the community's response to the commencement of Australia's first and only CoSA program (Richards & McCartan, 2018), suggests there is cause for concern in this regard. One reason for the public's resistance to CoSA was the erroneous belief that CoSA provide an avenue for people with sexual offence convictions to congregate together – a practice that was considered by some to be inappropriate and risky. As one member of the community (not cited in the research) commented: "putting them in contact with each other is an unacceptable risk" (see also Morrison et al., 2006). This need not preclude CoSA programs from supporting former core members to take on the role of wounded healer. It does, however, point to the need to approach this practice cautiously, as per Wilson and McWhinnie's (2017) guidance, outlined earlier in this chapter.

Note

1. Volunteer 1 had not formally participated in CoSA as a core member but has a conviction in relation to sexual offending.

References

Ashenden, S. (2002). Policing perversion: The contemporary governance of paedophilia. *Cultural Values*, *6*(1–2), 197–222. doi: https://doi.org/10.1080/1362517022019829

Blagden, N., Elliott, H., & Lievesley, R. (2018). Circles of Support and Accountability, assisted desistance and community transition. In H. Elliott, K. Hocken, R. Lievesley, N. Blagden, B. Winder, & P. Banyard (Eds.), *Sexual crime and Circles of Support and Accountability* (pp. 25–42). Palgrave Macmillan. doi: https://www.palgrave.com/gp/book/9783319748221

Brown, D. (1991). The professional ex: An alternative for exiting the deviant career. *The Sociological Quarterly*, *32*(2), 219–230. doi: https://www.tandfonline.com/doi/abs/10.1111/j.1533-8525.1991.tb00354.x

Corcoran, M., & Grotz, J. (2016). Deconstructing the panacea of volunteering in criminal justice. In A. Hucklesby, & M. Corcoran (Eds.), *The voluntary sector and criminal justice*, (pp. 93–116). Palgrave Macmillan. doi: https://www.palgrave.com/gp/book/9781137370662

Halsey, M., & Deegan, S. (2012). Father and son: Two generations through prison. *Punishment & Society*, *14*(3), 338–367. doi: https://journals.sagepub.com/doi/10.1177/1462474512442315

Harris, D. (2017). *Desistance from sexual offending: Narratives of retirement, regulation and recovery*. Palgrave Macmillan. doi: https://www.palgrave.com/gp/book/9783319631998

Hocken, K., Good, C., Elliott, H., Webb, C., O'Connor, H., & Cox, K. (2018). Future directions: Alternative Circles of Support and Accountability models and minority groups. In H. Elliott, K. Hocken, R. Lievesley, N. Blagden, B. Winder, & P. Banyard (Eds.), *Sexual crime and Circles of Support and Accountability* (pp. 171–200). Palgrave Macmillan. doi: https://www.palgrave.com/gp/book/9783319748221

Höing, M., Bogaerts, S., & Vogelvang, B. (2013). Circles of Support and Accountability: How and why they work for sex offenders. *Journal of Forensic Psychology Practice, 13*(4), 267–295. doi: https://www.tandfonline.com/doi/abs/10.1080/15228932.2013.808526

Le Bel, T., Richie, M., & Maruna, S. (2015). Helping others as a response to reconcile a criminal past: The role of the wounded healer in prisoner re-entry programs. *Criminal Justice and Behavior, 42*(1), 108–120. doi: https://journals.sagepub.com/doi/10.1177/0093854814550029

Maruna, S. (2001). *Making good: How ex-convicts reform and rebuild their lives.* American Psychological Association. doi: https://www.apa.org/pubs/books/431645A

Maruna, S., & LeBel, T. (2015). Strengths-based restorative approaches to re-entry: The evolution of creative restitution, reintegration and destigmatization. In N. Ronel, & D. Segev (Eds.), *Positive criminology* (pp. 65–84). Routledge. doi: https://www.routledge.com/Positive-Criminology/Ronel-Segev/p/book/9781138288454

McNeill, F., & Maruna, S. (2007). Giving up and giving back: Desistance, generativity and social work with offenders. In G. McIvor, & P. Raynor (Eds.), *Developments in social work with offenders* (pp. 224–239). Jessica Kingsley Publishers.

Morrison, W., Doucet, C., & Murray, J. (2006). *Ex-offenders as peer volunteers: Promising practices for community-based programs.* Imagine Canada. http://sectorsource.ca/sites/default/files/resources/files/JHoward_ExOffenders_Report.pdf

Nolte, P., & Dreyer, Y. (2010). The paradox of being a wounded healer: Henri J.M. Nouwen's contribution to pastoral theology. *Theological Studies, 66*(2), 1–8. doi: https://hts.org.za/index.php/HTS/article/view/861

Nouwen, H. (1972). *The wounded healer: Ministry in contemporary society.* Darton, Longman & Todd.

Perrin, C., Blagden, N., Winder, B., & Dillon, G. (2018). "It's sort of reaffirmed to me that I'm not a monster, I'm not a terrible person": Sex offenders' movements toward desistance via peer-support roles in prison. *Sexual Abuse, 30*(7), 759–780. doi: https://journals.sagepub.com/doi/10.1177/1079063217697133

Richards, K., Death, J., & McCartan, K. (2020). Toward redemption: Aboriginal and/or Torres Strait Islander men's narratives of desistance from sexual offending. *Victims & Offenders, 15*(6), 810–833. doi: https://www.tandfonline.com/doi/full/10.1080/15564886.2020.1754311

Richards, K., & McCartan, K. (2018). Public opinion about Circles of Support and Accountability: A qualitative analysis. *Deviant Behavior: An Interdisciplinary Journal, 39*(3), 400–416. doi: https://www.tandfonline.com/doi/abs/10.1080/01639625.2017.1304800

Scrutton, A. (2015). Suffering as potentially transformative: A philosophical and pastoral consideration drawing on Henri Nouwen's experience of depression. *Pastoral Psychology, 64*(1), 99–109. doi: https://link.springer.com/article/10.1007/s11089-013-0589-6

Smith, J. (2021). The formerly incarcerated, advocacy, activism, and community reintegration. *Contemporary Justice Review, 24*(1), 43–63. doi: https://www.tandfonline.com/doi/full/10.1080/10282580.2020.1755846

Sullivan, K. (2012). *Motivating and maintaining desistance from crime: Male Aboriginal serial offenders' experience of 'going good'* [PhD thesis, Australian National University]. Canberra.

Toby, J. (1957). Social disorganization and stake in conformity: Complementary factors in the predatory behavior of hoodlums. *Journal of Criminal Law, Criminology, and Police Science, 48*(1), 12–17. doi: https://psycnet.apa.org/record/1959-01797-001

Wacquant, L. (2009). *Punishing the poor: The neoliberal government of social insecurity*. Duke University Press. doi: https://www.jstor.org/stable/j.ctv11smrv3

White, W. (2000a). The history of recovered people as wounded healers I: From native America to the rise of the modern alcoholism movement. *Alcoholism Treatment Quarterly, 18*(1), 1–23. doi: https://www.tandfonline.com/doi/abs/10.1300/J020v18n01_01

White, W. (2000b). The history of recovered people as wounded healers II: The era of professionalization and specialization. *Alcoholism Treatment Quarterly, 18*(2), 1–25. doi: https://www.tandfonline.com/doi/abs/10.1300/J020v18n02_01

Wilson, R., & McWhinnie, A. (2017). *Circles of Support & Accountability: A "how to" guide for establishing CoSA in your location*. Counseling & Psychotherapy Center Inc.

Wylie, A. (2003). Why standpoint matters. In R. Figueroa, & S. Harding (Eds.), *Science and other cultures: Issues in philosophy of science and technology* (pp. 26–48). Routledge. doi: https://www.routledge.com/Science-and-Other-Cultures-Issues-in-Philosophies-of-Science-and-Technology/Harding-Figueroa/p/book/9780415939928

Zerubavel, N., & O'Dougherty Wright, M. (2012). The dilemma of the wounded healer. *Psychotherapy, 49*(4), 482–491. doi: https://doi.apa.org/doiLanding?doi=10.1037%2Fa0027824

Chapter 8

Implications for Practice

Delivering Circles of Support and Accountability as Desistance-Promotion

This chapter makes a series of suggestions about what the key findings outlined in the preceding chapters mean for the practise of Circles of Support and Accountability (CoSA) around the globe. It gives specific guidance on the main ways in which CoSA programs could adopt their key points to strengthen practice and improve outcomes in the future. The chapter will also be of relevance to professionals who engage with people with sexual offence convictions beyond CoSA, such as those who work in clinical/therapeutic and correctional capacities with people who have sexually offended, as it proposes innovative ways of supporting the desistance of people who have sexually offended.

The Key Arguments

This book has made four primary interrelated claims about how CoSA reduce sexual recidivism and how they might be harnessed to do so in future. First, it argued that CoSA reduce sexual reoffending by providing a platform for people with sexual offence convictions to create, practise, refine and maintain redemption scripts. It has been well-documented that former offenders who are able to adopt believable self-narratives about their past offending and subsequent shift away from crime are better positioned to successfully desist from crime. Chapter 4 documented the ways in which CoSA – however inadvertently – foster the development of redemption scripts among core members. Second, I have argued that CoSA provide core members with a platform to demonstrate their (hyper-)commitment to desistance in front of an audience and to have their desistant identities witnessed by supportive others and reflected back to them, thereby reinforcing these moves towards desistance (Chapter 5). Third, this book has argued that CoSA provide avenues for core members to perform generative acts and to capitalise on these in their development of desistant identities (Chapter 6). Finally, in Chapter 7, I argued that CoSA can facilitate the adoption of the wounded healer identity by empowering former core members to act as CoSA volunteers. In this way, CoSA can make a substantial contribution to shaping the desistant identities

DOI: 10.4324/9781003125532-9

of people who have sexually offended. This reconceptualisation of how CoSA work necessitates a reframing of the delivery of CoSA and especially of the relationship between core members and volunteers. The remainder of this chapter outlines how this might be achieved in practical terms.

Assisting Desistance in Practice

By way of broad background, the recent surge of interest in the desistance paradigm has begun to inform the practice of professionals in the offender management domain such as probation and parole officers (King, 2013; McNeill, 2006; McNeill et al., 2012; McNeill & Maruna, 2007). A key question that emerges in this context is how such professionals can "assist desistance". McNeill et al.'s (2012, pp. 46–47) review of the extant research on this topic identified seven central principles that ought to characterise professionals' work with (ex-)offenders:

1 Interventions with former offenders must recognise that desistance is an inherently individualised process, and as such, should focus on matters of the former offender's personal *identity* (Bullock et al., 2019; Richards et al., 2020);
2 Intervention should focus on the development and maintenance of *hope*. Importantly for current purposes, Rex (1999) identified that a sense that correctional authorities were *invested* in their desistance was vital for successful probationers;
3 *Relationships* are central to desistance, and as such, any intervention with former offenders must privilege the development of healthy relationships not only between professionals and former offenders (see King, 2013) but between former offenders and others in their social networks. Previous research highlights that successful relationships between correctional and (ex-)offenders are characterised by respect, fairness, reasonableness (Rex, 1999) and good quality communication, including an emphasis on the professional listening deeply to the former offender (McCulloch, 2005), the building of trust and rapport between parties (McCulloch, 2005; Trotter, 2012) and the encouragement of the former offender (Rex, 1999);
4 Intervention with former offenders should prioritise the identification, development and maintenance of personal *strengths*, rather than involving a primary focus on risks;
5 Interventions with former offenders must encourage agency and self-determination; professionals must work *with* former offenders, rather than *on* or *for* them. McCulloch's (2005) study of probationers in Scotland supports this principle. It found that probationers identified receiving guidance and advice from their probation officers about how best to resolve their life problems – rather than direct assistance – as critical. Probationers benefited from being able to talk through their problems

and receive advice on various options, but valued the autonomy to act themselves (see also Rex, 1999). Both McCulloch (2005) and Rex (1999) also identified that problem-solving should be participatory and led by the probationer – i.e., the former offender should be given the autonomy and authority to identify priorities;

6 Interventions with former offenders must address the development of *social* capital (i.e., resources that individuals possess because of their relationships, including support from and obligations to, groups to which they belong (McCartan & Kemshall, 2020, p. 90)), not solely *human* capital (i.e., personal resources, such as coping mechanisms, resilience, hope and goals (McCartan & Kemshall, 2020, p. 91)). This point was supported in McCulloch's (2005) research, which found that probationers value support from their probation officers to identify and strengthen healthy external relationships (e.g., with prosocial family members) and to make connections with community groups and services and

7 Former offenders' reform should be reinforced, certified or *recognised* in some way.

Individuals with convictions for sexual offending (indeed, any type of offending) can be expected to have distinctly different relationships with correctional authorities than with criminal justice volunteers (including CoSA volunteers). Indeed, the CoSA literature consistently reports that core members appreciate the voluntary nature of the support they receive in Circles (Hanvey et al., 2011; Höing et al., 2015) and distinguish between the nature of their relationships with correctional authorities and that of their relationships with CoSA volunteers, who they often refer to as "friends" (see for example Richards, 2011). While the above principles of effective professional support – such as encouragement, fairness and respect – apply also to how volunteers can best interact with (ex-) offenders, we must therefore ask how CoSA volunteers can most effectively assist desistance.

Höing et al.'s (2013) research helpfully outlined the characteristics of *unhelpful* CoSA volunteers. They studied a number of "dysfunctional" CoSA – i.e., those characterised by conflict and/or crisis – and found that volunteers were ineffectual (indeed, even inimical to Circle aims) where they excluded the core member from conversation, were frequently absent from the Circle, dominated the Circle and/or used the Circle for their own ends. Conversely, effective volunteers were those whose engagement with the core member was honest, open (involving sharing something of themselves and their personal lives with the core member and other volunteers) and accepting (Höing et al., 2013). The remainder of this chapter builds on this background and outlines specific practice implications based on the four key arguments outlined in this book.

Implications for Practice – Redemption Scripts

A number of practice implications stem from the finding that a previously overlooked aspect of CoSA is their ability to support core members to develop redemption scripts. As has already been recognised in the international CoSA literature, a key tenet of volunteers' interactions with core members must be based on the separation of the core members' previous acts of sexual harm from the core member as a person. In Höing et al.'s (2013, p. 276) words, volunteers must "express their rejection of the offense and their acceptance of the core member as a person". Höing et al.'s (2013, p. 277) research found that for core members, "being accepted and not being morally condemned as a person by the volunteers—while their offense is clearly not condoned—is crucial for their willingness to be open". It is also crucial to enable the core member to develop a redemption narrative; if the core member cannot envisage a non-offending self, they are unlikely to enact one. In practical terms, this means that volunteers could focus on supporting core members to develop a redemptive self-story.

There are a number of ways in which redemption scripts could be encouraged. Perhaps chief among these is that CoSA volunteers should both implicitly and explicitly communicate to core members their belief in core members' redeemability. This of course is reflected by the very existence of CoSA, but might also be communicated to core members in more tangible ways through, for example, an encouraging word or gesture. In more concrete terms, Circle activities could include an exercise with core members that aims to identify a true, good self. The core member and volunteers could each address the question: "what is one aspect of your character that you are proud of and why"? Circle volunteers might then look for further examples of those characteristics nominated by core members in their future behaviour as evidence to reinforce this with the core member over time. This has ramifications for the ways in which volunteers interact with core members and particularly in relation to how they respond to core members' expressions of "knifing off" (see Chapter 2) – i.e., that their offending former self is entirely separate from their current prosocial self. While it may be tempting for core members to present themselves as entirely disconnected from their offending pasts – and for volunteers to reinforce this type of self-expression – a more potent tool in fostering desistance is being able to identify and articulate enduring, fixed elements of a core member's good self.

Obversely, volunteers should resist accepting or reinforcing core members' condemnation or contamination scripts. For example, while core members may feel condemned by the societal and criminal justice response to their offending, the findings outlined above suggest that reinforcing core members' sense of powerlessness in this regard could be counter-productive. Instead, volunteers should highlight former core members' successes in building prosocial lives in the community and highlight the value to core members of the support that they receive through CoSA and other avenues. In general terms, responding to core members with optimism and hope (without being unrealistic about their prospects) could support narratives of redemption and resist narrative of condemnation.

If CoSA are to be used (explicitly) as an avenue for core members to develop redemption scripts, it follows that volunteers could support core members to make sense of their prior sexual offending by attributing it to an external cause (e.g., substance misuse) rather than construing it as internal and innate to the core member, since attributing offending to an external cause can support desistant moves (Kras, 2014; Kras & Blasko, 2016). As Maruna and Mann (2006, p. 164) argued:

> it may be better for an individual who has committed a crime to believe "I only did that because I was drunk and I was badly provoked" than to internalize the blame for the offence with the seemingly dangerous attribution "I did it because I wanted to" or "I did it because that is the type of person I am". Individuals making such internal attributions may take responsibility for their offence, but they also show a shocking lack of social awareness and provide little evidence that they should be reintegrated.

A corollary is that in appropriate instances, CoSA could become avenues via which core members' own experiences of childhood sexual abuse can be heard and their lack of natural justice in this regard validated. A careful balance must, however, be struck here. It would be neither appropriate nor effective to minimise or excuse the offending behaviour of core members, or to support the fabrication of a false or forced narrative. Indeed, honesty and holding to account those who have sexually offended are, and should remain, central principles of CoSA.

Finally, in supporting core members to develop redemption narratives, CoSA volunteers should validate core members' expressions of self-efficacy – i.e., that core members are the architects of their own successful desistance. In other words, volunteers should interact with core members in ways that support their desistance but (admittedly paradoxically) highlight core members' own role in this. Volunteer 17's method, which involves "try[ing] to let them solve it themselves, so it gives them a feel that they're...helping themselves" encapsulates this practice recommendation.

Moreover, volunteers could reinforce that core members' successful desistance has come about due to enduring positive character traits of the core member such as perseverance and resiliency.

Implications for Practice – 110 Percenters and Witnesses to Identity Transformation

The finding that CoSA provide core members with a platform to demonstrate their (hyper-)commitment to desistance in front of an audience, and to have their desistant identities witnessed by supportive others, thereby reinforcing these moves towards desistance, gives rise to a number of practice suggestions.

In general terms, positive reinforcement from witnesses (such as CoSA volunteers) should be used to reinforce desisters' identities as reformed and prosocial members of communities (see generally Maruna, Le Bel, et al., 2004; Sample et al., 2021). Volunteers might, for example, highlight to core members that the very fact of their participation in CoSA demonstrates their commitment to a prosocial life. CoSA volunteers should act as active witnesses to core members' desistance, reflecting verbally (and materially, as discussed below) to core members that they have faith in their desistance – where appropriate of course – and facilitating opportunities for core members' desistance to be witnessed by other "personal vouchers" (Maruna, 2001). Importantly, this should occur at the level of an individual's *self* rather than at the level of specific *acts* or *behaviours*; witnesses should ideally reinforce that a kind *act* reflects that the ex-offender is a kind *person* – that the act reflects an enduring good self – rather than positioning the act as singular or an aberration. (Somewhat paradoxically, then, CoSA ought to view a core member's past criminal acts as an aberration from his good character, but his current prosocial acts as reflective of it).

CoSA programs could also create ways of marking a core member's successful desistance – such as through awards and/or ceremonies that "decertify deviance" in Braithwaite's (1989, p. 163) terms. Maruna (2011, p. 19) highlighted the importance of such rituals in recognising desistance, and argued that:

> …rituals could be designed to recognize a person's efforts to "make good" after committing an offense. These might include immediate efforts to apologize or make amends to one's victims, a period of "good behaviour" on the outside, and efforts to recover from addiction, find productive work, "give something back" to one's community, or contribute to one's family responsibilities.
>
> (see further Braithwaite, 1989)

Maruna (2011) argued that ideally such rituals will not be one-off events but repeatedly reinforced over a period of time as necessary and also highlights the central role of members of the community as witnesses to such rituals. CoSA are a clear example of the type of process that Maruna (2011) champions here. Indeed, celebrating core members' successes had been of central importance to CoSA as they were initially devised; Harry Nigh (cited in Höing et al., 2015, p. 5) recalls "celebrating anniversaries, milestones and all the small advances in Charlie [Taylor]'s journey of reintegration". The findings presented in Chapter 5 demonstrated that core members who received recognition from their Circle in the form of an award or ceremony valued that recognition immensely. CoSA programs might thus give thought in future to expanding and/or amplifying the use of such rituals. Again, this should be approached with a degree of caution. Maruna (2011) stressed that reintegration rituals should not be entered into lightly, given that the more challenging it is to be accepted by a group, the more highly valued such acceptance is by the inductee. Furthermore, awards or ceremonies that recognise core members' reform are likely to carry the risk of public censure. Many media articles about CoSA have expressed outrage at the notion of people with sexual offence convictions being given "treats" or what the public might perceive as special privileges (see generally Richards & McCartan, 2018). An article about CoSA by Dean Herbert (2010b), for example, trumpeted that "Treats scheme for paedophiles sparks outrage". Another, by Pownall (2016) screamed "OUTRAGE OVER TREATS FOR SEX OFFENDERS" (see also Brennan, 2011; Herbert, 2010a; McLaughlin, 2004; Paterson, 2010). Nonetheless, in practice terms, measures that recognise core members' desistance can enhance community safety and should be cautiously considered on these grounds.

Where such rituals are not feasible, more quotidian aspects of CoSA – such as meeting with the core member for a meal or other activity – can "serve to normalize the offender within the community and testify to ordinary citizens' investment in offenders' humanity" (Fox, 2010, p. 348). As such, these practices might be used alongside or in place of more formal certification rituals. This type of activity may not carry the same symbolic import as a formal ceremony but does have the benefit of being reinforced over a period of time as per Maruna's (2011) suggestion.

As a corollary, CoSA programs might create opportunities for core members to demonstrate their desistance. This could be a simple as requiring a core member to show up to meetings on time, to respect Circle processes and to be respectful towards CoSA staff and volunteers. It could also be more involved than this, particularly as Circles mature over time. CoSA programs could, for example, create and/or support opportunities for core members to make good in a variety of ways, such as committing to a course of education and/or participating in community events. Such opportunities will enable core members to "go above and beyond", thus demonstrating their commitment to trustworthiness, and ultimately to desistance.

Implications for Practice – Generativity

In Chapter 6, I argued that CoSA can be usefully understood as a vehicle for supporting core members to develop and enact generativity. McNeill and Maruna (2007, p. 233) asserted that "the development, encouragement and facilitation of generativity should be at the heart of effective practice with [ex-]offenders"; although CoSA's capacity in this regard has not previously been recognised, they can (and I argue, should) support core members' generative journeys. McNeill and Maruna (2007, p. 236 italics added) further argued that "generativity…is a two-way process" and that "'giving back' will only make sense to offenders in *social contexts* within which they are offered the realistic prospect of 'getting back' (or perhaps enacting for the first time) their status as fully included citizens". Understanding CoSA as a vehicle for generativity highlights the critical role of the community – represented by volunteers in CoSA – in desistance-promotion.

A number of recommendations for CoSA practice emerge in this context. For example, CoSA volunteers might use Circle processes to elicit core members' projective interests – i.e., engage in discussions about ways in which core members desire to give back, however tangentially, in future. Such activity can be used to support core members' sense of themselves as fundamentally good and as desiring to be generative – to give back. Volunteers could be encouraged to verbally reinforce to core members that desiring to give back demonstrates their fundamentally good character, even if they are currently or permanently precluded from performing generative acts.

CoSA programs might also think creatively about ways – however seemingly insignificant – that core members might give back. These may be highly tangential given the restrictions that characterise the post-release lives of people with sexual offence convictions. Nonetheless, as Chapter 6 illustrated, even an act as seemingly inconsequential as engaging in conversation with an elderly person can be framed by a core member as generative and as indicative of his good character. CoSA volunteers could therefore support such endeavours, verbally reinforcing how these are demonstrative of core members' good selves. Volunteers might also reinforce that undertaking seemingly quotidian activities can be done with generative care. For example, a core member's banal work in a factory might be framed as generative if it benefits the community in some way (however tenuous).

Even managing one's own risks and trigger behaviours could be highlighted by volunteers as generative activity on the part of core members, and indeed, this may be all that is available to those core members with particularly restrictive release conditions. To be clear, I am not suggesting here that core members should merely be encouraged to manage their risk. Rather, a core member's efforts to do so might be helpfully construed as evidence of moves towards desistance. As Ward and Laws (2010, p. 20) argued:

> ...care should be taken when attempting to persuade individuals to give up crime to look to build strengths rather than simply eradicate, control, or manage risk. The research literature on motivation is clear that the best way to get people engaged in the process of behavior change is to focus on approach goals that are personally meaningful.... Simply demanding that offenders participate in challenging treatment or change programs so that they are less harmful is not an attractive option....What is also required is that there is a possibility of a more fulfilling life and the perception that practitioners care about them and are personally invested in assisting them with their journey.

Volunteers might also support core members' efforts towards "reintegration advocacy" (Flores & Cossyleon, 2017; LeBel, 2013; Smith, 2021) – by, for example, helping others subject to similarly restrictive criminal justice responses – and positioning these acts as generative. As argued in Chapter 6, other ex-offenders may be the only available (or most suitable) targets of a budding desister's generative efforts. This must, however, be approached cautiously and volunteers and CoSA staff should avoid positioning core members as the "real" victims. To this end, instructions to CoSA volunteers such as "Do not speak in derogatory terms about the criminal justice system (e.g., C[orrectional] S[ervice] C[anada], police) and other professionals to the Core Member"– contained in the Edmonton CoSA program's *Volunteer Code of Conduct* (https://www.edmontoncosa.org/volunteering-with-cosa/volunteer-code-of-conduct/) – are critical.

In sum, the findings presented in Chapter 6 suggested that CoSA volunteer training could explicitly equip volunteers to foster and support opportunities for core members to give back and to link core members to other avenues via which they can enact generativity particularly as individual Circles mature over time. When other targets of generative acts are unavailable to core members, volunteers could support core member desistance by themselves becoming potential targets of generativity. Again, this needs to be approached with prudence, and with appropriate regard given to safety and boundary-setting. As discussed in Chapter 6, however, even enabling core members to utilise their own experiences as former offenders to give back to Circle volunteers was experienced by core members as opportunities to enact generativity, and thus to establish a desistant identity.

Implications for Practice – Wounded Healers

It is perhaps most challenging to translate the findings outlined in Chapter 7 into recommendations for CoSA practice. Based on these findings, CoSA programs could consider allowing former core members to act as CoSA volunteers in line with Wilson and McWhinnie's (2017) guidelines. This approach, of course, will not be uniformly suitable or feasible and comes with an elevated level of complexity that not all CoSA programs will be willing or able to manage.

Nonetheless, some more general recommendations emerge from these findings. As Maruna et al. (2004, p. 228) argued, transforming former offenders from *recipients* of help to *providers* of help through encouraging voluntary and community service sends a critical message to both the former offender – that they have something important to offer others – and to the community – that the former offender is worthy of support. Supporting former offenders to see themselves as assets to the community – as individuals with strengths and talents – is especially important since this type of belief about one's self-efficacy is a key element of successful desistance (Maruna, 2001; Maruna, Porter, et al., 2004). Thus, although it may not be possible for all CoSA programs to provide opportunities for core members to act as wounded healers, other avenues might be found via which successful former core members could enact this role. CoSA programs could, for example, seek the input of successful core members into volunteer training and/or program development. In any case, a key practice recommendation in this regard is that CoSA volunteers could mirror back to successful core members their belief in their desistance and their value as wounded healers – however formal or informal their role in this regard might be.

Another general practice recommendation that emerges in this context is that CoSA volunteers communicate to wounded healers that they are similar moral subjects to themselves, thereby reinforcing wounded healers' desistant identities (where appropriate). To highlight "we-ness" (Weaver, 2015; Weaver & McNeill, 2015), Circle volunteers could reveal their own missteps or past acts of which they are not proud while demonstrating that these do not define how they see themselves as people. As I have argued elsewhere (Richards, in press), core members appreciate this aspect of their relationships with volunteers. Daniel, for example, was grateful that his volunteers had shared their own wayward actions as young people, and Terry was especially indebted to two of his volunteers who "weren't afraid to share their deficiencies or the things that they struggled with" (see further Richards, in press). Like many of the other suggestions outlined in this chapter, this ought to be approached with prudence. The *Volunteer Code of Conduct* developed by CoSA in Edmonton, Canada, cautions that "while sharing personal information with the Core Member is good for establishing rapport", volunteers should "keep Circle meetings focused on the Core Member and his issues" (https://www.edmontoncosa.org/volunteering-with-cosa/volunteer-code-of-conduct/). In some CoSA programs, volunteers are instructed not to reveal their surnames to core members, at least before a Circle formally concludes and transitions to an informal network of social relationships (Armstrong et al., 2008, p. 65). Such advice has developed over many years of CoSA practice and is undoubtedly astute. My recommendation that volunteers might reveal their own missteps in order to encourage core members to see themselves as redeemable subjects who are similar to volunteers in moral terms need not, however, contradict this advice. Such admissions need not involve revealing especially personal information and would rather be delivered in relatively abstract terms; for example, a volunteer could merely acknowledge that they themselves have committed acts that they are not proud of such as shoplifting as a young person. Such an admission could help minimise the moral distance between core members and the community – represented by CoSA volunteers – and powerfully communicate to core members their own redeemability. CoSA programs could also facilitate we-ness and develop other ways for core members to demonstrate their moral similarity to volunteers. This might include, for example, supporting core members to demonstrate a commitment to community safety by participating in community justice events, fundraising for victim services or social welfare initiatives and so on.

Conclusion

The practical recommendations put forward in this chapter flow from the primary findings of the study presented throughout this book and focus specifically on reframing CoSA as desistance-promotion. In particular, I have focused on the dynamics of the relationship between CoSA volunteers and core members, since this is at the heart of CoSA practice, and is one of the key factors that differentiates CoSA from other post-prison measures for people with convictions relating to sexual violence. The practice suggestions are by no means intended to be prescriptive or exhaustive, but rather to stimulate a conversation about the merits and practicalities of positioning CoSA in these terms.

References

Armstrong, S., Chistyakova, Y., Mackenzie, S., & Malloch, M. (2008). *Circles of Support & Accountability: Consideration of the feasibility of pilots in Scotland*. Scottish Centre for Crime & Justice Research. https://www.sccjr.ac.uk/publications/circles-of-support-accountability-consideration-of-the-feasibility-of-pilots-in-scotland/

Braithwaite, J. (1989). *Crime, shame and reintegration*. Cambridge University Press. doi: https://www.cambridge.org/core/books/crime-shame-and-reintegration/5F40BF6C9DFC3D5752888BC73034A1BA

Brennan, D. (2011, 13 December). €215k cinema trips to cure child abusers. Daily Mail, np.

Bullock, K., Bunce, A., & McCarthy, D. (2019). Making good in unpromising places: The development and cultivation of redemption scripts among long-term prisoners. *International Journal of Offender Therapy and Comparative Criminology*, *63*(3), 406–423. doi: https://journals.sagepub.com/doi/10.1177/0306624X18800882

Flores, E., & Cossyleon, J. (2017). "I went through it so you don't have to": Faith-based community organizing for the formerly incarcerated. *Journal for the Scientific Study of Religion*, *55*(4), 662–676. doi: https://onlinelibrary.wiley.com/doi/abs/10.1111/jssr.12294

Fox, K. (2010). Second chances: A comparison of civic engagement in offender re-entry programs. *Criminal Justice Review*, *35*(3), 335–353. doi: https://journals.sagepub.com/doi/abs/10.1177/0734016809360328

Hanvey, S., Philpot, T., & Wilson, C. (Eds.). (2011). *A community-based approach to the reduction of sexual reoffending*. Jessica Kingsley Publishers.

Herbert, D. (2010a, 6 December). Plans to treat abusers with trip to the movies. Daily Star, np.

Herbert, D. (2010b, 6 December). Treats scheme for paedophiles sparks outrage. Express, np.

Höing, M., Bogaerts, S., & Vogelvang, B. (2013). Circles of Support and Accountability: How and why they work for sex offenders. *Journal of Forensic Psychology Practice*, *13*(4), 267–295. doi: https://www.tandfonline.com/doi/abs/10.1080/15228932.2013.808526

Höing, M., Duke, L., & Völlm, B. (2015). *Circles of Support and Accountability European handbook*. Avans University of Applied Sciences Centre for Public Safety and Criminal Justice. https://www.circles-uk.org.uk/circles4eu/what-is-circles-4eu

King, S. (2013). Assisted desistance and experiences of probation supervision. *Probation Journal, 60*(2), 136–151. doi: https://journals.sagepub.com/doi/10.1177/0264550513478320

Kras, K. (2014). *Redemption or condemnation? A long-term follow-up of the desistance patterns of sex offenders* [PhD thesis, University of Missouri]. St Louis.

Kras, K., & Blasko, B. (2016). Pathways to desistance among men convicted of sexual offenses: Linking post hoc accounts of offending behavior and outcomes. *International Journal of Offender Therapy and Comparative Criminology, 60*(15), 1738–1755. doi: https://journals.sagepub.com/doi/abs/10.1177/0306624X16668178

LeBel, T. (2013). Formerly incarcerated persons' use of advocacy/activism as a coping orientation in the reintegration process. In B. Veyesy, J. Christian, & D. Martinez (Eds.), *How offenders transform their lives* (pp. 165–187). Willan. doi: https://doi.org/10.4324/9781843927310

Maruna, S. (2001). *Making good: How ex-convicts reform and rebuild their lives.* American Psychological Association. doi: https://www.apa.org/pubs/books/431645A

Maruna, S. (2011). Reentry as a rite of passage. *Theoretical Criminology, 13*(1), 3–28. doi: https://journals.sagepub.com/doi/10.1177/1462474510385641

Maruna, S., Le Bel, T., Mitchell, N., & Naples, M. (2004). Pygmalion in the reintegration process: Desistance from crime through the looking glass. *Psychology, Crime & Law, 10*(3), 271–281. doi: https://www.tandfonline.com/doi/full/10.1080/10683160410001662762

Maruna, S., & Mann, R. (2006). A fundamental attribution error? Rethinking cognitive distortions. *Legal and Criminological Psychology, 11*(2), 155–177. doi: https://bpspsychub.onlinelibrary.wiley.com/doi/abs/10.1348/135532506X114608

Maruna, S., Porter, L., & Carvalho, I. (2004). The Liverpool desistance study and probation practice: Opening the dialogue. *Probation Journal, 51*(3), 221–232. doi: https://journals.sagepub.com/doi/10.1177/0264550504045899

McCartan, K., & Kemshall, H. (2020). The potential role of recovery capital in stopping sexual offending: Lessons from Circles of Support and Accountability to enrich practice. *Irish Probation Journal, 17*, 87–106. doi: https://www.pbni.org.uk/wp-content/uploads/2020/11/Kieran-McCartan-and-Hazel-Kemshall.pdf

McCulloch, T. (2005). Probation, social context and desistance: Retracing the relationship. *Probation Journal, 52*(1), 8–22. doi: https://journals.sagepub.com/doi/10.1177/0264550505050623

McLaughlin, P. (2004, 29 November). Parties for perverts; Fury over scheme that rewards abusers to stop them reoffending. *Daily Mail*, 22.

McNeill, F. (2006). A desistance paradigm for offender management. *Criminology and Criminal Justice, 6*(1), 39–62. doi: https://journals.sagepub.com/doi/10.1177/1748895806060666

McNeill, F., Farrall, S., Lightowler, C., & Maruna, S. (2012). Reexamining evidence-based practice in community corrections: Beyond "A conflned view" of what works. *Justice Policy and Research, 14*(1), 35–60. doi: https://journals.sagepub.com/doi/10.3818/JRP.14.1.2012.35

McNeill, F., & Maruna, S. (2007). Giving up and giving back: Desistance, generativity and social work with offenders. In G. McIvor, & P. Raynor (Eds.), *Developments in social work with offenders* (pp. 224–239). Jessica Kingsley Publishers.

Paterson, K. (2010, 6 December). Cinema trips so paedophiles 'aren't lonely'. *Metro*, 2.

Pownall, S. (2016, 16 October). Outrage over treats for sex offender. *Sunday Mirror*, 1.

Rex, S. (1999). Desistance from offending: Experiences of probation. *The Howard Journal, 38*(4), 366–383. doi: https://onlinelibrary.wiley.com/doi/abs/10.1111/1468-2311.00141.

Richards, K. (2011). *The potential of Circles of Support and Accountability (COSA) to reduce child sexual abuse in Australia*. Winston Churchill Memorial Trust. https://www.churchilltrust.com.au/media/fellows/Richards_Kelly_2010.pdf

Richards, K. (in press). Circles of Support and Accountability: The role of social relations in core member desistance. *International Journal of Offender Therapy and Comparative Criminology*. doi: https://doi.org/10.1177/0306624X20964094

Richards, K., Death, J., & McCartan, K. (2020). Toward redemption: Aboriginal and/or Torres strait islander men's narratives of desistance from sexual offending. *Victims & Offenders, 15*(6), 810–833. doi: https://www.tandfonline.com/doi/full/10.1080/15564886.2020.1754311

Richards, K., & McCartan, K. (2018). Public opinion about Circles of Support and Accountability: A qualitative analysis. *Deviant Behavior: An Interdisciplinary Journal, 39*(3) 400–416. doi: https://www.tandfonline.com/doi/abs/10.1080/01639625.2017.1304800

Sample, L., Cooley, B., Ten Bensel, T., Hyter, C., & Hurley, B. (2021). Forced interactions with sheriff deputies over time and their influence on stigma and self-identities among individuals convicted of sex crimes. *Qualitative Criminology, 10*(1). doi: https://doi.org/10.21428/88de04a1.dcb307ab

Smith, J. (2021). The formerly incarcerated, advocacy, activism, and community reintegration. *Contemporary Justice Review, 24*(1), 43–63. doi: https://www.tandfonline.com/doi/full/10.1080/10282580.2020.1755846

Trotter, C. (2012). *Trends & issues in crime and criminal justice no. 448: Effective community-based supervision of young offenders*. Australian Institute of Criminology. https://www.aic.gov.au/publications/tandi/tandi448

Ward, T., & Laws, R. (2010). Desistance from sex offending: Motivating change, enriching practice. *International Journal of Forensic Mental Health, 9*(1), 11–23. doi: https://www.tandfonline.com/doi/abs/10.1080/14999011003791598

Weaver, B. (2015). *Offending and desistance: The importance of social relations*. Routledge. doi: https://www.routledge.com/Offending-and-Desistance-The-importance-of-social-relations/Weaver/p/book/9781138062610

Weaver, B., & McNeill, F. (2015). Lifelines: Desistance, social relations, and reciprocity. *Criminal Justice and Behavior, 42*(1), 95–107. doi: https://journals.sagepub.com/doi/10.1177/0093854814550031

Wilson, R., & McWhinnie, A. (2017). *Circles of Support & Accountability: A "how to" guide for establishing CoSA in your location*. Counseling & Psychotherapy Center Inc.

Conclusion

When the Reverend Harry Nigh gathered together a group from his church congregation to support Charlie Taylor to rejoin the community in 1994, he could scarcely have imagined the impacts that his act of "accidental courage" (Wilson, 2006: np) would have across the world in the intervening two-and-a-half decades. Not only have Circles of Support and Accountability (CoSA) spread across the West – albeit somewhat haphazardly – but this practice continues to defy the primary thrust of the criminal justice landscape towards increased punitivism, particularly for people with sexual offence convictions (Bartels et al., 2019).

A number of attempts have previously been made to explicate CoSA in theoretical terms. While each of these has limitations, I am not proposing that they be abandoned. Rather, situating CoSA within the theoretical landscape of desistance, as I have done here, offers a complimentary perspective and approach to understanding both how Circles work and how they might work better. In particular, situating CoSA as desistance-promotion allows an understanding of the relationships between core members and volunteers that prior theoretical explanations (especially the Risk Needs Responsivity and Good Lives Models) lack. It has long been recognised that relationships are at the heart of CoSA (Almond et al., 2015; Heise et al., 1996; McCartan & Kemshall, 2020; Richards, in press); here, I have begun to explicate how the relationships central to CoSA practice translate into reduced sexual reoffending. As such, this book has sought to start a conversation about the role of CoSA in core members' desistance journeys among the international community of CoSA scholars and practitioners.

I have made four interrelated arguments in this regard:

- That CoSA reduce sexual reoffending by providing an avenue for core members to develop redemption scripts;
- That CoSA give core members an opportunity to display their (hyper-) commitment to desistance in front of a supportive "audience" of Circle volunteers and staff, who in turn both shape and reinforce core members' moves towards building desistant identities;

DOI: 10.4324/9781003125532-10

- That CoSA provide opportunities for core members to perform generative acts and to build on these in their development of desistant identities and
- That CoSA (in some locations at least) can facilitate the adoption of the wounded healer identity by empowering former core members to act as CoSA volunteers.

While CoSA were not explicitly designed to achieve these outcomes, I argue that they often do so – however inadvertently – and that understanding CoSA in these terms – as a form of "assisted desistance" (Blagden, Elliott et al., 2018) that offers core members a turning point, hook for change and/or opportunity to knife off a former offending self– could inform our understanding of their efficacy in future.

Limitations of the Study

Like all research, the study presented here has a number of limitations that should be borne in mind. While the study was conducted with CoSA programs in specific local contexts, it should be acknowledged that CoSA programs in different parts of the world vary considerably from one another (Höing et al., 2013) and that the locations at which data were collected cannot represent all CoSA programs. The research was conducted with CoSA programs in California and Canada, and it has been recognised that CoSA practice in these locations differ, for example, from CoSA in the United Kingdom (Richards, 2011). Furthermore, CoSA *within* national boundaries vary significantly from one another. The arguments made in this book will likely be of most relevance to CoSA in the North American context, although CoSA practitioners from other parts of the world may find the material presented here of utility as well. In addition, CoSA practice continues to evolve and it is possible that the practice dynamics I have captured here are different from those that currently characterise CoSA.

As noted in Chapter 3, the average age of core members was 55 years. It is possible that their narratives of redemption, generativity and so on would not have emerged from younger core members with more limited life experience. However, differences were not noted across the core members of varying ages in the current research. The sampling approach used likely also has favoured core members with long histories of involvement with CoSA. The findings may thus better reflect outcomes from more stable, longer-term Circles and the relational dynamics described between core members and volunteers may reflect CoSA that have been especially successful. This is not necessarily a weakness of the research but rather underscores that such dynamics are aspirational in supporting core members on their desistance journeys. Whether and how these dynamics would assist core members who are less well-suited to CoSA remains to be seen and could form the focus of future research (see further below). The development of redemptive narratives, generativity and so on also takes considerable time and cannot be expected to occur rapidly or early in a core member's desistance process (see also Harris, 2014). Again, this need not detract from the claims made in this book but rather highlights the need for appropriate resourcing and support for CoSA programs over the longer-term.

Future Research Directions

There is consensus in the literature that longitudinal research (rather than, or in addition to, cross-sectional research) is required to capture the complex dynamics of desistance (Doekhie & Van Ginneken, 2020; Maruna, 2001). Cross-sectional research refers to studies undertaken at a specific point in time; in contrast, longitudinal studies (also referred to as "cohort" or "panel" studies) involve the collection of data about the same participants over time (Cohen et al., 2017). In Maruna's (2001) terms, in desistance research it is critical to capture the "going" part of "going straight". A longitudinal approach presents difficulties for researchers due to the complexities involved in following a cohort of people – especially those whose lives are often characterised by profound instability – over time. Nonetheless, documenting core members' desistance *journeys* as they unfold presents a logical next step to the research presented here. Future research could thus involve deep ethnographic engagement with core members during their involvement in Circles (and beyond) in order to flesh out the findings presented in the preceding chapters. To this end, a prospective research design – that is, a program of research that documents desistance narratives as they unfold, rather than capturing only *post hoc* accounts – would allow for a deeper understanding of the vicissitudes of desistance from sexual offending and the role of CoSA in this. A more representative sample of core members – i.e., those of varying ages and who have participated in Circles for varying lengths of time – would also enable a fuller picture of the role of CoSA in desistance from sexual offending to emerge.

As desistance has been found to be shaped by culture (Bracken et al., 2009; Calverley, 2013, 2016; Deane et al., 2007; Finestone, 1967; Glynn, 2014, 2016; Howell, 2008; Richards et al., 2020b; Sullivan, 2012), an explicit focus on understanding the role of culture in core members' desistance journeys would also contribute to our knowledge of both desistance generally and CoSA specifically. Future research could also explore cross-national differences and commonalities in core members' moves toward desistance. Such research would be invaluable for CoSA projects and would enable programs to articulate and capitalise on local strengths to encourage desistance among core members.

Finally, observational research of CoSA would overcome the limitations of interview-based research, which relies on participants' recollections. Observational research would usefully supplement participants' *post hoc* accounts of CoSA.

Victim/Survivor and Public Views of CoSA

I want to acknowledge before closing what many readers may be grappling with as they engage with the research presented in this book: that CoSA – and in particular the understanding of CoSA I have expounded – may be unpalatable (to say the least) to victims/survivors of sexual violence and the broader community. Why should people who have sexually harmed others be given the opportunity to "make good" (Maruna, 2001) at all? Certainly, there has been public resistance to CoSA. In Australia, a victim/survivor support group even launched an online petition against the Adelaide-based pilot CoSA program (Richards & McCartan, 2018). Importantly, however, a small body of research has also documented pockets of community support for CoSA alongside this resistance (Höing et al., 2016; McAvoy, 2012; Richards & McCartan, 2018; Wilson et al., 2007).

One of the main reasons that members of the public offer for their reluctance to endorse CoSA is that victims/survivors of sexual violence – not those responsible for perpetrating it – should be the beneficiaries of government funding designed to address this issue (Richards & McCartan, 2018). It is vital to acknowledge, however, that victims/survivors of sexual violence are heterogeneous and hold diverse and complex views (McGlynn & Westmarland, 2019). While (as noted earlier) victims/survivors of sexual violence even sometimes act as volunteers in CoSA (Wager & Wilson, 2017), most are (understandably) unlikely to opt to take on this role (Richards et al., 2020a, in press). My recent research (Richards et al., 2021) found, however, broad support for CoSA among a sample of 33 Australian victims/survivors of sexual violence. Victims/survivors were supportive of the monitoring aspects of CoSA but also supported people who have sexually harmed others getting the help they require in order to prevent harm to others in future (see also Jülich, 2006). This is perhaps unsurprising given that few have a more vested interest in the creation of "no more victims" than victims/survivors of sexual violence themselves.

Conclusion

In closing, I want to underscore that while it presents the self-narratives of core members, this book is not really about people who have sexually offended. Rather, it is about all of us. In other words, it is a call to action, arguing that if we desire safer communities for our children and ourselves, we, the community, ought to follow the path set by the Reverend Nigh. While we will not all be willing or able to volunteer in a CoSA, we all have a role to play if we are to achieve the aim of "no more victims". Understanding CoSA as desistance-promotion illuminates how we might begin.

References

Almond, P., Bates, A., & Wilson, C. (2015). Circles of Support and Accountability: Criminal justice volunteers as the 'deliberative public'. *British Journal of Community Justice, 13*(1), 25–40. doi: https://mmuperu.co.uk/bjcj/articles/circles-of-support-and-accountability-criminal-justice-volunteers-as-the-deliberative-public/

Bartels, L., Walvisch, J., & Richards, K. (2019). More, longer, tougher... or is it finally time for a different approach to the post-sentence management of sex offenders in Australia? *Criminal Law Journal, 43*(1), 41–57.

Blagden, N., Elliott, H., & Lievesley, R. (2018). Circles of Support and Accountability, assisted desistance and community transition. In H. Elliott, K. Hocken, R. Lievesley, N. Blagden, B. Winder, & P. Banyard (Eds.), *Sexual crime and Circles of Support and Accountability* (pp. 25–42). Palgrave Macmillan. doi: https://www.palgrave.com/gp/book/9783319748221

Bracken, D., Deane, L., & Morrisette, L. (2009). Desistance and social marginalization: The case of Canadian Aboriginal offenders. *Theoretical Criminology, 13*(1), 61–78. doi: https://journals.sagepub.com/doi/10.1177/1362480608100173

Calverley, A. (2013). *Cultures of desistance: Rehabilitation, reintegration and ethnic minorities.* Routledge. doi: https://www.routledge.com/Cultures-of-Desistance-Rehabilitation-Reintegration-and-Ethnic-Minorities/Calverley/p/book/9780415623483

Calverley, A. (2016). Different pathways for different journeys: Ethnicity, identity transition and *Transforming identities*, (pp. 121–151). Bristol: Bristol University Press. doi: https://www.jstor.org/stable/j.ctt1t88xzs

Cohen, L., Manion, L., & Morrison, K. (2017). *Research methods in education* (8th ed.). Routledge.

Deane, L., Bracken, D., & Morrissette, L. (2007). Desistance within an urban Aboriginal gang. *Probation Journal, 54*(2), 125–141. doi: https://journals.sagepub.com/doi/10.1177/0264550507077231

Doekhie, J., & Van Ginneken, E. (2020). House, bells and bliss? A longitudinal analysis of conventional aspirations and the process of desistance. *European Journal of Criminology, 17*(6), 744–763. doi: https://journals.sagepub.com/doi/10.1177/1477370818819702

Finestone, H. (1967). Reformation and recidivism among Italian and Polish criminal offenders. *American Journal of Sociology, 72*(6), 575–588. doi: https://www.journals.uchicago.edu/doi/abs/10.1086/224396

Glynn, M. (2014). *Black men, invisibility and crime: Towards a critical race theory of desistance.* Routledge. doi: https://www.routledge.com/Black-Men-Invisibility-and-Crime-Towards-a-Critical-Race-Theory-of-Desistance/Glynn/p/book/9781138933675

Glynn, M. (2016). Towards an intersectional model of desistance for black offenders. *Safer Communities, 15*(1), 24–32.

Harris, D. (2014). Desistance from sexual offending: Findings from 21 life history narratives. *Journal of Interpersonal Violence, 29*(9), 1554–1578. doi: https://journals.sagepub.com/doi/abs/10.1177/0886260513511532?journalCode=jiva

Heise, E., Horne, L., Kirkegaard, H., Nigh, H., Peters Derry, I., Steinmann, V., Yantzi, M., & Worth, D. (1996). *Community reintegration project: A pilot project meeting the needs of communities for enhanced safety by providing circles of support for released sex offenders discharged at warrant expiry from federal institutions.* Mennonite Central Committee Ontario.

Höing, M., Bogaerts, S., & Vogelvang, B. (2013).Circles of Support and Accountability: How and why they work for sex offenders. *Journal of Forensic Psychology Practice, 13*(4), 267–295.

Höing, M., Petrina, R., Duke, L., Völlm, B., & Vogelvang, B. (2016). Community support for sex offender rehabilitation in Europe. *European Journal of Criminology, 13*(4), 491–516. doi: https://journals.sagepub.com/doi/abs/10.1177/1477370816633259

Howell, T. (2008). *The point of no return: Aboriginal offenders' journey towards a crime free life* [PhD thesis, University of British Columbia]. Vancouver.

Jülich, S. (2006).Views of justice among survivors of historical child sexual abuse: Implications for restorative justice in New Zealand. *Theoretical Criminology, 10*(1), 125–138. doi: https://journals.sagepub.com/doi/10.1177/1362480606059988

Maruna, S. (2001). *Making good: How ex-convicts reform and rebuild their lives*. American Psychological Association. doi: https://www.apa.org/pubs/books/431645A

McAvoy, J. (2012). *Birds of a feather? Irish public attitudes towards sex crime and sex offender reintegration. Is there a publically perceived scale of sexual deviance?* [Master's thesis, Dublin Institute of Technology]. Dublin.

McCartan, K., & Kemshall, H. (2020). The potential role of recovery capital in stopping sexual offending: Lessons from Circles of Support and Accountability to enrich practice. *Irish Probation Journal, 17*, 87–106. doi: https://www.pbni.org.uk/wp-content/uploads/2020/11/Kieran-McCartan-and-Hazel-Kemshall.pdf

McGlynn, C., & Westmarland, N. (2019). Kaleidoscopic justice: Sexual violence and victim-survivors' perceptions of justice. *Social & Legal Studies, 28*(2), 179–201. doi: https://doi.org/10.1177/0964663918761200

Richards, K. (in press). Circles of Support and Accountability: The role of social relations in core member desistance. *International Journal of Offender Therapy and Comparative Criminology*. doi: https://doi.org/10.1177/0306624X20964094

Richards, K. (2011). *The potential of Circles of Support and Accountability (COSA) to reduce child sexual abuse in Australia*. Winston Churchill Memorial Trust. https://www.churchilltrust.com.au/media/fellows/Richards_Kelly_2010.pdf.

Richards, K., Death, J., & McCartan, K. (2020a). *Community-based approaches to sexual offender reintegration*. Australia's National Research Organisation for Women's Safety. https://www.anrows.org.au/project/community-based-approaches-to-sexual-offender-reintegration/

Richards, K., Death, J., & McCartan, K. (2020b). Toward redemption: Aboriginal and/or Torres Strait Islander men's narratives of desistance from sexual offending. *Victims & Offenders, 15*(6), 810–833. doi: https://www.tandfonline.com/doi/full/10.1080/15564886.2020.1754311

Richards, K., Death, J., & Ronken, C. (2021). What do victim/survivors of sexual violence think about Circles of Support and Accountability? *Victims & Offenders*, 16, 893–911.

Richards, K., & McCartan, K. (2018). Public opinion about Circles of Support and Accountability: A qualitative analysis. *Deviant Behavior: An Interdisciplinary Journal, 39*(3), 400–416. doi: https://www.tandfonline.com/doi/abs/10.1080/01639625.2017.1304800

Sullivan, K. (2012). *Motivating and maintaining desistance from crime: Male Aboriginal serial offenders' experience of 'going good'* [PhD thesis, Australian National University]. Canberra.

Wager, N., & Wilson, C. (2017). Circles of Support and Accountability: Survivors as volunteers and the restorative potential. In E. Zinsstag, & M. Keenan (Eds.), *Restorative responses to sexual violence: Legal, social and therapeutic dimensions* (pp. 265–282). Routledge. doi: https://www.routledge.com/Restorative-Responses-to-Sexual-Violence-Legal-Social-and-Therapeutic/Zinsstag-Keenan/p/book/9780367226480

Wilson, D. (2006 17 June). Saturday comment: The prison trick. *The Guardian*, 25.

Wilson, R., Picheca, J., & Prinzo, M. (2007). Evaluating the effectiveness of professionally facilitated volunteerism in the community based management of high-risk sexual offenders: Part one – effects on participants and stakeholders. *The Howard Journal of Criminal Justice*, *46*(3), 289–302. doi: https://psycnet.apa.org/record/2007-09392-006

Index

Made in the USA
Las Vegas, NV
05 November 2024

388cebf7-f040-487a-8657-1f57c298621bR01